Bullying

Recent Titles in the
CONTEMPORARY WORLD ISSUES
Series

Books in the **Contemporary World Issues** series address vital issues in today's society such as genetic engineering, pollution, and biodiversity. Written by professional writers, scholars, and nonacademic experts, these books are authoritative, clearly written, up-to-date, and objective. They provide a good starting point for research by high school and college students, scholars, and general readers as well as by legislators, businesspeople, activists, and others.

Each book, carefully organized and easy to use, contains an overview of the subject, a detailed chronology, biographical sketches, facts and data and/or documents and other primary source material, a forum of authoritative perspective essays, annotated lists of print and nonprint resources, and an index.

Readers of books in the Contemporary World Issues series will find the information they need in order to have a better understanding of the social, political, environmental, and economic issues facing the world today.

Bullying

A REFERENCE HANDBOOK

Jessie Klein

ABC-CLIO®

An Imprint of ABC-CLIO, LLC
Santa Barbara, California • Denver, Colorado

Library of Congress Cataloging-in-Publication Data

Names: Klein, Jessie, author.
Title: Bullying : a reference handbook / Jessie Klein.
Description: Santa Barbara, CA : ABC-CLIO, 2020. | Series: Contemporary world issues | Includes bibliographical references and index.
Identifiers: LCCN 2019042640 (print) | LCCN 2019042641 (ebook) | ISBN 9781440855221 (hardcover) | ISBN 9781440855238 (ebook)
Subjects: LCSH: Bullying. | Bullying—Prevention. | Cyberbullying—Prevention.
Classification: LCC BF637.B85 K54 2020 (print) | LCC BF637. B85 (ebook) | DDC 302.34/3—dc23
LC record available at https://lccn.loc.gov/2019042640
LC ebook record available at https://lccn.loc.gov/2019042641

ISBN: 978-1-4408-5522-1 (print)
 978-1-4408-5523-8 (ebook)

24 23 22 21 20   1 2 3 4 5

This book is also available as an eBook.

ABC-CLIO
An Imprint of ABC-CLIO, LLC

ABC-CLIO, LLC
147 Castilian Drive
Santa Barbara, California 93117
www.abc-clio.com

This book is printed on acid-free paper ∞

Manufactured in the United States of America

For my great loves, Justin, Lev, and Susan, and for my inspiring and loving mother, Daisy, and father, Louis.

And to you readers: Keep researching and sharing kindness and compassion.
We need all hands on deck to stop bullying.

Preface

As a parent, I have seen the impact of bullying and the parallel agony caregivers experience when their children endure persistent teasing, social exclusion, pushing, name-calling, assault, and more—sometimes for years. When it comes close to home, I am also reminded of my own difficult childhood experiences and the havoc bullying wreaked.

School staff sometimes look the other way, discounting the behavior as "normal" growing pains. Other times, they work hard to make things better, and in spite of best efforts, it sometimes gets worse. Parents may give up and leave their school, only to find their children in similar circumstances elsewhere.

Bullying: A Reference Handbook is a launching pad for youths, families, school staff, college and university students and faculty, and others who want to understand more about what bullying is, why it occurs, and what schools and families can do to prevent and stop it.

You may be surprised by much of what you learn here, including causes related to emotional abuse, trauma-induced brain imbalances, and the role of social, economic, and racial inequalities.

Almost every recommended solution involves building empathy, trust, and connection, which makes sense given that since the 1980s, empathy and trust among youths and adults have decreased, and depression, anxiety, and social isolation have nearly tripled. People gripped by relationships (or lack of relationships) increasingly mediated by technology are disconnected from support and community.

School bullying is an international health crisis that contributes to short- and long-term mental and physical illness and that plays a role in school shootings and suicides. Between one in three and one in four K–12 students are bullied, approximately one in three admit to bullying others, and three-fourths of students say they have witnessed bullying. The Federal Bureau of Investigation (FBI) states that 75 percent of school shootings are linked to bullying and harassment; and 64 percent of those bullied don't report it, often fearing social or other retaliation.

Chapter 1, "Background and History," discusses the common definition of bullying and cyberbullying, most targeted student groups, as well as the impact of bullying and some of its causes.

Chapter 2, "Problems, Controversies, and Solutions," introduces disputes about the definition of bullying and its roots in social problems. It offers school solutions, including restorative justice circles, trauma-sensitive education, and systemic social-emotional learning, as well as what families can do to prevent their children from bullying others and being bullied.

Chapter 3, "Perspectives," is a series of essays by scholars, experts, and bullying-prevention facilitators including a parent, a school counselor, and a student. These essays cover many topics, such as addressing prejudice based on looks (looksism), facilitating "Kindness Conversations," teaching mindfulness, and administering effective restorative justice circles.

Chapter 4, "Profiles," provides accounts of youth and adult activists, empathy-focused programs, and victims associated with bullycides, including a teen who runs the anti-bullying website Ask Jamie and Phoebe Prince, age fifteen, whose suicide following brutal sex-shaming inspired Massachusetts legislation that requires school reports on bullying, whether on or off school property.

Chapter 5, "Data and Documents," provides a set of graphs and statistics that explain rates and types of bullying, places where it occurs, and differences by gender, with charts that show relationships between bullying and school shootings. The chapter also includes excerpts from policies, court cases, influential speeches, and other reports.

Chapter 6, "Resources," is an annotated bibliography of books, journal articles, popular writings, organizations, and media to help further your study.

Chapter 7, "Chronology," is a timeline of important events, including high-profile cases and legislation.

Finally, a glossary is provided with definitions of important terms.

I hope you find this information useful for your research. Now is a critical moment in history, and your work can make a difference and save lives.

More Information

If you are in danger of hurting yourself (or you know of anyone in danger of hurting themselves), call 911 immediately. You can also get support and referrals by calling this twenty-four-hour phone number for the National Suicide Prevention Hotline: 1-800-273-8255.

If you are hurt by bullying or anything else, ask for help from trusted people in your family, school, and community.

The Centers for Disease Control and Prevention provide information and critical resources for some of the youths most at risk for being bullied:

- LGBTQI+: https://www.cdc.gov/lgbthealth/youth-resources .htm
- Those perceived to have disabilities: https://www.cdc.gov /ncbddd/disabilityandsafety/bullying.html

ConnectSafely offers tips to stop cyberbullying at https:// www.connectsafely.org/tips-to-help-stop-cyberbullying.

Mental Health America provides steps you can take if you are bullied at http://www.mentalhealthamerica.net/bullying -what-do-if-im-bullied. Always get help!

StopBullying.gov is the U.S. government website providing comprehensive information on school bullying. It includes suggestions for parents, educators, community members, and youths who want bullying to stop at https://www.stopbullying .gov/what-you-can-do/index.html.

Robin Tutt, manager of editorial operations at ABC-CLIO, went above and beyond. While I dealt with family emergencies, Robin was understanding and compassionate, provided consistently excellent editorial feedback, and worked tirelessly, directly and indirectly, especially for chapters 4 and 5, in the service of this book. She is the phenomenal backbone of the project, and I am grateful for and awed by her contributions.

Catherine M. Lafuente, ABC-CLIO acquisitions editor, Michelle Scott, ABC-CLIO production editor, Angel Daphnee, Amnet project manager, and Hollianna Bryan, copyeditor, did exceptional work in their respective roles and made this a better book.

The ABC-CLIO marketing team continues to get the word out about this important topic and adjusted to new timetables as needed.

I am grateful to my research assistants, Anara Katz and Ashley Ajay, remarkable high school students, and to my A+ Adelphi University student, now graduate, Victoria Caracci, who worked quickly to make messy notes into crisp references, found missing information, and checked over the whole of them.

Tracy Wuischpard and Jean Casella were devoted editors on early drafts. Jean Casella, friend and mentor, also contributed crucial insights. David Callahan, my loving, loyal, and erudite friend, offered critical guidance and advice.

John Sanbonmatsu, animal rights activist and scholar at Worchester Polytechnic University, treasured and esteemed friend, mentored me on the relationship between animal abuse and bullying, with resources, references, links, articles, books, and videos.

Adelphi University granted a year-long sabbatical, a faculty development grant, and funds from the Center for Health Innovation for my research on this and related work and for my bullying prevention/intervention program, Creating Compassionate Communities. I am especially grateful to Liz Cohn, former director of the Center for Health Innovation, and Meghan McPherson, assistant director of the Center for Health Innovation; and to Susan Briziarelli, assistant provost for global affairs; Catherine Cleaver, executive director of the American Association of University Professors; Perry Greene, former vice president for diversity and inclusion; Sam Grogg, interim provost and executive vice president; and the members of my Sociology/Criminal Justice Department: department chair Jacqueline Johnson; director of the Criminal Justice Program Stephanie Lake; Professors Giovani Burgos, Melanie Bush, Deborah Little, Jackie Olvera, and Sal Primeggia, administrative assistant Sarah Avery, and also our wonderful adjunct professors.

Claudia Heilbrunn continues to be my outstanding and brilliant bedrock with the extraordinary Craig Katz and sharp Christine Foertsch.

Shayna Caul's powerful, otherworldly direction is beyond words.

Roberta Malles is a wonderful friend and daily support. The world is better for her compassion, humor, and loyal heart, and I am too.

I am grateful to the people who contributed essays in chapter 3 and whom I interviewed for chapter 4. They work hard in programs, scholarship, and activism to transform bully societies into compassionate communities.

I thrive on the care and love I experience in Maine, the poetic life there, the culture of generosity and kindness, and my warm and wonderful "friend-family."

The late Russ Lancaster and Roger Tripp Sr., noble and generous, contributed friendship and sustenance. I miss Roger's gardens, wisdom, and stop-by-talks. Russ's love, encouragement, companionship, and understanding often kept me going. I am grateful to their families for helping to keep their spirits alive.

My mother, Daisy Menkes Klein, is proud and enthusiastic about my endeavors, even in the midst of her medical setbacks. A holocaust refugee/survivor, one of the first U.S. female electrical engineers, a leader in women's rights and peace movements, and a runner of six marathons until she was seventy, she continues to enliven me.

The memories of my father, Louis Klein, and Uncle Milty are a blessing. I know my father would be moved by these efforts to stop bullying, and I feel his love, support, and care and my uncle's warm enthusiasm.

My brother, Franklin Klein, also made this book possible. Together we care for our mother, and our partnership allowed me the time to complete this book. A kind, ethical, and loving man, so much like our gentle father, he heartens me daily. And to Kathy and Elias Klein, for being our family.

Judith Canada, Eva Bitter, Marjorie Anderson, Carol Percival, Jae Lopez, Andria and Bridget Nelson, and my childhood friend Jeremy Rosen go above and beyond with extraordinary care to help our mother. And of course, Anna Panurach contributes clarity, order, and warmth.

Tiffany Vasilchik and Paul Heubeck, who by making life happier, easier, and friendlier, free up some mind clutter and help me focus.

My husband, Justin Leites, and my children, Lev and Susan, are my greatest joys. Lev and Susan's wise souls, kind and empathetic ways, sharp wit, creative and righteous ideas, fierce independence, and sweet precious love—each in their own beautiful ways—strengthen me more than they know.

I am grateful for the love they share with me every day. With them; our dog, Pokey; our cat, Seymour; the rabbits, Cutie and Frannie (and our beloved late Isabelle); and the two hamsters,

I consider myself blessed to have such a large and happy inter-species family.

Most gratitude goes to my husband. In addition to being a gentle and uplifting soul, he is my steadfast loving base, ethical underpinning, and supportive and devoted partner who keeps me laughing and on my toes. He read over every page of this manuscript in its late stages with his widely celebrated editing care. Thank you Pookie.

Bullying

What is school bullying? Why does it happen? What will stop it? There are no simple answers. We do know that bullying is a serious public health concern, frequently undermining students' physical and mental health and ability to learn. In the worst cases bullying culminates in suicide and murder.

Bullying: A Reference Handbook is an aid to researching crucial questions and concerns. This chapter presents information on ways to communicate about bullying; its history and definition(s); some of its impact; statistics; and biological, psychological, and social explanations.

Terminology

The language used to discuss bullying is important. Calling students "bullies" or "victims" is problematic because using these terms can affect how students perceive themselves and how others see them. No one, though, is just one thing. To see youth as the complex beings that humans are and to encourage and guide them, scholars and experts suggest that the language used to discuss bullying refer to *behaviors* rather than *identity*.

As stated on the federal government bullying-prevention website StopBullying.gov, "Labels suggest that behavior is fixed

---

A male youth feels unhappy because his school friends are gossiping about him. Contrary to popular opinion, males are involved in relational aggression as much as females, including spreading rumors and excluding others. (Katie Nesling/Dreamstime.com)

and is unlikely to improve over time" (Reiney & Limber 2013). People do change, though, and prior experiences do not determine the future. Students involved in bullying, especially with constructive school and family interventions, can even become leaders in helping to build more peaceful schools and stop others from bullying.

"When you're given a positive label, you're afraid of losing it, and when you're hit with a negative label, you're afraid of deserving it," writes Dweck (2007: 75–76). Judging others does little to foster constructive behaviors, and it limits understanding about the behaviors. Calling youths "bullies" suggests that the behavior is their fault. The label allows "us to ignore other factors that contribute to bullying behavior . . . [including] family dynamics, peer influences, and school climates" (Reiney & Limber 2013).

Bullying Language

The labels "bully," "bully-victim," "victim," and even "bystander" suggest that people in those categorizes always behave in the same way and for similar reasons. Dan Olweus, considered the pioneer of bullying research, describes four bullying types: those who initiate bullying; those who actively copy or support someone else's bullying; those who passively bully, for instance by laughing; and those who like the bullying, even though their support or encouraging behavior is less visible (Olweus & Limber 2010; Olweus 2016). The sheer variety of bullying types makes it problematic to attribute a specific set of behaviors to the static label "bully."

The term "bystander" is also troubling. Padgett and Notar (2013) note that there are contradictory definitions, including "Bystanders are individuals who are neither victims nor perpetrators of bullying" and "The bystander usually accepts or even participates in the bullying or they may try to stop the bully and take up for the target" (33). So, a bully and a bystander can be polar opposites or one and the same.

"Victim" can send a message that students who are bullied are helpless and can't do anything to change their circumstances, or that they are weak or deserving of pity, when what they may actually need is help to stop the bullying. The term's rigidity obscures the different responses people have to being bullied. While one might feel devastated, another may brush off the same behaviors (Rigby 1996).

Olweus (2003) suggests that some differences among those who are bullied warrant distinct categories. He refers to a "passive" and "provocative" victim. Passive victims, the most common, do not actively incite those who bully. Provocative victims may behave in ways that "elicit negative reactions" (50). These terms, then, raise other concerns; the term "passive victim" implies that the people bullied did nothing to stop the behavior. And yet they might have actively but unsuccessfully tried to stop it. A "provocative victim" suggests that the bullying may be at least partly the fault of the person bullied, but bullying is not okay under any circumstances. Researchers refer to other types of victims too, including "vicarious victim" or "surrogate victim"—those who witness or hear about bullying and become consumed with fear that they will be next (Besag 1989).

There are also students who in one moment may be a bully, in a second are bullied, and in a third manage to be uninvolved. The term "bully-victim" refers to someone who is both being bullied and bullying others.

These labels objectify and blame students involved in bullying, obscure the complex explanations that foster the behaviors, and create a perception of homogeneity in each role that doesn't exist.

Writing for StopBullying.gov about the importance of referring to actions and refraining from judgment, Reiney and Limber (2013) say, "Rather than calling a child a 'bully,' our website refers to 'the child who bullied.'" Instead,

[Even though] the labels *bully*, *victim*, and *target* are used often by media, researchers and others to refer to children who bully others, and children who are bullied . . . you won't find these terms used in this way on StopBullying .gov. . . . The next time you are tempted to use the terms "bully," "victim" or even "bully-victim" as shorthand labels for children involved in bullying . . . don't. Focus on behavior, not on the label.

As much as possible, this book replaces the label "bully" with a phrase such as "youth who bullied," "victims" with "those who were bullied," and "bully-victims" with "youth who bullied and were bullied." Because the latter is cumbersome and can be confusing, sometimes the "bully-victim" term is still used. Instead of using the term "bystanders," this book refers to students present when bullying takes place as "witnesses."

Scholars and experts do use many different terms. When discussing their work, the words they use are generally prioritized.

Gender

References to "boys" and "girls" are also complicated. The Human Rights Campaign's *Glossary of Terms* (2019) includes over thirty genders and sexualities including "gender-fluid, of or relating to a person having or expressing a fluid or unfixed gender identity"; "transgender, an umbrella term for people whose gender identity and/or expression is different from cultural expectations based on the sex they were assigned at birth"; and "cisgender, a person whose gender identity aligns with those typically associated with the sex assigned to them at birth."

Schools, universities, and workplaces are raising awareness about the many ways people identify themselves. Adelphi University's (AU) "Guide to Inclusive Language," for instance, suggests avoiding gender pronouns. Instead of stating, "Each author was chosen based on his or her research," the website recommends, "Authors were chosen based on their research."

When studies examine binary gender categories, this book uses these terms and otherwise avoids gender pronouns.

Youths

This book is primarily about students in kindergarten through twelfth grade (K–12) and college. To encompass this wide age range, the word most often used is "youth."

Defining Bullying

What is school bullying? How is bullying different from other hurtful behaviors? A brief history of the evolution of this term illuminates why researchers have different perspectives on these questions.

"Boele"

Considering the anguish around bullying in schools and society, it may be strange to learn that the word "bully" originally meant "sweetheart." It was used as early as 1538, according to *Merriam-Webster*, and likely came from "boele," a Middle Dutch word that means "lover." In the 1600s, the term was used as an endearment for the way male friends might address one another, such as "fine fellow" or "fine chap." By the end of the seventeenth century, the meaning darkened. In the 1700s, the term connoted a "ruffian," or a tough, lawless, or brutal person—closer to today's "bully."

Mobbing

In Sweden, the word "mobbing" morphed into what is considered a form of bullying today. Peter Paul Heinemann, a holocaust survivor and physician living in Sweden, used the word "mobbing" to describe his community's hostile reaction to his black adopted son, David. The name came from Konrad Lorenz, an Austrian ethologist (1966), who wrote about "mobbing" as an animal behavior that happens when stronger members in a species assault weaker ones. Heinemann (1972) applied the meaning to large group aggression against a particular child. "Mobbing" among people became a subject of Swedish public debates.

Olweus's Definition

In 1972, Olweus began to study verbal and physical aggression in a group of one thousand Swedish twelve- to sixteen-year-old boys. Heinemann's theory of "mobbing" framed the problem as an anonymous group picking on others, or "crowd behavior." Olweus observed, though, that among school children, the perpetrators were most often a small group of two or three students.

He first published his research in Sweden in 1973, and the 1978 English translation became *Aggression in the Schools: Bullying and Whipping Boys*. Here, Olweus analyzed the results he collected from his "self-report questionnaire," releasing the first systemic large-scale study of bullying. "Bullying," he explained, includes *three* traits among the parties involved: "verbal or physical abuse," "repetition," and a "power imbalance."

School bullying still received little public policy attention until 1982, when classmates severely tormented three fourteen-year-old boys in Norway. The youths wrote notes about the abuse and then committed suicide. The Norway Ministry of Education spearheaded a national campaign against bullying, and Olweus developed the Olweus Bullying Prevention Program (OBPP), still the most well-known evidence-based bullying intervention.

The OBPP was instituted in every primary and secondary school in Norway and expanded rapidly in many languages throughout Europe. The definition of bullying evolved in the 1990s to include indirect or relational aggression such as spreading rumors and gossip and making unkind gestures and facial expressions (Olweus 1999; Koo 2007).

The idea that "teasing" and "roughhousing" are normal parts of childhood still prevailed for most of the twentieth century (Lawrence 1998) until the late 1990s, when increasing numbers of school shootings and suicides revealed roots in bullying (Klein & Chancer 2000; Kimmel & Mahler 2003). A report from the National Center for Education Statistics highlighted the shift from perceiving bullying to be normal to considering it a serious public concern, stating, "Researchers increasingly find that bullying is a problem that can be detrimental to students' well-being" (Türkmen et al. 2013: 143).

Over and again, school shooting perpetrators left notes, testified in courts, and explained that they targeted students who bullied them. They also shot their peers whom they believed did nothing to help or who egged on their abuse as well as school authorities they believed looked the other way (Klein 2012a, 2012b).

In the *Journal of Pediatric Healthcare* (2018), Hornor writes,

Despite generations of doubt about the true impact of bullying, it is now clear that childhood bullying can have significant lifelong consequences for victims and bullies alike. Recent school shootings and suicides by students who have been victims of bullying have helped to solidify public awareness of the gravity of the problem of childhood bullying. (399)

Federal Definition

In 2004, the Centers for Disease Control and Prevention (CDC) published a formal definition for school bullying, derived from Olweus' three conditions (physical/verbal/relational aggression, repetition, and power imbalance). The U.S. Department of Education uses this explication for research and surveillance purposes. StopBullying.gov (2019) states, "Bullying is unwanted, aggressive behavior among school aged children that involves a real or perceived power imbalance. The behavior is repeated, or has the potential to be repeated, over time. Both kids who are bullied and who bully others may have serious, lasting problems.

In order to be considered bullying, behavior must be aggressive and include:

- An imbalance of power: Kids who bully use their power—such as physical strength, access to embarrassing information, or popularity—to control or harm others. Power imbalances can change over time and in different situations, even if they involve the same people.
- Repetition: Bullying behaviors happen more than once or have the potential to happen more than once.

Bullying includes actions such as making threats, spreading rumors, attacking someone physically or verbally, and excluding someone from a group on purpose."

Definition Controversies

The formal definition helps schools recognize bullying and respond appropriately per state regulations (Bazelon 2013), and having an agreed-upon meaning helps many researchers isolate bullying as specific behaviors in order to observe, understand, and seek solutions (Patchin & Hinduja 2016). Many researchers, though, suggest that this definition is too narrow and that rather than contributing a uniform meaning, it leaves too much to subjective interpretation. School officials, scholars, and others involved will more than likely assess the same behaviors differently when trying to determine what constitutes intent, aggression, repetition, and power imbalance (Carrera et al. 2011).

And what about the many different definitions used in myriad dictionaries and by organizations and academics across the world? In the United States, many states list variations of the definition in their anti-bullying laws and "the definitions are not fungible" (Waldman 2018: 140); some do not explicitly mention cyberbullying; and one doesn't define bullying in its statute at all.

While how to define bullying is disputed, researchers tend to agree that bullying is a subset of aggression (Smith & Thompson 1991; Olweus 1993; Rivers & Smith 1994). This book often highlights reactive and proactive school aggression that may or may not specifically meet the federal definition criteria.

Reactive and Proactive Aggression

Reactive aggression is characterized by anger and hostility and is understood as a reaction to feeling angry or frustrated (Dollard et al. 1939; Berkowitz 1962). Proactive aggression can be a means to instrumentally acquire an external reward, such as property, popularity, power, recognition, or affiliation (Bandura 1973).

Aggression may be direct, in the presence of the person being bullied, or indirect, not in the person's company. Indirect bullying may be relational aggression, such as damaging someone's relationship(s), including social exclusion. Schools authorities often overlook indirect aggression and consider it to be friendship squabbles, even as studies show that these behaviors can be as damaging as, if not more devastating than, direct bullying (Wang et al. 2010; Wei 2017).

Cyberbullying

School bullying occurs everywhere—in classrooms where teachers are present, in stairways and recess yards, on after-school routes home where adults are less present, and, in this era, in cyberspace. Youths bully others electronically using phones, texts, email, chat rooms, social media, instant messaging, and online posts. Cyberbullying can take the form of verbal aggression (making threatening or harassing comments), relational aggression (excluding and spreading rumors), or property damage (the modification, dissemination, damage, or other destruction of a person's electronically stored information).

StopBullying.gov gives specific examples:

- Posting comments or rumors about someone online that are mean, hurtful, or embarrassing.
- Threatening to hurt someone or telling them to kill themselves.

- Posting a mean or hurtful picture or video.
- Pretending to be someone else online in order to solicit or post personal or false information about someone else.
- Posting mean or hateful names, comments, or content about any race, religion, ethnicity, or other personal characteristics online.
- Creating a mean or hurtful webpage about someone.
- Doxing, an abbreviated form of the word documents, is a form of online harassment used to exact revenge and to threaten and destroy the privacy of individuals by making their personal information public, including addresses, social security, credit card and phone numbers, links to social media accounts, and other private data.

Sexting is sending, receiving, or forwarding sexually explicit messages, photographs, or images via technology. Ringrose et al. (2013) write that more often than males, females are bullied via sexting. U.S. statistics suggest that approximately 15 percent of teens send sexual messages, and 27 percent of teens receive them (Madigan et al. 2018).

Some cyberbullying definitions parallel face-to-face bullying—including repetition, power imbalance, and harm—through electronic means (e.g., Vandebosch & Cleemput 2008). Other research suggests that this ignores factors specific to cyberbullying. Singular, high-profile public attacks, such as hostile comments on a social forum or blog, can be repetitive, in that they reach dozens or even hundreds of others. People may also see one post multiple times (Langos 2012).

Impact on Those Involved in Bullying

Bullying can cause physical injuries and mental illness that last into adulthood. In the worst cases, it has culminated in homicide, and suicide associated with bullying is frequent enough that it has its own word: "bullycide."

Since the late twentieth century, the tragic consequences of bullying have escalated, with increasing cases of reactive school shootings. These tragedies take place in the midst of a more widespread crisis: a "culture of misery," characterized by significant decreases in empathy and trust and a rapid rise in depression, anxiety, and social isolation. Students who are depressed are also at risk for being involved in bullying as victims, bullies, and bully-victims (Kaltiala-Heino et al. 1999; Rigby & Slee 1999; Swearer et al. 2001; Fekkes et al. 2005; Ivarsson et al. 2005; Fekkes et al. 2006; Copeland et al. 2013; Lereya et al. 2013; Wang & Kenny 2014).

Between 1985 and 2004, across demographics, social isolation, closely linked to depression and anxiety, tripled. Neighborhoods are more fragmented and organic communities less present. According to analyses of the General Social Survey during this time, people have fewer confidants then they did in earlier generations. The number of friends—people the average person speaks to about important matters in their life, who they can trust to be genuinely happy for them in good times and compassionate in hard ones—has decreased. People, including youths, have much fewer nonfamilial connections and support. This surge in loneliness is one factor contributing to the growth in depression (McPherson et al. 2006).

Seven percent of adults had a major depressive episode in 2017, according to the National Survey on Drug Use and Health. Depression is so high today that some studies suggest it has become an epidemic (Hidaka 2012). In 2007, college and high school students were six to eight times more likely to experience a clinical depression compared with youth in 1938, and depression afflicts youth at increasingly younger ages (Twenge 2006; Twenge et al. 2010, 2018).

Anxiety has also increased. Thirty percent of college freshmen report being anxious, twice as many as in the 1980s (Twenge 2006: 105–107, 146, 180). Antidepressant use in the United States among teens and adults increased 400 percent between 1998 and 2008, according to the National Center for Health

Statistics (Wehrwein 2011). Others self-medicate with alcohol, illicit drugs, and other addictions, including food, gambling, and online gaming (Ko et al. 2009; Alavi et al. 2012; Zhang et al. 2012).

As people become more depressed, anxious, and disconnected from themselves and others, empathy has plummeted. People born before 1986 tend to be more empathetic than those born after 1986 (Perry & Szalavitz 2011).

Taken together, these findings suggest that the average young and older American is lonelier, more depressed, more anxious, and less empathetic. This contributes to a critical environment that predicts school bullying and being bullied with a high proportion of emotionally unavailable adults. Alone and grappling with bullying-related pain, anger, humiliation, shame, and isolation, students' physical and mental health are at serious risk.

Physical/Mental Health

Being involved in bullying (bullying others, being bullied, witnessing bullying, and/or cyberbullying) is often traumatic and is considered an adverse childhood experience (ACE) in the National Academies of Sciences, Engineering, and Medicine's report "Preventing Bullying Through Science, Policy, and Practice" (StopBullying.gov 2017, August). The CDC-supported ACEs study involved over 13,000 people and examined the relationship between childhood trauma and health-risk behaviors and adult diseases (Felitti et al. 1998).

Being bullied is associated with poor self-esteem, depression, low body satisfaction, substance use, and self-harm behaviors (Bucchianeri et al. 2016). Being cyberbullied can create emotional injuries that affect how youths view the world, how they relate to people, and if they feel safe and understood (StopBullying.gov 2017, August). The impact is often immediate, indefinite, and sometimes permanent. Long term, students who are bullied are at risk for physical difficulties including sleep and eating disorders (anorexia and bulimia) and heart disease. They are more susceptible to colds, physical injury, headaches, rashes, sore throats, and dizziness (Rigby 1998, 2003). Almost 10 percent of seriously injured students report that their injuries came from bullying-related assaults (Peyton et al. 2017).

These students are also more likely to suffer from generalized anxiety, panic disorder, post-traumatic stress disorder (PTSD), psychotic symptoms, and agoraphobia—an anxiety disorder that entails fearing and avoiding places where the student might panic or feel trapped, helpless, or embarrassed (Kaltiala-Heino et al. 1999; Swearer et al. 2001; Ivarsson et al. 2005; Copeland et al. 2013; CDC 2014, April).

Those who are bullied are at increased risk for developing early maladaptive schemas (EMS). Calvete (2014) writes,

> As a consequence of being bullied, adolescents may develop schemas involving thoughts and feelings of being rejected and abused by others (disconnection/rejection), feelings of being defective to some extent (disconnection/rejection), a sense of vulnerability and failure (impaired autonomy), and the need to satisfy the desires of others in an attempt to gain acceptance (other-directedness) and eventually to avoid bullying. (743)

Students who bully others and are also bullied (bully-victims) may experience severe anxiety and depression, social isolation, changes in sleep and eating patterns, loss of interest in activities, low self-esteem, poor school achievement, alcohol and drug abuse, aggression, and suicidal ideation. This group of students is often perceived to be the most impaired group with respect to depression and anxiety (Kaltiala-Heino et al. 1999; Swearer et al. 2001; Ivarsson et al. 2005; Copeland et al. 2013).

Bullying others is also an ACE. "Violence is an ACE from any perspective," states the StopBullying.gov fact sheet "Bullying as an Adverse Childhood Experience" (2017, August). Youth involved in bullying are more often involved in violence, fights, vandalizing, and crime. Males, in particular, may have "externalizing symptoms" like delinquency and aggression, oppositional defiant disorder (ODD), and attention deficit disorder (ADD). Additionally, they suffer with depression as much as students who are bullied. As adults, students who bully are also at greater risk for being delinquent, having an antisocial personality disorder, and participating in criminal behavior (Kaltiala-Heino et al. 1999; Swearer et al. 2001; Ivarsson et al. 2005; Swearer 2008; Copeland et al. 2013).

Those who are involved in bullying are at greater risk than students uninvolved in bullying for "depression, anxiety, involvement in interpersonal violence or sexual violence, substance abuse, poor social functioning, and poor school performance, including lower grade point averages, standardized test scores, and poor attendance" (CDC 2014, April).

Witnessing bullying can also be a traumatic ACE. Students who see their peers bullied have a higher rate of drug, tobacco, and alcohol use, and they are at higher risk for many serious mental and physical health challenges (StopBullying.gov 2017, August). Compared with youth who haven't witnessed bullying, those who do witness it report feeling more helpless and less connected to their families and schools. Being involved in bullying also increases the risk for suicidal behavior (CDC 2014, April).

Bullycide

Youth who bully others are at a high and long-term risk for suicide-related behaviors. In some studies, suicidal ideation occurs most often among those who bully (Kaltiala-Heino et al. 1999). In other research, youths who report both being bullied and bullying others (bully-victims) have the highest rates of negative mental health outcomes, including depression, anxiety, and suicide-related behaviors, suicidal ideation, suicide attempts, and suicide. This is especially prevalent in males. One study found that students who were bully-victims were two to nine times more likely to consider suicide than those who have not been bullied.

Youth who report being frequently bullied by others are also at increased risk for suicide-related behaviors as well as other negative physical and mental health outcomes (Kaltiala-Heino et al. 1999; Swearer et al. 2001; Ivarsson et al. 2005; Copeland et al. 2013; CDC 2014, April; Holt et al. 2015; StopBullying .gov 2017, August).

A CDC report (2014, April) on bullying and suicide suggests that while suicide is more common among students involved in bullying, it may be difficult to ascertain whether being involved in bullying directly causes suicide-related behavior. These tragedies often occur when youths are grappling with additional difficulties. Students involved in bullying who also reported sexual abuse, a mental health problem, or running away from home in the last year were more likely than others to report suicidal thinking or behavior.

Among students who are bullied and bully others (bully-victims), suicidal ideation or attempted suicide was more likely for more than half of the youths who also witnessed family violence, had a history of physical abuse, smoked cigarettes, used marijuana, skipped school because of safety concerns, or carried a weapon in school (Borowsky et al. 2013).

Murder/Mass Murder

In rare cases, bullying culminates in homicide. While people are understandably scared of and devastated by mass-murder shootings against school children, the FBI reports in their 1999–2002 National Center for the Analysis of Violent Crime report that it is unlikely that any student will die at school because of school violence—"one in a million." However, in a growing spate of school shootings since 1979, students who were bullied brought guns and bombs to school in order to commit retaliatory mass murder. Three-fourths of perpetrators, according to this report, planned the shooting because they felt bullied, persecuted, and/or threatened.

School shootings, where a gun was fired on school property, more than doubled just before the turn of the century, according to Klein (2012a, 2012b), from 27 in the decade ending in 1988 to 55 by 1998. There were 66 shootings from 1998 through 2008, or a total of 148 shootings over these thirty years (Klein 2012b). Looking at news reports over the next decade from 2009 through 2018, there were 175 school shootings, more than the three previous decades combined. In 2018, there were more school shootings (37) than in any prior year.

For instance, on May 18, 2018, seventeen-year-old Dimitrios Pagourtzis killed ten students and school staff in his Texas high school. Students reported afterwards that Pagourtzis's peers and football coaches "constantly teased" him. The coaches told Pagourtzis that he "smelled," and the other students laughed at him. His father said that his son had been bullied and was lashing out even before he brought the guns to school (Fox News 2019; Lasker 2018).

Statistics

According to the StopBullying.gov "Statistics" page, between one in four and one in three youths report being bullied. Bullying in the United States is especially common in middle school, and decreases slightly in high school (Espelage & Swearer 2003; Van Cleemput et al. 2014; Jones et al. 2015). The actual numbers are likely even higher, since many students do not report bullying, sometimes because they are ashamed or because they don't believe anyone will help them. In one study, only 20 to 30 percent of bullied youth reported what happened to them (Ttofi & Farrington 2011).

In a large one-month study assessing fourth grade through twelfth grade students that was posted on the StopBullying .gov "Statistics" page, 49 percent of students reported being bullied. Nine percent of sixth- through twelfth-grade students report being cyberbullied. Thirty percent of students admit bullying others. Almost three-fourths of students and teachers say they have witnessed bullying (Bradshaw et al. 2007).

Vulnerable Populations

According to some research, three groups of students are bullied most: students who are perceived to have disabilities, students who identify as LGBTQI+ (lesbian, gay, bisexual, transgender, queer, intersex, and others), and students who are targeted because of their weight.

In a large Midwestern study, weight-appearance-based harassment was more prevalent than other targeted bullying among both females (25.3%) and males (19.8%). Students perceived to be overweight experienced the severest harassment (Bucchianeri et al. 2016).

In other research, youth with disabilities are bullied three times more often than those in the general population. Those with developmental disorders (e.g., autism spectrum) experience the most bullying, followed by learning disabilities (e.g., dyslexia), sensory disorders (e.g., difficulty processing things seen, heard, felt, or tasted), and psychological difficulties (e.g., depression, anxiety) (McNicholas & Orpinas 2016: A158).

LGBTQI+ students are at much greater risk than heterosexual students for bullying (Olsen et al. 2014). The GLSEN (2005) National School Climate Survey reported that among these students, 75 percent report hearing homophobic comments frequently, making this the most common form of biased language at schools. Over a one-year study, about 65 percent of LGBTQI+ students were verbally harassed because of their sexual orientation, and 40 percent were physically harassed; 46 percent were verbally harassed because of their gender expression, 25 percent of these students were physically harassed (Kosciw & Diaz 2006).

Unless they have hyper-masculine characteristics, cisgender male youth are often called derogatory names associated with homosexuality whether or not they identify as gay. These comments target their height, body weight, affect, and lack of participation in male-associated activities, like sports (Klein & Chancer 2000; Messerschmidt 2000; Connell 2005; Kimmel 2008; Klein 2012a, 2012b).

Cisgender female youth are similarly attacked when their sexual or gender expression is thought to be less traditional. Peers and school authorities often blame girls for the bullying assaults they endure if the girls are perceived to be dressing or acting "too sexual" (Ringrose & Rawlings 2015; Pickel & Gentry 2017; Rawlings 2017).

Being bullied due to gender identity is often a retaliatory motive in school shootings. Many male perpetrators reported that they launched these attacks because they were teased and called "gay." In close to 50 percent of the shootings between 1979 and 2008, masculinity challenges were involved. Perpetrators used guns and violence to prove their manhood, when they were bullied about their sexuality, lack of athletic ability, and ability to fight. In his 1997 shooting, Michael Carneal in Kentucky said the boys teased him because he was "too nice to girls." Many shooters retaliated when they were ridiculed for their weight or appearance, either because they were perceived to be too "skinny," "lanky," "wiry," or "pudgy" (Klein 2012a, 2012b).

Males and females are frequently sexually assaulted, and related violence is chronic on college campuses. Due to its high frequency, dating-violence and sexual-harassment prevention now starts in some elementary schools (Hand & Sanchez 2000; Ottens & Hotelling 2000; Sanchez et al. 2001; Espelage et al. 2007).

Another study found that after weight-based harassment, harassment focused on race was the second most common form of bullying, especially against nonwhite males (Bucchianeri et al. 2016). According to the U.S. Justice and Education departments, Asian American teens are bullied more than any other racial groups (Izadi 2011). Arab American students report being bullied because of their ethnic, racial, and religious background (Albdour et al. 2017). The Council on American Islamic Relations found that 55 percent of Muslim students were bullied because of their religion; 29 percent were bullied for wearing hijabs, which included other students trying to pull them off or touching them offensively. Twenty percent of

Muslim students said that a school staff member discriminated against them.

Males and females from lower socioeconomic groups tend to be bullied by those with higher socioeconomic status (Bucchianeri et al. 2013). Across thirty-five European and North American countries, adolescents from less wealthy families were targeted more often than affluent youth. Economic inequality is also associated with a greater likelihood for school bullying. The more extreme the economic inequality, the higher the rate of bullying (Due et al. 2009; Pickett & Wilkinson 2010; Garandeau et al. 2014).

In the Bucchianeri et al. study (2016), those perceived to be overweight report the highest rates of multiple forms of harassment. Males perceived to be overweight are also more likely to be sexually harassed, and females experience weight-based and sexual harassment most often. Low-socioeconomic-status females were most likely to report weight-based harassment when compared with members of other groups. Asian males report the highest levels of race, weight, and socioeconomic harassment (Bucchianeri et al. 2013).

Students who are already depressed and tend to self-blame are also vulnerable to being bullied, especially in middle school. Depression heightens the risk for being bullied, and youth who are bullied tend to become depressed (Kochenderfer-Ladd & Wardrop 2001; Sweeting et al. 2006; Reijntjes et al. 2010; Copeland et al. 2013; Schacter et al. 2015).

This phenomenon is particularly alarming, as depression among youth has escalated exponentially over the last few decades (Twenge 2006; Twenge et al. 2010, 2018). Depression is associated with being involved in bullying in each capacity: bullying, being bullied, and being a bully-victim (Kaltiala-Heino et al. 1999; Rigby & Slee 1999; Swearer et al. 2001; Fekkes et al. 2005; Ivarsson et al. 2005; Copeland et al. 2013; Lereya et al. 2013; Wang & Kenny 2014). The role depression plays in bullying is often overlooked and is a critical component for understanding the high rates of bullying today.

Types of Bullying

More than other types, young people experience verbal and relational bullying. In one study, middle school students experienced the following: name-calling (44%); teasing (43%); spreading rumors or lies (36%); pushing or shoving (32%); hitting, slapping, or kicking (29%); leaving out (29%); threatening (27%); stealing belongings (27%); sexual comments or gestures (24%); and hurtful email or blogging (10%) (Espelage & Swearer 2003).

According to one StopBullying.gov report (2015), more females (23%) than males (21%) were bullied. Popular opinion and some studies suggest that bullying among girls tends to be relational (social exclusion and rumors) and bullying among boys is more often physical; other research, though, suggests that boys are more relationally aggressive than girls (Zimmer-Gembeck et al. 2012).

In Juvonen and Graham's (2014) study, boys used verbal assaults and social exclusion as well as other forms of relational aggression as often as girls. In the Wang et al. (2012) study, boys also perpetuated more social exclusion (boys 25%; girls 24%), rumor spreading (boys 13%; girls 11%), and cyberattacks (boys 11%; girls 7%). Boys also committed more physical bullying (boys 19%; girls 9%) and verbal bullying (boys 41%; girls 35%).

In a Child Trends (2016) report, males (13%) were only slightly more likely to experience physical harm (being slapped, hit, or pushed) than females (12%), and males experienced more harassment via internet or cell phone (males 5%; females 4%). In this study, females were more likely to experience relational aggression (females 38%; males 33%).

In terms of lifetime exposure, another study found that females experienced "all types of bullying" more than males. Female-perpetuated physical violence is also increasing and escalating at a faster rate than boys' violence. Males are still most likely to participate in violent bullying (Garbarino 2007) and are exponentially more likely to commit related school shootings. Between 1979 and 2008, of 148 school shootings, females committed less than 7 percent (Klein 2012b).

International

In a study of bullying in forty countries (2006), for both males and females ages eleven, thirteen, and fifteen, the United States landed roughly in the middle. Sweden had the least bullying (females 5%; males 9%), and other Scandinavian countries, including Iceland and Finland, also have much less bullying. Lithuanian students reported the highest rate of bullying (females 36%; males 45%), and the other Baltic states were similarly high. Latvia had the second-highest rate of bullying. In the United States, 17 percent of females reported bullying, as did 22 percent of males (Harel-Fisch et al. 2009).

In this study, countries economically structured around private enterprise and small government had mostly higher bullying rates, while social democracies with strong welfare states had less. Do economic systems that guarantee (often free) prenatal, child, health, and elder care, as well as higher education, contribute to a sense of communal responsibility and support that results in lower bullying scores? Do less regulated capitalist economies, which are dependent on competition and an aggressive pursuit of profit, create zero-sum rivalries and contribute to high bullying scores?

Derber and Malgrass (2016) suggest in their book *Bully Nation: How the American Establishment Creates a Bullying Society* that an imbalance of power in the form of extreme hierarchies and repeated exploitation are made to seem natural in the United States and predict interpersonal bullying. Klein (2012a) discusses a similar concern in the chapter "The Bully Economy" in her book *The Bully Society*. When hyper-competition and aggression are integral to financial and professional success, a "bully society" may be an expected outcome. Espelage and Swearer (2010) found that perceiving aggression positively predicts bullying. Perhaps countries that nurture combative competition as integral for financial and professional success inadvertently breed bullying. U.S. workplace bullying is also a significant problem; some studies report that between 38 and 90 percent of U.S. workers experience bullying (Glendinning 2001: 272–273).

Explanations

Researchers have found many different kinds of explanations for bullying triggers. A Violence Prevention Works OBPP fact sheet (2007) states, "There is no single or simple 'cause' of bullying behavior."

Brain imbalances, family problems, and social influences are among the issues raised to explain why youths bully. Some who bully believe that they should dominate and control others, perhaps because of family or social expectations. Messerschmidt (2000) found that boys were more likely to commit physical assault when they were influenced by strong male figures in their lives, including fathers, uncles, and grandfathers, who valorized violence as an essential aspect of masculinity.

The Violence Prevention Works OBPP overview flags students with difficult home situations. These students may be motivated to take out their frustrations by causing other students to suffer, especially if their behaviors are reinforced with positive peer attention that increases their status and prestige.

Students who bully may also have parents who are authoritarian and use physical punishment or other "power-assertive" child-rearing methods. Their caregivers may also be embroiled in interpersonal violence. This kind of background can become a model for using violence to solve problems and may contribute to a proclivity to bully others.

None of these circumstances conclusively predict bullying. Many students with similar backgrounds are not aggressive or involved in bullying at all.

Biological

Bullying may also occur when, due to prolonged family or social stresses, the sympathetic fight part of the fight-or-flight autonomic nervous system becomes overactive; youths may then feel provoked by even minor or unintentional slights or criticism and respond with aggression. Students who bully may even be unaware when they feel threatened by other students.

Emotionally or physically abusive peers, families, school staff, or other authorities who chronically criticize and hurt youths may be overstimulating the students' defensive sympathetic reactions. These students may then bully others and *fight* to try to feel powerful, rather than helpless, as they have felt when they were originally attacked (Brown & Gerberg 2012, 2017; Brown et al. 2013; Gerberg & Brown 2015; Porges & Carter 2017; Miller 2018; Gerberg et al. 2019).

The parasympathetic, self-soothing part of the autonomic nervous system can become similarly unbalanced, making it difficult for these students to make compassionate choices when confronted by a perceived threat. An overactive *fight* part of the sympathetic system, coupled with the underactive empathetic parasympathetic part, decreases the ability to feel and behave with empathy toward others and can increase the proclivity to hurt them.

An underactive parasympathetic system can also undermine bonding, compassion, and cooperation. People who bully may seem popular or socially connected, but there is usually an underlying sense of inadequacy and difficulty for them to feel close to others. Students contending with stressful circumstances outside school are then more likely to feel triggered in schools contextualized by social climbing, envy, competition, and aggressive posturing, rather than supportive relationships (Brown & Gerberg 2012, 2017; Brown et al. 2013; Gerberg & Brown 2015, 2016; Porges & Carter 2017; Miller 2018; Gerberg et al. 2019; personal oral communication, Gerberg 2019, Sept. 18).

Autonomic imbalances are exacerbated by an inability to respond constructively to perceived threats or difficulties. Youths who experience stressful circumstances can become stuck in a cycle of affronts to their nervous system. The initial stress is compounded by responses to subsequently perceived threats. An overactive nervous system can also trigger more anxiety, aggression, delinquent behavior, other behavioral disorders, and autonomic imbalance (Miller 2018).

Students who are subjected to authoritative parenting, repeated yelling, verbal or emotional aggression, physical or sexual abuse, and other forms of violence are likely to have central autonomic brain imbalances and are also at risk for being involved in bullying (Sutherland 2006; personal oral communication, Gerbarg 2019, Sept. 18).

Psychological

Almost 50 percent of Americans in the ACEs study survived chronic childhood stresses and traumas that can have serious consequences. About 25 percent of people have two or more ACEs. Having multiple ACEs increases risks for problems with mental and physical health. Youths who experience ACEs are also at risk for being bullied and bullying others (Vaughn et al. 2011; StopBullying.gov 2017, August; Sacks & Murphey 2018). In one study of youths who had at least one ACE, 40 percent were perpetrators; 37 percent were victims; and 63 percent were bully-victims. Nineteen percent did not perpetuate any violence (Forster et al. 2017).

The original ACEs study includes five personal traumas: emotional abuse or neglect; physical abuse or neglect; and sexual abuse; and five traumas related to family members, including parents who are experiencing interpersonal violence, abusing substances, struggling with a mental illness, spending time in jail, or who have disappeared due to divorce, death, or abandonment. ACEs also include homelessness, discrimination, economic hardship, and any form of witnessing or experiencing of violence (Felmlee & Faris 2016; Sacks & Murphey 2018). Other ACEs are still being identified. At a 2018 ACEs conference called Action to Access, a panel on race and health equity raised awareness of traumas that include experiencing disproportionate suspensions and expulsions and the impact from being involved in juvenile justice, foster care, and deportation (White 2018, November 14).

ACEs make it more likely that youths will struggle in peer relationships both as aggressors and victims. Trauma tends to lead to difficulty regulating emotions and is associated both with "higher externalizing symptomatology," including "delinquency and violence against peers," and "higher internalizing symptomatology," including depression, anxiety, and loneliness associated with being involved in bullying. Youths exposed to abuse may also lack social skills and have relationship difficulties due to their insecure attachments (Kim & Cicchetti 2010; Eastman et al. 2018).

Extreme conflict among siblings may also predict being involved in bullying. If siblings find a need to compete with one another to gain status or leadership in the family and then bring these unresolved feelings to school, they may bully others (Kumpulainen et al. 1999).

Youths are particularly at risk for being involved in bullying if they experience emotional abuse or neglect. *Emotional abuse* (also called psychological abuse, psychological aggression, and psychological maltreatment) and emotional neglect are ACEs that can cause trauma and PTSD and are linked to bullying (Rogers et al. 2003; Lereya et al. 2013; Bethell et al. 2014; Zottis et al. 2014).

Emotional abuse includes frequent yelling, swearing, and putting youths down; blaming; and threatening, isolating, rejecting, degrading, isolating, or otherwise engaging in exploitative caregiving. Emotional neglect is the failure to respond to youths' emotional needs. As a result of these abuses, youths can receive messages that they are flawed or valued only when they meet the parent's or others' needs (Leeb et al. 2008; Briere et al. 2012; CDC 2014, April; Park et al. 2016).

When parents emotionally abuse children, it increases the risk that these youths will be involved in peer-related aggression or victimization (Hutchinson & Mueller 2008) and that they will become depressed and socially anxious (Gibb et al. 2003, 2007; Simon et al. 2009; Bruce et al. 2012; Calvete 2013). Being depressed and anxious, in turn, predicts and is often a consequence of being involved in bullying (Hoglund 2007; Cook et al. 2010; Blake et al. 2016).

Some caregivers engage in authoritarian parenting as a means to help children develop accountability and to teach them to discern good behavior from bad. Authoritarian parenting is high on control but low on responsiveness, emphasizing rigid behavior and prioritizing obedience. The style tends to be emotionally distant and unresponsive (Baumrind 1971). Authoritarian parenting may also approve of and use corporal and physical punishment (Friedson 2016). Parents who engage in authoritative parenting tend to ascribe hostile intent to youths and are more likely to feel negative in response to perceived transgressions (Crouch et al. 2017). This form of parenting puts children at risk for being involved in bullying (Georgiou et al. 2013; Martínez et al. 2019). Authoritative parenting can also be emotionally abusive.

Parents' "harsh verbal discipline" has been found to be as damaging to developing adolescents as physical discipline. Caregivers sometimes shift from physical discipline to verbal discipline when youths enter adolescence. Approximately 90 percent of American parents report one or more instances of harsh verbal discipline toward their children, and 50 percent report "severe verbal discipline," such as swearing, cursing, and name-calling (Wang & Kenny 2014).

Youths whose parents humiliate them are more likely to demonstrate behavior challenges that include bullying others, engaging in other antisocial and aggressive behaviors, and experiencing serious depression, anxiety, and low self-esteem. These youths may develop difficulties defending themselves, become unable to thwart peer-led aggression, and become trapped in a violent bully-victim cycle (Kaltiala-Heino et al. 1999; Swearer et al. 2001; Ivarsson et al. 2005; Estévez et al. 2007; Ellenbogen 2008; Hodgdon et al. 2009; Espelage & Swearer 2010; Copeland et al. 2013; Taillieu & Brownridge 2013; Wang & Kenny 2014).

Youths who bully others are often grappling with these and other forms of family or school stressors. Their caregivers may be poor role models for managing conflict. The caregiver-child relationship may suffer from a poor or insecure attachment and become a relationship based on fear, with an absence of trust (Salmivalli et al. 1996; Schwartz et al. 1997; Kaltiala-Heino et al. 1999; Swearer et al. 2001; Ivarsson et al. 2005; Espelage and Swearer 2010; Nickerson et al. 2010; Copeland et al. 2013).

Many caregivers use harsh verbal discipline to try to stop their children from engaging in the behaviors that concern them, including bullying. However, yelling, shouting, and insulting can aggravate depression and aggressive tendencies, and the undesirable behaviors are more likely to increase (Wang & Kenny 2014).

Screaming and attacking youths during their adolescence can have other negative personal and social consequences. It is a "sensitive developmental period," write Moretti and Craig (2013), when abusive experiences can undermine neurobiological, cognitive, and socioemotional shifts, resulting in debilitating symptoms including depression that may linger into late adulthood. Attachment is essential to support adolescent adjustment. Teens often turn to their primary caregivers for the secure and safe base they need for both emotional soothing and learning how to cope with difficult emotional experiences. Frequent yelling and attacking undermines secure attachment (Moretti & Craig 2013).

Caregivers may be kind and loving in between bouts of rage and yelling, but the intermittent closeness does not mitigate the damage and may be more confounding to the adolescent, who is then more likely to self-blame and feel shame. Parental warmth, the degree of love, emotional support, and affection a parent shows, does not decrease the detrimental impact of harsh verbal discipline. Even if there is a strong parent-child bond and a warm and loving relationship, the hostile screaming can trigger aggressive and self-harming behaviors (Wang & Kenny 2014).

Emotional abuse predicts psychopathology even more than physical or sexual abuse. Emotional abuse can occur in isolation, but "frequently accompanies other types of abuse, making it the most common type of maltreatment" (Berzenski & Yates 2013: 181). In one study, between 45 percent and 86 percent of parents reported engaging in emotionally abusive behaviors including yelling, insulting, and threatening; 38 percent of females and 45 percent of males experienced psychological neglect (Briere et al. 2012).

Helping youths who are being psychologically maltreated can be challenging. Even when they struggle with symptoms like depression, anxiety, anger, and aggression and they can describe the painful experiences, they are often unable to acknowledge that they are being abused. Youths may instead adapt to their abusive circumstances (Goldsmith & Freyd 2005; Wang & Kenny 2014). Caregivers may also be unaware that their yelling and insulting is abusive and that it puts their children at increased risk for being aggressive, depressed, and involved in bullying.

As adults, survivors of psychological aggression often find abusive partners in efforts to subconsciously work through childhood issues with their original parent abusers. They may not know any other way of being with others, as people tend to repeat early childhood dynamics in their adult relationships. It can feel too painful to let go of the wish that the abusive parent might one day meet their needs. The abusive adult relationship is a way for the person to continue to try, again and again, to get their needs met—sadly while staying stuck in the bully-victim cycle. People from abusive families often find themselves in adulthood acting as the victim (bullied) and/or aggressor (bully) (Crawford & Wright 2007).

Some children grow up trying to appease a parent, placing the caregiver's needs above their own, as a way to stave off the parent's rage. As adults, this compulsive caregiving for their partner and chronic self-sacrificing puts these survivors at risk for being emotionally abused and bullied in their adult interpersonal relationships.

Those who experience physical abuse are more likely to be aggressors in adult interpersonal relationships and less likely to experience adult intimate-partner victimization. Instead, they may grow up to rage at and bully a more passive partner. Male survivors of emotional abuse are more likely than females to be either aggressors/bullies or victims/bullied in their adult relationships (Berzenski & Yates 2013).

Physical abuse is also associated with being involved in school bullying (Estévez et al. 2007; Espelage & Swearer 2010). Youths are more likely to be involved in bullying, often as aggressors, if their parents' authoritative discipline methods include physical punishment, especially when parents push, slap, punch, or use objects like belts, brooms, and sticks to beat a child (Espelage et al. 2000; Swearer & Doll 2001; Smith 2004; Duong et al. 2009; Hodgdon et al. 2009; Lereya et al. 2013; Gómez-Ortiz et al. 2016). When youths are physically punished, they often come to believe that violence is a legitimate way to interact (Orue & Calvete 2012).

Physical and emotional abuse are the ACEs that most predict youth aggression (neglect and sexual abuse, in one study, were not linked to bullying). Youth aggression increases when they endure severe and frequent abuse and when they experience the common combination of both emotional and physical abuse simultaneously (Hodgdon et al. 2009). When parents abuse children, bullying others and being bullied are predictable outcomes (Sutherland 2006).

Intergenerational abuse also impacts bullying. Since youths who are emotionally and physically abused at home or at school are also at risk for being involved in bullying in their adult interpersonal relationships, there is also concern about an intergenerational cycle of trauma. Statistics likely underestimate rates of trauma associated with bullying. Intergenerational abuse, not just through individual families but also due to systemic domination and oppression of different peoples, can create cyclical dynamics of abuse and victimization that affect students' relationships with themselves, their peers, and school staff (Rieder 2013).

Adults who physically, emotionally, and otherwise abuse young people are mostly themselves damaged by their own childhood traumas and/or generations of trauma, pain, and anxiety that developed from surviving oppressive social structures, such as wars, forced slavery, and attempted genocides. ACEs occur from witnessing or experiencing horrific political and cultural violence and from suffering severe psychological harm, which can then be unwittingly transmitted from one generation to the next.

In the multicultural United States, many adults and children grapple with intergenerational trauma—centuries of oppression that contribute to a cycle of debilitating ACEs. Among many others surviving social, economic, and political oppression are American Indians (Brave Heart & DeBruyn 1998; Evans-Campbell 2008); ancestors descending from U.S. slavery (DeGruy 2005; Graff 2014); and immigrants from Africa and Latin America's war-torn countries (Perreira & Ornelas 2013). Intergenerational trauma is present in Armenians (Kupelian et al. 1998) and Croatians (Klain & Pavić 2002) who survived attempted genocide; Japanese American internment survivors (Nagata 1991); and first, second, and third generation Jewish holocaust survivors (Felsen 1998; Kahane-Nissembaum 2011).

School staff who were bullied in their youth can also get caught in a bully-victim cycle where they then bully their students and put these students at risk for bullying other youths. Teachers who were bullied in their childhood are both more likely to bully their students and to experience bullying by students in and outside of their classroom. The youths they bully are at risk for bullying their students if they become teachers themselves (Twemlow et al. 2006).

According to the FBI's National Center for the Analysis of Violent Crime (1999–2002), the bully-victim cycle is in part responsible for almost three-fourths of school shootings, where perpetrators attacked their schools because they felt bullied, persecuted, or threatened. After school shootings, surviving students are often traumatized and consumed with anxiety and survivor's guilt, like the two students who killed themselves a year after the Parkland shooting (Mazzei 2019, March), tragically attacking themselves after surviving the horror.

Social Environment

School environments can undermine students' mental health when staff and peers look the other way if violence takes place and when the community hosts widespread might-makes-right belief systems, multifaceted prejudices, hyper-masculinity pressures, and rigid social hierarchies.

Mental health: Emotional stability can be compromised for students grappling with bullying and other ACEs, recently inflicted or endured over generations. Where youths and adults need support to thrive and to make positive and constructive contributions, they often contend instead with aggressive, hyper-competitive, and painful social conditions (Klein 2012a). Many students who are shamed in society because of issues like their weight, gender, sexual expression, mental illness, or disability also find that they are emotionally and physically bullied at school.

The United States has tended to charge mental health problems as the most significant factor in determining why some people commit violence, including school shootings (Rocque & Duwe 2018). If so, mental health support and constructive mental illness intervention in schools are that much more imperative to preventing violence.

A "social-ecological" framework shifts focus from blaming individuals to examining and addressing interrelationships among school, family, and community, including levels of social support (Swearer & Doll 2001; Espelage & Swearer 2003, 2010; Nickerson et al. 2010; Swearer et al. 2010). Tendencies toward aggression manifest in social environments that feel threatening, and such tendencies can remain dormant or transform in cultures that create safety and support kindness and cooperation (Orpinas & Horne 2006; Klein 2012a; Dewitt & Slade 2014; Gerbarg & Brown 2016; Porges & Carter 2017).

Often, though, schools increase rather than decrease students' already overstimulated fight-or-flight reactions, PTSD, and other maladaptive social responses. Students who may have mental health challenges are more likely to get worse when they are judged, blamed, and bullied instead of being supported and helped to heal as therapeutic models recommend (McNicholas & Orpinas 2016).

Look the other way: The destructive aspects of many school environments are so pervasive and normalized that they can seem invisible and desensitize community members to this everyday violence. Students become accustomed to school staff and students who look the other way when so called low-level violence takes place.

Desensitization to violence is likely evident in the statistic that only 20 to 30 percent of bullied students even notify adults. While there are multiple concerns about why students don't report, one piece is that aggressive behavior is often overlooked and has come to seem normal (Ttofi & Farrington 2011). Cruel interactions become common. Without help and support to make other choices, students are more likely to join in the various forms of bullying, including cyberbullying, if they see their peers supporting this behavior (Bastiaensens et al. 2015).

How spectators respond to bullying is critical to curbing it (Cowie 2000; Nickerson et al. 2008; Swearer et al. 2010). When witnesses do nothing, their behavior tends to support and increase the bullying (Cowie 2000; Gini et al. 2008) and increase others' passivity (Espelage et al. 2007), and when they egg on the abuse, bullying escalates (Swearer et al. 2009).

If administrators, school staff, coaches, and families don't notice or don't intervene until conflicts escalate into more conspicuous bullying, they may be sending implicit messages that some violence is acceptable. Relational violence is routinely misdiagnosed as "relatively harmless" or a "girl problem," even as it creates a decreased "health-related quality of life" (Chester et al. 2017) and can feel devastating for people across gender and other demographics (Simmons 2011; Juvonen & Graham 2014; Wiseman 2016).

Bullying often persists in public view. Just as authoritative parental screaming is relatively accepted, when certain forms of school violence are perceived to be commonplace or intractable, there may be reduced physiological arousal and external emotional reactions as well as a more positive attitude toward acts that harm others (Funk et al. 2004; Bushman & Huesmann 2006; Carnagey et al. 2007; Scharrer 2008; Fanti et al. 2009; Fraser et al. 2012; Guo et al. 2013; Mrug et al. 2015). And when any form of abuse is perceived to be normal, a "might-makes-right" belief system is more likely to manifest.

Might-makes-right: Schools may unintentionally embolden a "might-makes-right perspective" that legitimates bullying (Weinhold 2000). Those who have more power in a social environment may believe that they have the right to control and bully those whom they believe are subordinate. Unequal status can create these conditions (Vega & Comer 2005), like in the workplace, when subordinates feel afraid "to express disagreement with management," there often exists an implicit might-makes-right culture. Similar to those who witness school bullying, many workers refuse to support mistreated peers because they fear retaliation (Hofstede 1997; Ahmed 2008).

High levels of inequality in income or status predicts greater tolerance for hierarchy, authoritarian values, and frequent bullying. A large power distance anticipates a proclivity toward social conditions informed by might makes right, a philosophy that power is based on the use of force and that autocracy is valid (Vega & Comer 2005). In these kinds of environments, prejudiced supremacy can also poison social relationships.

Multi-faceted prejudices: As do many adults, students may come to believe that they are more important than others whom they disdain for being different. Youths are often bullied when they have different attributes than those associated with an Anglo-Saxon prototype, including being tall, large boned, and muscular, with a long angular face, pale skin, straight blond or light brown hair, and blue or light-colored eyes (Shore 1906: 333–334). This model of beauty is so accepted that the multifaceted prejudices it breeds can appear invisible, further desensitizing students to violence.

Multifaceted prejudices propel bullying against students who are not like this Anglo ideal, especially against students who are short or less muscular (perceived to be too heavy or skinny) or who look "ethnic," including having darker or differently textured hair, facial features, and skin and eye color. Adulation of this prototype also devalues those with mental or physical challenges and disabilities as well as students with less traditional emotional and sexual expression. Students try to contort themselves and their bodies to emulate the dominant white Anglo characteristics in order to win peer approval and avoid being bullied—often going to great lengths to attain the supremacist images.

At increasingly younger ages, youths get nose jobs, ear surgery, breast augmentation and reduction, and acne scar treatment. The American Society of Plastic Surgeons (2019) writes that through these procedures, teens can "reverse the social withdrawal that so often accompanies teens who feel different." Instead of helping students to accept and appreciate themselves and one another in many different shapes, sizes, colors, genders, ways of self-expression, learning, and the like, youths feel compelled to erase their differences and often develop an alienated and often abusive relationship with themselves and others.

Masculinity pressures: Another way people are desensitized to violence develops from conventional masculinity pressures. Gender expectations are so seamlessly woven into social life that the violence they create can seem natural, including the widespread existence of school cultures that glorify gay-bashing and rape (Kimmel 2008).

High-profile crimes against LGBTQI+ youths receive national attention, including the brutal 1998 gay-bashing murder of college student Matthew Shepard in Laramie, Wyoming, and the 2008 school shooting where 14-year-old Brandon Mc-Inerney targeted and killed 15-year-old Larry King because King was transgender (Klein 2012b; Rozsa et al. 2018). One of the two students who killed a classmate and wounded eight others in their 2019 Denver, Colorado, shooting identified as transgender and reportedly sought revenge after being bullied for it (Coffman 2019).

The term "rape culture" refers to a school environment where young men are expected to define and encourage one another to perform masculinity in the form of sexual conquest, including sexual assault and rape. The failure on the part of schools and universities to support victims, prevent recurrences, and hold perpetrators accountable contributes to the belief that these kinds of masculinity behaviors are normal. Reports reveal that out of every one hundred women on a college campus, twenty are survivors of attempted or completed sexual assault or rape. Of these twenty survivors, approximately seventeen do not report the assault (Gourley 2016: 198).

People who are sexually assaulted are so often held responsible for the crime committed against them that the phrase "blame the victim" was created to describe this phenomenon. Many films document these pervasive conditions, such as *The Hunting Ground* (2015), *It Happened Here* (2015), and the TV docudrama, *Our Guys: Outrage at Glen Ridge* (1999) that chronicled the 1989 high school football players' gang rape of a seventeen-year-old girl in Glen Ridge, New Jersey (1999).

A masculinity-femininity heterosexual binary informs and fuels bullying, enforcing conformity to heterosexism (prejudice against those who are not perceived to be traditionally heterosexual) by creating and maintaining a sexuality surveillance. LGBTQI+ students are among the most typically bullied, but students who identify as heterosexual but do not meet current cisgender expectations are often abused, as in what happened to many of the school shooters who sought revenge (Connell 2005; Klein 2012a; Olsen et al. 2014).

Males tend to gain status when they demonstrate heterosexual promiscuity and flaunt their sexual exploits with females, while females are still often punished and sexually shamed if they are used in a male person's real or imagined sexual bragging. Females are bullied with sexually derogatory names if they are perceived to be too sexual, not sexual enough, overly masculine, or to have failed to be feminine in some anticipated way (Ringrose & Rawlings 2015).

This sexual shaming involves multiple prejudices when used against females from minority groups (Connell & Pearse 2015). Since early colonial and slave-trading days, nonwhite females have been preemptively shamed as being too sexual (Cossins 2003), and low-income females' sexual behaviors have been referred to as "trashy." When white and wealthier females engage in comparable activities, their behaviors have a better chance of being referred to as "classy" (Armstrong et al. 2014: 100).

Masculinity norms also encourage males to laugh with others about their sexual exploits and the humiliation they inflict (Lefkowitz 1997; Messerschmidt 2000; Connell 2005; Kimmel 2008; Klein 2012a, 2012b). This hegemonic masculinity performance helps males rise to the top of their school's rigid hierarchies, but also undermines their potential to develop close relationships with others (Connell 2005).

Rigid status-hierarchies: Bullying is also motivated by a desire for acceptance. Students find they have to contort themselves in many different ways to be accepted and to rise in their schools' social hierarchies, and sometimes that means putting others down to raise themselves up.

Some youth who bully make friends easily, especially with others who endorse violence and bullying. Once students reach middle school or early adolescence, bullying others is more likely to help them gain their peers' fear, respect, and admiration (Nansel et al. 2001; Juvonen et al. 2003; Cillessen & Mayeux 2004; Rose et al. 2004; Keisner & Pastore 2005). In schools with rigid status-hierarchies, youths often find that they raise their position in the caste system by hurting others.

Some students who bully are perceived to be socially unskilled and unaccepted by their peers (Crick & Dodge 1999, Arsenio & Lemerise 2001). Others seem to use their social skills to dominate their school's social life and peer relationships (Sutton et al. 1999; Vaillancourt et al. 2003). While roles vary, often it is those perceived to be popular who bully more socially isolated or marginalized students (Farmer et al. 2010).

Such a hostile school culture can undermine students' sense of safety among most students, and often those who bully have an even poorer perception of the school climate than those who are bullied and who are bully-victims (Espelage & Swearer 2010). School status hierarchies can dominate students' sense of themselves and one another, and youths may find themselves immersed in power dynamics that prevent them from developing fulfilling friendships. Tolerance for school hierarchies also predicts bullying (Garandeau et al. 2014).

"I see them as a platoon of soldiers who have banded together to navigate the perils and insecurities of adolescence," writes Wiseman (2016) about the female social cliques she studied. Wiseman sees a "chain of command," including the "Queen Bee," "Sidekick," and "Banker" (who "sells others' secrets" in return for more social power) (19). Social exclusion, rumors, and gossip are some of the weapons used in the jockey for power on the social ladder.

Even if they feel conflicted about participating in hurtful behaviors, students often feel pressured to be popular by any means necessary rather than be ostracized. Popularity doesn't usually mean warm connections with others, but it makes it less likely that a student will be made into a pariah.

Popularity often requires befriending powerful peers and working to accrue "body," "economic," "cultural," and "social capital."

In many schools, students gain peer acceptance when they have "body capital"; usually males are expected to be big and muscular and females are expected to be skinny and toned. Youths also acquire body capital when they resemble a perfectionistic version of the Anglo-Saxon model of beauty, including being white, thin, and tall—part of the reason so many get nose jobs and ear surgery, wear high heel shoes, and diet compulsively. Bodies that fail to meet these criteria may be tormented and scorned, a prejudice Chancer refers to in her essay in chapter 3 and in other research (1998) as "looksism." Students may then feel negatively about their own and others' bodies if they are "ethnic," smaller, rounder, or any number of other culturally different qualities.

In the 1600s, the thin, muscular bodies that people work tirelessly to achieve today were considered unattractive. Historically the rich woman was fat and the poor thin, while now the opposite is true (Servadio 2005). The shifts in history may help youths know, at least cognitively, that the pressure to meet a contemporary version of an Anglo-Saxon model of beauty is culturally specific and not the definition of objective beauty.

Another form of popularity currency that students acquire to help them rise in their schools' hierarchies is "economic capital," which generally refers to the family's socioeconomic status. High-end consumer products are no longer the main indicator of economic status. Due to technological advances and globalization, people from many different classes can purchase high-end consumer products (e.g., smartphones via payment plans, or designer clothes on eBay). Wealthier people today accrue status from purchasing expensive experiences, services, vacations, and elitist educations at expensive private schools (Currid-Halkett 2017). Youths may be bullied, ostracized, or otherwise looked down upon, even pitied, when they are perceived to have low economic capital, without the funds to participate in these kinds of activities (Klein 2006, July).

"Cultural capital" includes valued practices that build social currency. For instance, males are often rewarded for being leaders in contact sports. Being smart or having an interest in computers or academic subjects can deprive them of this kind of value. Students may also attain cultural capital if they are aggressive and prone to bullying (Evans & Eder 1993; Merten 1997; Farmer et al. 2003; Xie et al. 2003; Klein 2006; Vaillancourt & Hymel 2006).

Students find they have more social power—"social capital"—if they associate with students who already have high social status and if they avoid and objectify those perceived to have low status (Gerth & Mills 1946: 188–189; Bourdieu 1986; Klein 2006). Extroverted and outgoing personalities tend to accrue social capital and popularity, while quieter students can be demonized or pathologized as loners, outsiders, and outcasts or discarded as too shy or timid.

Since the beginning of the twentieth century in the United States, introverted people have been more likely to be vilified and ostracized and less likely to be included in popular groups. Being contemplative, modest, thoughtful, serious, introspective, and virtuous used to be the highest-praised qualities, writes Cain, in *Quiet* (2012). Today being loud and energetic is valued instead (41). In schools, students are expected to be outgoing if they want to be popular (O'Dell et al. 2018). Those who bully in the United States are often aggressive and loud, and they tend to be seen as having more social competence and peer-reported social acceptance (Reijntjes et al. 2013).

Not every culture champions these attributes. There is the "soft power" of Asian Americans, writes Cain (2012), typified by Gandhi, who said, "In a gentle way, you can shake the world" (181). Many Asian cultures still prioritize quiet contemplation, restraint, listening, and refraining from interrupting or speaking loudly (Axtell 1990). This may explain, then, why in one study Asian Americans, who have a culture perhaps most different from Western extroverted pressures, were bullied more than any other race or ethnicity (Bucchianeri et al. 2013).

Students are socially rewarded for conforming to external barometers regarding how they should look, who their families are, what they should be interested in, and how (and with whom) they should interact (Vaillancourt & Hymel 2006). Different schools have some variations in social currency expectations. Some schools value academics over athletics, middle-class status or urban poor over elitist wealth, or different body features. Cultural, economic, social, and body capital can shift in different environments (Bourdieu 1986). The result though is the same: students are not accepted and helped to thrive in their own skin.

Simmons (2011) writes that competition for popularity is as dangerous for youth as anxieties over weight, appearance, or sexuality. Some young people starve themselves to be thin, and others destroy peers to attain popularity. Peers may bully others if they feel jealous of their valued attributes (e.g., wealth, clothing, Anglo-Saxon beauty characteristics) or of their social or romantic relationships (Land 2003; Jan & Husain 2015).

Pressure to be popular and to avoid ostracism can steer students away from building mutually supportive friendships. Such connections, though, are considered critical for adults and youths to build emotional and medical health, especially at a time when social isolation is so high (McPherson et al. 2006; Masi et al. 2011).

Many parents and caregivers limit the time their children can spend developing social relationships in the interests of focusing on school and getting ahead. Among some students, the culture of academic competition also creates a "mental habit of hierarchically ranking individuals," writes Zhao (2011). Students judge potential friends on their social and academic success.

Here again, they are encouraged to base their self-esteem on being better than others. The competition incites "jealousy, distrust, and antagonism" and prevents mutuality and close friendships. Exams also reward self-advancement, rather than "mutual benefit." The hyper-assessment culture of the twenty-first century can prevent support and connection. Adolescent friendships are often mired in stress, fierce hierarchies, and "competition between friends" (Zhao 2011: 155).

Capital-related school shootings magnify the bullying many students endure daily, which is accompanied by reactive despair and rage. As motives for their crimes, school shooters repeatedly reported that they felt dehumanized because they did not (or could not) conform to their school's valued attributes. Many of these victims-turned-mass-murder bullies cited multiple insults and indignities.

School shootings magnify the bullying many students endure daily around "rigid status-hierarchies," "might-makes-right" belief systems, "hyper-masculinity pressures," "multi-faceted prejudices," and when school members "look the other way" if violence takes place (Klein 2012b).

"Look the other way": In 1997 in Bethel, Alaska, Evan Ramsey, age 16, killed his principal, one student, and wounded two others. News reports said Ramsey explained: "I figured since the principal and the dean weren't doing anything that was making any impression, that I was gonna have to do something, or else I was gonna keep on getting picked on."

Might-makes-right belief systems: In 1997 in Pearl, Mississippi, Luke Woodham, age 16, killed his ex-girlfriend, her friend, and his mother. He was called "short, little fat boy," "pudgy," and "poor." He commented about the students who bullied him: "They'd always talk about me and push me around and start fights with me and stuff. . . . They'd call you gay or call you stupid or fat or whatever. Kids would sometimes throw rocks at me and push and kick me."

Woodham and his friends turned the tables and became the most powerful. They called themselves the "Third Reich" for Hitler. After the shooting, Woodham said: "One second I was some kind of heartbroken idiot, and the next second I had the power over many things."

Before his school shooting, Woodham left a note that seemed to sum up these perpetrators' reactive rage: "I am not insane, I am angry. I killed because people like me are mistreated every day."

Multi-faceted prejudices: In 2007 at Virginia Tech University, a twenty-three-year-old South Korean immigrant, Cho Seung-Hui, killed twenty-seven students, five teachers, and wounded ten students before killing himself. He said he was enraged at "rich kids" and that he hated the wealthy. He was bullied because of his speech difficulties and mocked because he was shy and for the strange way he talked. Students told him to "go back to China."

Hyper-masculinity issues: In 2001 in Santee, California, Charles Andrew Williams, age fifteen, killed two male students and wounded thirteen. He was picked on for being "skinny" and called "Anorexic Andy" and "a little kid." News reports commented that other students would light their lighters and press the hot metal against his neck. He was also called vile, anti-gay slurs.

The weekend before the shooting Williams told some students that he was going to "pull a Columbine" on Santana High. Two students called him a girl and dared him to do it. After the shooting, one student said, "There's a lot of hate around here. . . . This is a school that was waiting for something like this to happen. But who would have guessed that it would be the skinny, jug-eared, timid freshman wearing a silver necklace with the name MOUSE."

Rigid status-hierarchies:

- In March 1987 in Dekalb, Missouri, Nathan Harris, age twelve, killed one student before killing himself. He was an honor student and called an "overweight loner" and a "walking dictionary." He was bullied from a young age because he was smart. He said he was "tired of being teased" and he killed the boy who bullied him that day in class.

- In March 2001 in Williamsport, Pennsylvania, Elizabeth Catherine Bush, age fourteen, had been called "idiot, stupid, fat, and ugly." Other students "barked at her as if she was a dog." In her shooting she wounded the "popular cheerleader" whom she said had told other students some of her secrets.

Technological Alienation

Perhaps no other aspect of the twenty-first-century social environment contributes more to increased bullying than technological alienation. Technology has replaced face-to-face relationships, making it possible for bullying to be constant and relentless. Ninety-five percent of teens have a mobile device. As recently as 2012, face-to-face communication was the preferred way of connecting. By 2018, it had become texting. Seventy percent of teens check social media several times during the day. Six years ago, it was 34 percent (Common Sense Media 2018).

Online, students tell each other that they are unattractive, unpopular, sexually unacceptable, boring, or otherwise not okay. The rise of smartphones and social media use is thought to be a significant factor in the deterioration of teens' mental health. Students go to SNS like Facebook to seek popularity, compare themselves to others, and receive peer feedback. "Fear of missing out" on SNS increases risks for depression, anxiety, suicidal ideation, and suicide (Allen et al. 2014; Nesi & Prinstein 2015; Ophir 2017).

To cushion themselves against cyberbullying, students perfect their SNS images, going to great lengths to get followers and likes and to curate their digital profile to project popularity and an exciting social life, sometimes even purchasing hundreds of likes through a website or using computer programs for a digital nose job. Students often make comments to others to try to make them feel badly about themselves in comparison (Wallace 2018, May). When youths compare themselves to the

Anglo idealized bodies on highly visual social media, like Snapchat and Instagram, they face risks for poor body image issues and mental health difficulties, including depression (Marengo et al. 2018).

By regularly using social media, young people are more likely to feel ostracized, ignored, and excluded (Pharo et al. 2011) as well as socially disconnected and isolated (Williams 2007) and to experience "cyberostracism" (D'Amato et al. 2012). According to a Pew study, 53 percent reported that they have seen people post events that they weren't invited to on social media (Lenhart 2015). They can be socially excluded in school and also shut out and ignored online (Zadro et al. 2004; Gonsalko-rale & Williams 2007). Students are excluded from Facebook groups and defriended, blocked, and prevented from following others on Twitter (Allen et al. 2014).

Bullying also takes the form of posting humiliating photos, gay-bashing, ridicule, texting rumors, and pretending to befriend a person thought to be lonely. Cyberaggression can occur among strangers, acquaintances, friends, former friends, and dating partners. As in face-to-face bullying, non-cis-gender, nonheterosexual students are bullied more than most other students—in cyberspace, at four times the rate (Felmlee & Faris 2016).

High school dating is often competitive in cyberspace too. Students undermine peers' chances with those perceived to be the "most valued romantic partners" by trying to "humiliate and scare them via a nasty, threatening text message" or by posting an embarrassing photo on Facebook. When a breakup occurs, some might post "a cruel comment on an ex's Facebook page" to "wound someone back, avenge a wrong, or attempt to shame and coerce a former partner into reuniting" (Felmlee & Faris 2016: 16).

While school policies are now more likely to hold administrators and teachers responsible for reporting and intervening in cyberbullying, it is sometimes difficult for students to find adults who will help them. Some teachers bully students and others may feel too downtrodden themselves due to being bullied by other staff and even their students.

Teachers Bully

As in many workplaces, teachers may be embroiled in their own popularity contests, painful social exclusion, and demeaning workplace bullying, making it even more difficult for them to help students who need assistance and support. And teachers, as other adults, are also less available because many are struggling with the increased depression, anxiety, and social isolation endemic to the twenty-first century (McPherson et al. 2006; Twenge 2006; Twenge et al. 2010).

Teachers may also degrade students in front of their peers, call them names, and put them down. When teachers bully students, those who witness this abuse can receive the message that the bullied students deserve this treatment. They emulate the teachers' negative behavior and bully the classmates picked on by teachers (James et al. 2008; Farmer et al. 2011).

If adults in the school feel secure in their work environment, they are more likely to intervene on behalf of bullied students, yet almost 20 percent of workers are bullied, including school staff (Namie 2017). Teachers may also reap social rewards for bullying students. Whereas power may shift from one to another peer (Olweus 1995), teachers who bully tend to maintain power in the student-teacher relationship (McEvoy 2005).

If teachers believe a student is popular, they are also more likely to assess this student's behavior as less objectionable and respond less harshly than if an "unpopular" student acts similarly (Nesdale & Pickering 2006). Like students, teachers who bully tend to target disadvantaged students, such as those who are disabled (McNicholas & Orpinas 2016).

In schools with high suspension rates, one study found that teachers bullied more students, reported that they worked with more teachers who bully, and witnessed more teachers bully students (Twemlow & Fonagy 2005). According to 64 percent of students surveyed in another study, being bullied by an adult is even more detrimental than peer bullying. When teachers bully students, it is often considered part of a legitimate authoritative pedagogy, including when teachers belittle, humiliate, and harass them (Whitted & Dupper 2008).

Sometimes teachers bully students by excessively punishing them, and these students respond with reactive behavior (Twemlow & Fonagy 2005; Twemlow et al. 2006). They may use the school's disciplinary response as an implicit defense for punishing others when they feel wronged.

Retribution "Justice"

Suspended students may take out their rage on the school authorities they blame for disciplining them. Sometimes they attack the student they believe is responsible for getting them punished (even if they had initiated the assault), or they let out their rage by "punishing" a different student.

Defiance theory suggests that there is a link between bullying and a youth's angry reactions to being punished. Bullying becomes the "auxiliary device" or "indirect defiance" youth use to "administer justice" for what they perceive to be unfair sanctions imposed on them. Their target represents the "unfair sanctioning agent" (Ttofi & Farrington 2008: 306). In her study of girls, Wiseman discussed this kind of justification in relational bullying: "They believe their actions are justified because of something done to them first" (2016: 26).

Students who bully others tend to believe in aggressive retaliation (Bradshaw et al. 2008). According to the FBI, school shooting perpetrators were often seeking retribution. "The justifications and excuses offered indicated this stemmed not from an absence of values," the FBI explained, "but from a well-developed value system in which violence was acceptable." Sixty-one percent were motivated by a "desire for revenge" (NCAVC 1999–2002). Many shooters targeted administrators and teachers they blamed for unfairly disciplining them (Klein 2012b).

In the late 1990s, zero-tolerance policies were implemented widely in the United States following the Columbine High School, Colorado, school shooting, when Eric Harris, age seventeen, and Dylan Klebold, age eighteen, killed thirteen people and wounded twenty-four others. Both the number and length of suspensions increased for large and small infractions, including fights, wearing hats, and failing to complete homework. Lawmakers increased school security measures (e.g., metal detectors and police presence), hoping that strong enforcement would deter other disruptive students. The "get tough" policies came out of the "broken window" theory that punishing minor disruptions would send a strong message.

Severe discipline for minor incidents, in many cases, contributed instead to more student resentment and retaliatory rage. Instead of reducing bullying, studies concluded that suspension and expulsion began to exacerbate the violence (Skiba & Knesting 2001; Skiba 2014). Of 148 school shootings between 1979 and 2008, approximately 25 percent related to student resentment about what perpetrators perceived to be the school behaving unjustly, especially when meting out punishments (Klein 2012b).

Studies found that suspensions and expulsions were also administered against black students two to three times more than when white students committed the same misbehaviors. Black students were also more frequently subjected to other punitive measures, including corporal punishment (Skiba & Knesting 2001; Skiba 2014).

Since 2012, zero-tolerance policies have fallen out of favor, in part because of students' devastating retaliatory responses and also because of growing awareness of the school-to-prison pipeline, where mostly minors from disadvantaged backgrounds are incarcerated after being disproportionately suspended or expelled. Many of those students are disabled, come from poverty, and survived traumas like abuse or neglect. The American Civil Liberties Union (ACLU) (2019) writes that these youth "would benefit from additional educational and counseling services. Instead, they are isolated, punished, and pushed out." Many states have restorative justice options now, according to the StopBullying.gov website on bullying policies. Colorado led the zero-tolerance movement in the late 1990s, but it is now at the national forefront for implementing school restorative justice practices (PBS News Hour 2014).

References

Ahmed, E. (2008, December). "Stop it, that's enough": Bystander intervention and its relationship to school connectedness and the shame management. *Vulnerable Children and Youth Studies, 3*(3), 203–213. doi:10.1080 /17450120802002548

Alavi, S. S., Ferdosi, M., Jannatifard, F., Eslami, M., Alaghemandan, H., & Setare, M. (2012). Behavioral addiction versus substance addiction: Correspondence of psychiatric and psychological views. *International Journal of Preventive Medicine, 3*(4), 290–294.

Albdour, M., Lewin, L., Kavanaugh, K., Hong, J. S., & Wilson, F. (2017). Arab American adolescents' perceived stress and bullying experiences: A qualitative study. *Western Journal of Nursing Research, 39*(12), 1567–1588. doi:10.1177/0193945916678214

Allen, K. A., Ryan, T., DeLeon, L. G., McInerney, D. M., & Waters, L. (2014). Social media use and social connectedness in adolescents: The positives and the potential pitfalls. *Australian Educational and Developmental Psychologist, 31*(1), 18–31.

American Civil Liberties Union. (2019). School-to-prison pipeline. Retrieved from https://www.aclu.org/issues /racial-justice/race-and-inequality-education/school -prison-pipeline

American Society of Plastic Surgeons. (2019). Briefing paper: Plastic surgery for teenagers. Retrieved from https://www.plasticsurgery.org/news/briefing-papers/briefing-paper-plastic-surgery-for-teenagers

Armstrong, E. A., Hamilton, L. T., Armstrong, E. M., & Seeley, J. L. (2014). "Good girls": Gender, social class, and slut discourse on campus. *Social Psychology Quarterly, 77*(2), 100–122. doi:10.1177/0190272514521220

Arsenio, W. F., & Lemerise, E. A. (2001). Varieties of childhood bullying: Values, emotion processes, and social competence. *Social Development, 10*(1), 59–73. doi:10.1111/1467-9507.00148

Axtell, R. E. (1990). *Gestures: The do's and taboos of hosting international visitors.* Hoboken, NJ: John Wiley & Sons.

Bandura, A. (1973). *Aggression: A social learning analysis.* Englewood Cliffs, NJ: Prentice-Hall.

Bastiaensens, S., Pabian, S., Vandebosch, H., Poels, K., Van Cleemput, K., & DeSmet, A. (2015). From normative influence to social pressure: How relevant others affect whether bystanders join in cyberbullying. *Social Development, 25*(1), 1–19.

Baumrind, D. (1971). Current patterns of parental authority. *Developmental Psychology Monographs, 4*(1–2), 1–103. Retrieved from https://psycnet.apa.org/record/1971-07956-001

Bazelon, E. (2013). *Sticks and stones: Defeating the culture of bullying and rediscovering the power of character and empathy.* New York: Random House.

BBC News. (2004, August). Teen depression on the increase. Retrieved from http://news.bbc.co.uk/go/pr/fr/-/2/hi/health/3532572.stm

Berkowitz, L. (1962). *Aggression: A social psychological analysis.* New York: McGraw-Hill.

Berzenski, S. R., & Yates, T. M. (2013). Preschoolers' emotion knowledge and the differential effects of harsh punishment. *Journal of Family Psychology, 27*(3), 463–472. doi:10.1037/a0032910

Besag, V. E. (1989). *Bullies and victims in schools: A guide to understanding and management.* Milton Keynes, England: Open University Press.

Bethell, C. D., Newacheck, P., Hawes, E., & Halfon, N. (2014, December). Adverse childhood experiences: Assessing the impact on health and school engagement and the mitigating role of resilience. *Health Affairs, 33*(12), 2106–2115. Retrieved from https://www.healthaffairs.org/doi/full/10.1377/hlthaff.2014.0914

Blake, J. J., Zhou, Q., Kwok, O.-M., & Benz, M. R. (2016). Predictors of bullying behavior, victimization, and bully-victim risk among high school students with disabilities. *Remedial and Special Education, 37*(5), 285–295. doi:10.1177/0741932516638860

Borowsky, I. W., Taliaferro, L. A., & McMorris, B. J. (2013, July). Suicidal thinking and behavior among youth involved in verbal and social bullying: Risk and protective factors. *Supplement, 53*(1), S4–S12.

Bourdieu, P. (1986). The forms of capital. In J. Richardson (Ed.), *Handbook of theory and research for the sociology of education* (pp. 241–258). New York: Greenwood.

Bradshaw, C. P., O'Brennan, L. M., & Sawyer, A. L. (2008). Examining variation in attitudes toward aggressive retaliation and perceptions of safety among bullies, victims, and bully/victims. *Professional School Counseling, 12*(1), 10–21.

Bradshaw, C. P., Sawyer, A. L., & O'Brennan, L. M. (2007, September). Bullying and peer victimization at school: Perceptual differences between students and school staff. *School Psychology Review, 36*(3), 361–382.

Brave Heart, M., & DeBruyn, L. (1998). The American Indian holocaust: Healing historical unresolved grief. *American Indian and Alaska Native Mental Health Research, 8*, 60–82.

Briere, J., Godbout, N., & Runtz, M. (2012). The psychological maltreatment review (PMR): Initial reliability and association with insecure attachment in adults. *Journal of Aggression, Maltreatment & Trauma, 21*(3), 300–320. Retrieved from https://psycnet.apa.org/record /2012-10160-004

Brown, R. P., & Gerbarg, P. L. (2012). *The healing power of breath* (E-Book and Sound Track). New York, NY: Shambhala Press.

Brown, R. P., & Gerbarg, P. L. (2017). Breathing techniques in psychiatric treatment. In P. L. Gerbarg, R. P. Brown, & P. R. Muskin (Eds.), *Complementary and integrative treatments in psychiatric practice* (pp. 241–250). Washington, DC: American Psychiatric Association.

Brown, R. P., Gerbarg, P. L., & Muench, F. (2013). Breathing practices for treatment of psychiatric and stress-related medical conditions. In P. R. Muskin, P. L. Gerbarg, & R. P. Brown (Eds.), *Complementary and integrative therapies for psychiatric disorders*. Philadelphia, PA: Elsevier.

Bruce, L. C., Heimberg, R. G., Blanco, C., Schneier, F. R., & Liebowitz, M. R. (2012). Childhood maltreatment and social anxiety disorder: Implications for symptom severity and response to pharmacotherapy. *Depression and Anxiety, 29*, 131–138. doi:10.1002/da.20909

Bucchianeri, M. M., Eisenberg, M. E., & Neumark-Sztainer, D. (2013, July). Weightism, racism, classism, and sexism: Shared forms of harassment in adolescents. *Journal of Adolescent Health, 53*(1), 47–53.

Bucchianeri, M. M., Gower, A. L., McMorris, B. J., & Eisenberg, M. E. (2016, August). Youth experiences with multiple types of prejudice-based harassment. *Journal of Adolescence, 51*, 68–75.

Bushman, B. J., & Huesmann, L. (2006). Short-term and long-term effects of violent media on aggression in children and adults. *Archives of Pediatrics & Adolescent Medicine, 160*(4), 348–352.

Cain, S. (2012). *Quiet: The power of introverts in a world that can't stop talking.* New York: Crown Publishers.

Calvete, E. (2014). Emotional abuse as a predictor of early maladaptive schemas in adolescents: Contributions to the development of depressive and social anxiety symptoms. *Child Abuse & Neglect, 38*(4), 735–746. Retrieved from https://psycnet.apa.org/record/2013-40866-001

Carnagey, N. L., Anderson, C. A., & Bushman, B. J. (2007). The effect of video game violence on physiological desensitization to real-life violence. *Journal of Experimental Social Psychology, 43*(3), 489–496.

Carrera, M., Depalma, R., & Lameiras, M. (2011). Toward a more comprehensive understanding of bullying in school settings. *Educational Psychology Review, 23*(4), 479–499. doi:10.1007/s10648-011-9171-x

Centers for Disease Control and Prevention. (2014, April). The relationship between bullying and suicide: What we know and what it means for schools. Retrieved from https://www.cdc.gov/violenceprevention/pdf/bullying-suicide-translation-final-a.pdf

Centers for Disease Control and Prevention. (2014, May). *The adverse childhood experiences (ACE) study.* Atlanta, GA: Centers for Disease Control and Prevention. Archived from the original on December 27, 2015.

Chancer, L. S. (1998). *Reconcile differences: Confronting beauty, pornography, and the future of feminism.* Berkeley: University of California Press.

Chester, K. L., Spencer, N. H., Whiting, L., & Brooks, F. M. (2017). Association between experiencing relational bullying and adolescent health-related quality of life. *Journal of School Health, 87*(11), 865.

Child Trends Databank. (2016). Bullying. Retrieved from https://www.childtrends.org/?indicators=bullying

Cillessen, A. H. N., & Mayeux, L. (2004, January–February). From censure to reinforcement: Developmental changes in the association between aggression and social status. *Child Development, 75*(1), 147–163. Retrieved from https://www.ncbi.nlm.nih.gov/pubmed/15015681

Coffman, K. (2019, June 20). Transgender teen accused in deadly Colorado school shooting wanted revenge. Reuters. Retrieved from https://www.reuters.com/article/us-colorado-shooting/transgender-teen-accused-in-deadly-colorado-school-shooting-wanted-revenge-idUSKCN1TM09T

Common Sense Media. (2018). Social media, social life: Teens reveal their experiences. Retrieved from https://www.commonsensemedia.org/sites/default/files/uploads/research/2018_cs_socialmediasociallife_fullreport-final-release_2_lowres.pdf

Connell, R., & Pearse, R. (2015). *Gender: In world perspective* (3rd ed.). Cambridge: Polity.

Connell, R. W. (2005). *Masculinities.* Oakland: University of California Press.

Cook, C. R., Williams, K. R., Guerra, N. G., Kim, T. E., & Sadek, S. (2010). Predictors of bullying and victimization in childhood and adolescence: A meta-analytic investigation. *School Psychology Quarterly, 25*(2), 65–83. doi:10.1037/a0020149

Copeland, W. E., Wolke, D., Angold, A., & Costello, E. J. (2013, April). Adult psychiatric outcomes of bullying and being bullied by peers in childhood and adolescence. *JAMA Psychiatry, 70*(4), 419–426. Retrieved from https://jamanetwork.com/journals/jamapsychiatry/fullarticle/1654916

Cossins, A. (2003). Saints, sluts and sexual assault: Rethinking the relationship between sex, race and gender. *Social & Legal Studies, 12*(1), 77–103. doi:10.1177/0964663903012001845

Cowie, H. (2000). Bystanding or standing by: Gender issues in coping with bullying in English schools. *Aggressive Behavior, 26*(1), 85–97.

Crawford, E., & Wright, M. O. (2007). The impact of childhood psychological maltreatment on interpersonal schemas and subsequent experiences of relationship aggression. *Journal of Emotional Abuse, 7*(2), 93–116. Retrieved from https://psycnet.apa.org/record/2008-01102-006

Crick, N. R., & Dodge, K. A. (1999). "Superiority" is in the eye of the beholder: A comment of Sutton, Smith, and Swettenham. *Social Development, 8*, 128–131.

Crouch, J. L., Irwin, L. M., Milner, J. S., Skowronski, J. J., Rutledge, E., & Davila, A. L. (2017, May). Do hostile attributions and negative affect explain the association between authoritarian beliefs and harsh parenting? *Child Abuse & Neglect, 67*, 13–21. Retrieved from https://www.ncbi.nlm.nih.gov/pubmed/28236774

Currid-Halkett, E. (2017). *The sum of small things: A theory of the aspirational class.* Princeton, NJ: Princeton University Press.

D'Amato, G., Cecchi, L., Liccardi, G., Pellegrino, F., D'Amato, M., & Sofia, M. (2012). Social networks: A new source of psychological stress or a way to enhance self-esteem? Negative and positive implications in bronchial asthma. *Journal of Investigational Allergology and Clinical Immunology, 22*(6), 402–405. Retrieved from http://www.ncbi.nlm.nih.gov/pubmed/23101183

DeGruy, J. (2005). *Post traumatic slave syndrome: America's legacy of enduring injury and healing.* Milwaukie, OR: Uptone Press.

Derber, C., & Malgrass, Y. R. (2016). *Bully nation: How the American establishment creates a bullying society.* Lawrence: University Press of Kansas.

DeWitt, P., & Slade, S. (2014). *School climate change: How do I build a positive environment for learning?* Alexandria, VA: ASCD Arias.

Dollard, J., Doob, L., Miller, N., Mowrer, O., & Sears, R. (1939). *Frustration and aggression.* New Haven, CT: Yale University Press.

Due, P., Merlo, J., Harel-Fisch, Y., Damsgaard, M. T., Soc, M. S., Holstein, B. E., & Lynch, J. (2009). Socioeconomic inequality in exposure to bullying during adolescence: A comparative, cross-sectional, multilevel study in 35 countries. *American Journal of Public Health, 99*(5), 907–914. doi:10.2105/AJPH.2008.139303

Duong, M. T., Schwartz, D., Chang, L., Kelly, B. M., & Tom, S. R. (2009). Association between maternal physical discipline and peer victimization among Hong Kong Chinese children: The moderating role of child aggression. *Journal of Abnormal Child Psychology, 37*, 957–966.

Dweck, C. S. (2007). *Mindset: The new psychology of success.* New York: Random House.

Eastman, M., Foshee, V., Ennett, S., Sotres-Alvarez, D., McNaughton Reyes, H. L., Faris, R., et al. (2018). Profiles of internalizing and externalizing symptoms associated with bullying victimization. *Journal of Adolescence, 65*, 101–110. doi:10.1016/j.adolescence.2018.03.007

Ellenbogen, S. (2008). *From physical abuse victim to aggressor: Exploring the relationship.* Monteal, Quebec: Gill Library and Collections. Masters in Social Work thesis, Retrieved from ProQuest Central; ProQuest Dissertations & Theses Global. (Order No. NR66294.) http://digitool.library .mcgill.ca/R/?func=dbin-jump-full&object_id=115674 &local_base=GEN01-MCG02

Espelage, D. L., Bosworth, K., & Simon, T. R. (2000). Examining the social context of bullying behaviors in early adolescence. *Journal of Counseling and Development, 78,* 326–333.

Espelage, D. L., Holt, M. K., & Isaia, A. (2007). Dating violence among adolescents—Understanding the roles of attachment, self-esteem, dominance, and need for interpersonal control. In K. A. Kendall-Tackett & S. M. Giacomoni (Eds.), *Intimate partner violence* (pp. 14–15). Kingston, NJ: Civic Research Institute.

Espelage, D. L., & Swearer, S. M. (2010). A social-ecological model for bullying prevention and intervention: Understanding the impact of adults in the social ecology of youngsters. In S. R. Jimerson, S. M. Swearer, & D. L. Espelage (Eds.), *Handbook of bullying in schools: An international perspective* (pp. 61–72). New York: Routledge.

Espelage, D. L., & Swearer Napolitano, S. M. (2003). Research on school bullying and victimization: What have we learned and where do we go from here? *School Psychology Review, 32*(3), 365–383. Retrieved from http://digitalcommons.unl.edu/edpsychpapers/154

Estévez, E., Murgui, S., Moreno, D., & Musitu, G. (2007). Family communication styles, attitude towards institutional authority and adolescents' violent behaviour at school. *Psicothema, 19,* 108–113.

Evans, C., & Eder, D. (1993, July). "No exit": Processes of social isolation in the middle school. *Journal of Contemporary Ethnography, 22*(2), 139–170.

Evans-Campbell, T. (2008, March). Historical trauma in American Indian/Native Alaska communities. *Journal of Interpersonal Violence, 23*(3), 316–338. Retrieved from https://www.ncbi.nlm.nih.gov/pubmed/18245571

Fanti, K. A., Vanman, E., Henrich, C. C., & Avraamides, M. N. (2009). Desensitization to media violence over a short period of time. *Aggressive Behavior, 35*(2), 179–187.

Farmer, J., Phillip, L., King, G. J., Farrington, J., & MacLeod, M. (2010). Territorial tensions: Misaligned management and community perspectives on health services for older people in remote rural areas. *Health Place, 16*(2), 275–283.

Farmer, T. W., Estell, D. B., Bishop, J. L., O'Neal, K. K., & Cairns, B. D. (2003, November). Rejected bullies or popular leaders? The social relations of aggressive subtypes of rural African American early adolescents. *Developmental Psychology, 39*(6), 992–1004. Retrieved from https://www.ncbi.nlm.nih.gov/pubmed/14584980

Farmer, T. W., Lines, M. M., & Hamm, J. V. (2011, September–October). SI teachers and classroom social dynamics. *Journal of Applied Developmental Psychology, 32*(5), 247–312. Retrieved from https://www.sciencedirect.com/journal/journal-of-applied-developmental-psychology/vol/32/issue/5

Fekkes, M., Pijpers, F. I., Fredriks, A. M., Vogels, T., & Verloove-Vanhorick, S. P. (2006, May). Do bullied children get ill, or do ill children get bullied? A prospective cohort study on the relationship between bullying and health-related symptoms. *Pediatrics, 117*(5), 1568–1574. Retrieved from https://www.ncbi.nlm.nih.gov/pubmed/16651310

Fekkes, M., Pijpers, F. I. M., & Verloove-Vanhorick, S. P. (2005). Bullying: Who does what, when and where? Involvement of children, teachers and parents in bullying behavior. *Health Education Research, 20*(1), 81.

Felitti, V. J., Anda, R. F., Nordenberg, D., Williamson, D. F., Spitz, A. M., Edwards, V., et al. (1998). Relationship of childhood abuse and household dysfunction to many of the leading causes of death in adults: The Adverse Childhood Experiences (ACE) Study. *American Journal of Preventive Medicine, 14*(4), 245–258. doi:10.1016/S0749-3797(98)00017-8

Felmlee, D., & Faris, R. (2016). Toxic ties: Networks of friendship, dating, and cyber victimization. *Social*

Psychology Quarterly, 79(3), 243–262. doi:10.1177 /0190272516656585

Felsen, I. (1998). Transgenerational transmission of effects of the Holocaust. In Y. Danieli (Ed.), *International handbook of multigenerational legacies of trauma* (pp. 43–68). New York: Plenum.

Forster, M., Gower, A. L., McMorris, B. J., & Borowsky, I. W. (2017, January). Adverse childhood experiences and school-based victimization and perpetration. *Journal of Interpersonal Violence.* doi:10.1177/0886260517689885

Fox News Associated Press. (2019, May). Texas school shooter's father suspects bullying caused him to snap. Retrieved from https://www.foxnews.com/us /texas-school-shooters-father-suspects- bullying-caused -him-to-snap

Fraser, A. M., Padilla-Walker, L. M., Coyne, S. M., Nelson, L. J., & Stockdale, L. A. (2012). Associations between violent video gaming, empathic concern, and prosocial behavior toward strangers, friends, and family members. *Journal of Youth and Adolescence, 41*(5), 636–649.

Friedson, M. (2016, January). Authoritarian parenting attitudes and social origin: The multigenerational relationship of socioeconomic position to childrearing values. *Child Abuse & Neglect, 51*(1), 263–275. Retrieved from https://www.sciencedirect.com/science/article/abs/pii /S0145213415003592

Funk, J. B., Baldacci, H. B., Pasold, T., & Baumgardner, J. (2004). Violence exposure in real-life, video games, television, movies, and the internet: Is there desensitization? *Journal of Adolescence, 27*(1), 23–39.

Garandeau, C. F., Lee, I. A., & Salmivalli, C. (2014, July). Inequality matters: Classroom status hierarchy and adolescents' bullying. *Journal of Youth Adolescence, 43*(7), 1123–1133. doi:10.1007/s10964-013-0040-4

Garbarino, J. (2007). *See Jane hit: Why girls are growing more violent and what we can do about it.* New York: Penguin.

Georgiou, S. N., Fousiani, K., Michaelides, M., & Stavrinides, P. (2013). Cultural value orientation and authoritarian parenting as parameters of bullying and victimization at school. *International Journal of Psychology, 48*(1), 69–78.

Gerberg, P. L., & Brown, R. P. (2015). Yoga and neuronal pathways to enhance stress response, emotion regulation, bonding, and spirituality. In E. G. Horowitz & S. Elgelid (Eds.), *Yoga therapy: Theory and practice* (pp. 49–64). New York: Routledge.

Gerberg, P. L., & Brown, R. P. (2016, November). Neurobiology and neurophysiology of breath practices in psychiatric care. *Psychiatric Times, 33*(11), 22–25. Retrieved from https://www.psychiatrictimes.com/special-reports /neurobiology-and-neurophysiology-breath-practices -psychiatric-care

Gerberg, P. L., Brown, R. P., Streeter, C. C., Katzman, M., & Vermani, M. (2019). Breath practices for survivor and caregiver stress, depression, and post-traumatic stress disorder: Connection, co-regulation, compassion. *OBM Integrative and Complementary Medicine.*

Gerth, H. H., & Wright Mills, C. W. (Eds.). (1946). *From Max Weber: Essays in sociology.* Oxford: Oxford University Press.

Gibb, B. E., Alloy, L. B., & Abramson, L. Y. (2003). Global reports of childhood maltreatment versus recall of specific maltreatment experiences: Relationships with dysfunctional attitudes and depressive symptoms. *Cognition and Emotion, 17*, 903–915.

Gibb, B. E., Chelminski, I., & Zimmerman, M. (2007). Childhood emotional, physical, and sexual abuse, and diagnoses of depressive and anxiety disorders in adult psychiatric outpatients. *Depression and Anxiety, 24*(4), 256–263. doi:10.1002/da.20238

Gini, G., Albiero, P., Benelli, B., & Altoe, G. (2008). Participants: Determinants of adolescents' active defending and passive bystanding behavior in bullying. *Journal of Adolescence, 31*(1), 93–105. doi:10.1016/j.adolescence.2007.05.002

Glendinning, P. M. (2001, September). Workplace bullying: Curing the cancer of the American workplace. *Public Personnel Management, 30*(3), 269–286. doi:10.1177/009102600103000301

Goldsmith, R. E., & Freyd, J. J. (2005, April). Awareness for emotional abuse. *Journal of Emotional Abuse, 5*(1), 95–123.

Gómez-Ortiz, O., Romera, M., & Ortega-Ruiz, R. (2016, January). Parenting styles and bullying: The mediating role of parental psychological aggression and physical punishment. *Child Abuse & Neglect, 51*, 132–143.

Gonsalkorale, K., & Williams, K. D. (2007). The KKK won't let me play: Ostracism even by a despised outgroup hurts. *European Journal of Social Psychology, 37*, 1176–1186. doi:10.1002/ejsp.392

Gourley, E. C. (2016). Getting to yes-means-yes: Re-thinking responses to rape and rape culture on college campuses. *Washington University Journal of Law & Policy, 52*, 195.

Graff, G. (2014). The intergenerational trauma of slavery and its aftermath. *Journal of Psychohistory, 41*(3), 181–197.

Guo, X., Zheng, L., Wang, H., Zhu, L., Li, J., Wang, Q., & Yang, Z. (2013). Exposure to violence reduces empathetic responses to other's pain. *Brain and Cognition, 82*(2), 187–191.

Hand, J. Z., & Sanchez, L. (2000, December). Badgering or bantering?: Gender differences in experience of, and reactions to, sexual harassment among U.S. high school students. *Gender and Society, 14*(6), 718–746. doi:10.1177/089124300014006002

Harel-Fisch, Y., Walsh, S. D., Fogel-Grinvald, H., Dostaler, S., Hetland, J., Simons-Morton, B., & Pickett, W. (2009). A cross-national profile of bullying and victimization among adolescents in 40 countries. *International Journal of Public Health, 54*, 216–224.

Heinemann, P.-P. (1972). *Gruppvåld bland barn och vuxna [Group violence among children and adults].* Stockholm: Natur och kultur.

Hidaka, B. H. (2012). Depression as a disease of modernity: Explanations for increasing prevalence. *Journal of Affective Disorders, 140*(3), 205–214. doi:10.1016/j.jad.2011.12.036

Hodgdon, C., Tondkar, R. H., Adhikari, A., & Harless, D. W. (2009). Compliance with International Financial Reporting Standards and auditor choice: New evidence on the importance of the statutory audit. *International Journal of Accounting, 44*(1), 33–55.

Hofstede, G. (1997). *Cultures and organizations: Software of the mind.* New York: McGraw-Hill.

Hoglund, W. L. G. (2007). School functioning in early adolescence: Gender-linked responses to peer victimization. *Journal of Educational Psychology, 99*(4), 683–699.

Holt, M. K., Vivolo-Kantor, A. M., Polanin, J. R., Holland, K. M., DeGue, S., Matjasko, J. L., & Reid, G. (2015). Bullying and suicidal ideation and behaviors: A meta-analysis. *Pediatrics, 135*(2), e496.

Hornor, G. (2018, July–August). Bullying: What the PNP needs to know. *Journal of Pediatric Health Care, 32*(4), 409–410. Retrieved from https://www.jpedhc.org/article/S0891-5245(18)30079-8/fulltext

Human Rights Campaign. (2019). Glossary of terms. Retrieved from https://www.hrc.org/resources/glossary-of-terms

Hutchinson, L., & Mueller, D. (2008). Sticks and stones and broken bones: The influence of parental verbal abuse on peer related victimization. *Western Criminology Review, 9*(1), 17–30.

Ivarsson, T., Broberg, A. G., Arvidsson, T., & Gillberg, C. (2005). Bullying in adolescence: Psychiatric problems in victims and bullies as measured by the Youth Self Report (YSR) and the Depression Self-Rating Scale (DSRS). *Nordic Journal of Psychiatry, 59*(5), 365–373. Retrieved from https://www.ncbi.nlm.nih.gov/pubmed /16757465

Izadi, E. (2011, November). Bullying by race: Which teens get picked on most. DCentric. Retrieved from http://dcentric .wamu.org/2011/11/bullying-by-race-which-teens-get -picked-on-most/index.html

James, D. J., Lawlor, M., Courtney, P., Flynn, A., Henry, B., & Murphy, N. (2008, May). Bullying behaviour in secondary schools: What roles do teachers play? *Child Abuse Review, 17*(3), 160–173. doi:10.1002/car.1025

Jan, A., & Husain, S. (2015). Bullying in elementary schools: Its causes and effects on students. *Journal of Education and Practice, 6*(19), 43–56.

Jones, L. M., Mitchell, K. J., & Turner, H. A. (2015, December). Victim reports of bystander reactions to in-person and online peer harassment: A national survey of adolescents. *Journal of Youth and Adolescence, 44*(12), 2308–2320.

Juvonen, J., & Graham, S. (2014, January). Bullying in schools: The power of bullies and the plight of victims. *Annual Review of Psychology, 65*, 159–185.

Juvonen, J., Graham, S., & Schuster, M. A. (2003, December). Bullying among young adolescents: The strong, the weak, and the troubled. *Pediatrics, 112*(6), 1231–1237. Retrieved from https://www.ncbi.nlm.nih.gov /pubmed/14654590

Kahane-Nissembaum, M. (2011). Exploring intergenerational trauma in third generation holocaust survivors. *Doctorate in*

Social Work (DSW) Dissertations, 16, 1–81. Retrieved from https://repository.upenn.edu/edissertations_sp2/16

Kaltiala-Heino, R., Rimpela, M., Marttunen, M., Rimpela, A., & Rantanen, P. (1999, August). Bullying, depression, and suicidal ideation in Finnish adolescents: School survey. *British Medical Journal, 319*(7206), 348–351. Retrieved from https://www.bmj.com/content/319/7206/348.full

Keisner, J., & Pastore, M. (2005, November–December). Differences in the relationships between antisocial behavior and peer acceptance across contexts and across adolescence. *Child Development, 76*(6), 1278–1293. Retrieved from https://www.ncbi.nlm.nih.gov/pubmed/16274440

Kim, J., & Cicchetti, D. (2010). Longitudinal pathways linking child maltreatment, emotion regulation, peer relations, and psychopathology. *Journal of Child Psychology and Psychiatry, 51*(6), 706–716.

Kimmel, M. (2008). *Guyland: The perilous world where boys become men.* New York: HarperCollins.

Kimmel, M., & Mahler, M. (2003, June). Adolescent masculinity, homophobia, and violence: Random school shootings, 1982–2001. *American Behavioral Scientist, 46*(10), 1439–1458.

Klain, E., & Pavić, L. (2002). Psychotrauma and reconciliation. *Croatian Medical Journal, 43*(2), 126–137.

Klein, J. (2006, July). Cultural capital and high school bullies: How social inequality impacts school violence. *Men and Masculinities, 9*(1), 53–75.

Klein, J. (2012a). *The bully society: School shootings and the crisis of bullying in America's schools.* New York: NYU Press.

Klein, J. (2012b). *For educators: The Bully society: School shootings and the crisis of bullying in America's schools.* New York: NYU Press. Retrieved from https://nyupress.org /resources/for-educators/ or jessieklein.com

Klein, J., & Chancer, L. S. (2000). Masculinity matters: The role of gender in high-profile school violence cases. In S. U. Spina (Ed.), *Smoke and mirrors: The hidden context of violence in schools and society* (pp. 129–162). New York: Rowman and Littlefield.

Ko, C., Liu, G., Hsiao, S., Yen, J., Yang, M., Lin, W., Yen, C., & Chen, C. (2009). Brain activities associated with gaming urge of online gaming addiction. *Journal of Psychiatric Research, 43*(7), 739–747. doi:10.1016/j.jpsychires.2008.09.012

Kochenderfer-Ladd, B., & Wardrop, J. L. (2001). Chronicity and instability of children's peer victimization experiences as predictors of loneliness and social satisfaction trajectories. *Child Development, 72*, 134–151. doi:10.1111/1467-8624.00270

Konrath, S. H., O'Brien, E. H., & Hsing, C. (2011) Changes in dispositional empathy in American college students over time: A meta-analysis. *Personality and Social Psychology Review, 15*(2), 180–198. doi:10.1177/1088868310377395

Koo, H. (2007). A time line of the evolution of school bullying in differing social contexts. *Asia Pacific Education Review, 8*(1), 107–116. Retrieved from https://files.eric.ed.gov/fulltext/EJ768971.pdf

Kosciw, J. G., & Diaz, E. M. (2006). The 2005 National School Climate Survey: The experiences of lesbian, gay, bisexual and transgender youth in our nation's schools. New York: GLSEN. Retrieved from https://www.glsen.org/sites/default/files/2005%20National%20School%20Climate%20Survey%20Full%20Report.pdf

Kumpulainen, K., Räsänen, E., & Henttonen, I. (1999). Children involved in bullying: Psychological disturbance and the persistence of the involvement. *Child Abuse & Neglect, 23*(12), 1253–1262. doi:10.1016/S0145-2134(99)00098-8

Kupelian, D., Kalayjian, A., & Kassabian, A. (1998). The Turkish genocide of the Armenians: Continuing effects on survivors and their families eight decades after massive trauma. In Y. Danieli (Ed.), *International handbook of multigenerational legacies of trauma* (pp. 191–210). New York: Plenum.

Land, D. (2003, May). Teasing apart secondary students' conceptualizations of peer teasing, bullying and sexual harassment. *School Psychology International, 24*(2), 147–165. doi:10.1177/0143034303024002002

Langos, C. (2012, June). Cyberbullying: The challenge to define. *Cyberpsychology, Behavior, and Social Networking, 15*(6), 285–289.

Lasker, A. (2018, May). Santa Fe high school student claims students and coaches "emotionally bullied" suspected shooter. Retrieved from https://www.aol.com/article/news/2018/05/18/santa-fe-high-school-shooting-suspect-dimitrios-pagourtiz-emotionally-bullied/23438298/

Lawrence, R. (1998). *School crime and juvenile justice.* New York: Oxford University Press.

Leeb, R. T., Paulozzi, L. J., Melanson, C., Simon, T. R., & Arias, I. (2008, January). Child maltreatment surveillance: Uniform definitions for public health and recommended data elements. Centers for Disease Control and Prevention. Retrieved from https://www.cdc.gov/violenceprevention/pdf/CM_Surveillance-a.pdf

Lefkowitz, B. (1997, July). *Our guys: The Glen Ridge rape and the secret life of the perfect suburb.* Berkeley: University of California Press.

Lereya, S. T., Samara, M., & Wolke, D. (2013, December). Parenting behavior and the risk of becoming a victim and a bully/victim: A meta-analysis study. *Child Abuse & Neglect, 37*(12), 1091–1108. Retrieved from https://www.ncbi.nlm.nih.gov/pubmed/23623619

Levine, M. (2008, July). *The price of privilege: How parental pressure and material advantage are creating a generation of disconnected and unhappy kids.* New York, NY: Harper Perennial.

Madigan, S., Ly, A., Rash C. L., Van Outsyel, J., & Temple, J. R. (2018, February 26). Prevalence of multiple forms of sexting behavior among youth: A systematic review and meta-analysis. *JAMA Pediatrics.* doi:101001/jamapediatrics.2017.5314

Marengo, D., Longobardi, C., Fabris, M. A., & Settanni, M. (2018). Highly-visual social media and internalizing symptoms in adolescence: The mediating role of body image concerns. *Computers in Human Behavior, 82,* 63–69.

Martínez, I., Murgui, S., Garcia, F., & Garcia, O. F. (2019). Parenting in the digital era: Protective and risk parenting styles for traditional bullying and cyberbullying victimization. *Computers in Human Behavior, 90,* 84–92.

Masi, C. M., Chen, H. Y., Hawkley, L. C., & Cacioppo. J. T. (2011). A meta-analysis of interventions to reduce loneliness. *Personality and Social Psychology Review, 15,* 219–266. doi:10.1177/1088868310377394

Mazzei, P. (2019, March 24). After 2 apparent student suicides, Parkland grieves again. *New York Times.* Retrieved from https://www.nytimes.com/2019/03/24/us/parkland-suicide-marjory-stoneman-douglas.html

McEvoy, A. (2005). Teachers who bully students: Patterns and policy implications. Retrieved from http://www.s3az.org/updates/Summer_2012/Bullying/Teachers.pdf

McNicholas, C. I., & Orpinas, P. (2016, September). Prevalence of bullying victimisation among students with disabilities in the United States. *Injury Prevention, 22*(Suppl. 2), A1–A397.

McPherson, M., Smith-Lovin, L., & Vrashears, M. E. (2006, June). Social isolation in America: Changes in core discussion networks over two decades. *American Sociological Review, 71*(3), 353–375.

Merten, D. E. (1997, July). The meaning of meanness: Popularity, competition, and conflict among junior high school girls. *Sociology of Education, 70*(3), 175–191.

Messerschmidt, J. W. (2000). *Nine lives: Adolescent masculinities, the body, and violence.* New York: Westview.

Miller, J. G. (2018). Physiological mechanisms of prosociality. *Current Opinion in Psychology, 20*, 50–54.

Moretti, M. M., & Craig, S. G. (2013). Maternal versus paternal physical and emotional abuse, affect regulation and risk for depression from adolescence to early adulthood. *Child Abuse & Neglect, 37*(1), 4–13. doi:10 .1016/j.chiabu.2012.09.015

Mrug, S., Madan, A., Cook, E. W., & Wright, R. A. (2015). Emotional and physiological desensitization to real-life and movie violence. *Journal of Youth and Adolescence, 44*(5), 1092–1108.

Nagata, D. K. (1991). Transgenerational impact of the Japanese-American internment: Clinical issues in working with children of former internees. *Psychotherapy: Theory, Research, Practice, Training, 28*(1), 121–128.

Namie, G. (2017). 2017 WBI U.S. workplace bullying survey. Workplace Bullying Institute. Retrieved from https://www.workplacebullying.org/wbiresearch/wbi-2017 -survey/

Nansel, T. R., Overpeck, M., Pilla, R. S., Ruan, W. J., Simons-Morton, B., & Scheidt, P. (2001, April). Bullying behaviors among US youth: Prevalence and association with psychosocial adjustment. *JAMA, 285*(16), 2094–2100.

National Center for Analysis of Violent Crime. (1999–2002). The school shooter: A quick reference guide. Retrieved from https://www.homelandsecurity.iowa.gov/documents /misc/FBI_School_Shooter_Guide.pdf

Nesdale, D., & Pickering, K. (2006). Teachers' reactions to children's aggression. *Social Development, 15*(1), 109–127.

Nesi, J., & Prinstein, M. J. (2015). Using social media for social comparison and feedback-seeking: Gender and popularity moderate associations with depressive symptoms. *Journal of Abnormal Child Psychology, 43*(8), 1427–1438.

Nickerson, A. B., Bryant R. A., Steel Z., Silove, D., & Brooks, R. (2010). The impact of fear for family on mental health in a resettled Iraqi refugee community. *Journal of Psychiatric Research, 44*(4), 229–235.

Nickerson, A. B., Mele, D., & Princiotta, D. (2008). Attachment and empathy as predictors of roles as defenders or outsiders in bullying situations. *Journal of School Psychology, 46*, 687–703. doi:10.1016/j.jsp.2008.06.002

O'Dell, L., Bertilsdotter-Rosqvist, H., & Brownlow, C. (2018). *Different childhoods: Non/normative development and transgressive trajectories.* London and New York: Routledge.

Olsen, E. O., Kann, L., Vivolo-Kantor, A., Kinchen, S., & McManus, T. (2014, September). School violence and bullying among sexual minority high school students, 2009–2011. *Journal Adolescent Health, 55*(3), 432–438.

Olweus, D. (1993). *Bullying at school: What we know and what we can do.* Hoboken, NJ: Wiley-Blackwell.

Olweus, D. (1995). Bullying or peer abuse at school: Facts and intervention. *Current Directions in Psychological Science, 4*(6), 196–200. doi:10.1111/1467-8721.ep10772640

Olweus, D. (1999). Bullying in Norway. In P. K. Smith, Y. Morita, J. Junger-Tas, D. Olweus, R. Catalano, & P. Slee (Eds.), *The nature of school bullying: A cross-national perspective* (pp. 28–48). London and New York: Routledge.

Olweus, D. (2003, March). A profile of bullying at school. *Bullying: A Research Project*. Retrieved from https://lhsela .weebly.com/uploads/7/9/0/8/7908073/_olweus_profile_of _bullying.pdf

Olweus, D. (2016, June). School bullying: Basic facts, intervention, and long-term effects. Olweus Group Against Bullying. Retrieved from http://cyfs.unl.edu/cyfsprojects /videoPPT/4be692cfe65fcc54603331b9a484208c/160613 -BPC-Olweus.pdf

Olweus, D., & Limber, S. P. (2010). Bullying in school: Evaluation and dissemination of the Olweus Bullying Prevention Program. *American Journal of Orthopsychiatry, 80*(1), 124–134. doi:10.1111/j.1939-0025.2010.01015.x

Ophir, Y. (2017). SOS on SNS: Adolescent distress on social network sites. *Computers in Human Behavior, 68*, 51–55.

Orpinas, P., & Horne, A. M. (2006). *Bullying prevention: Creating a positive school climate and developing social competence*. Washington, DC: American Psychological Association.

Orue, I., & Calvete, E. (2012). Justification of violence as a mediator between exposure to violence and aggressive behavior in children. *Psicothema, 24*, 42–47.

Ottens, A. J., & Hotelling, K. (2000, December). *Sexual violence on campus: Policies, programs, and perspectives*. New York: Springer.

Pabian, S., Vandebosch, H., Poels, K., Van Cleemput, K., & Bastiaensens, S. (2016, September). Exposure to cyberbullying as a bystander: An investigation of desensitization effects among early adolescents. *Computers in Human Behavior, 62*, 480–487.

Padgett, S., & Notar, C. E. (2013). Bystanders are the key to stopping bullying. *Universal Journal of Educational Research, 1*(2), 33–41.

Park, S., Shih, W., Presson, A. P., Mayer, E. A., & Chang, L. (2016, August). Adverse childhood experiences are associated with irritable bowel syndrome and gastrointestinal symptom severity. *Gastroenterology, 28*(8), 1252–1260. Retrieved from https://www.ncbi.nlm.nih.gov/pmc/articles /PMC4956522/

Patchin, J. W., & Hinduja, S. (2016, April). *Bullying today: Bullet points and best practices.* Thousand Oaks, CA: Corwin.

PBS News Hour (2014, February 20). Colorado high school replaces punishment with "talking circles." Retrieved from https://www.youtube.com/watch?v=g8_94O4ExSA

Perreira, K. M., & Ornelas, I. (2013). Painful passages: Traumatic experiences and post-traumatic stress among U.S. immigrant Latino adolescents and their primary caregivers. *International Migration Review, 47*(4), 976–1005.

Perry, B. D., & Szalavitz, M. (2011). *Born to love: Why empathy is essential—and endangered.* New York: William Morrow Paperbacks.

Peyton, R. P., Ranasinghe, S., & Jacobsen, K. H. (2017, March). Injuries, violence, and bullying among middle school students in Oman. *Oman Medical Journal, 32*(2), 98–105. Retrieved from https://europepmc.org/abstract /med/28439379

Pharo, H., Gross, J., Richardson, R., & Hayne, H. (2011). Age-related changes in the effect of ostracism. *Social Influence, 6*(1), 22–38. doi:10.1080/15534510.2010.525852

Pickel, K. L., & Gentry, R. H. (2017). Slut shaming in a school bullying case: Evaluators ignore level of harm when the victim self-presents as sexually available. *Sex Roles, 76*(1), 89–98. doi:10.1007/s11199-016-0662-6

Pickett, K., & Wilkinson, R. (2010, November). *The spirit level: Why equality is better for everyone.* East Rutherford, NJ: Penguin.

Porges, S. W., & Carter, C. S. (2017). Polyvagal theory and the social engagement system: Neurophysiological bridge between connectedness and health. In P. L. Gerbarg, R. P. Brown, & P. R. Muskin (Eds.), *Complementary and Integrative Treatments in Psychiatric Practice* (pp. 221–240). Washington, DC: American Psychiatric Association.

Rawlings, V. (2017). *Gender regulation, violence, and social hierarchies in school: Sluts, gays, and scrubs.* London: Palgrave Macmillan.

Reijntjes, A., Kamphuis, J. H., Prinzie, P., & Telch, M. J. (2010). Peer victimization and internalizing problems in children: A meta-analysis of longitudinal studies. *Child Abuse and Neglect, 34,* 244–252. doi:10.1016/j.chiabu .2009.07.009

Reijntjes, A., Vermande, M., Olthof, T., Goossens, F. A., van de Schoot, R., Aleva, L., & van der Meulen, M. (2013). Costs and benefits of bullying in the context of the peer group: A three wave longitudinal analysis. *Journal of Abnormal Child Psychology, 41,* 1217–1229.

Reiney, E., & Limber, S. P. (2013, October 23). Why we don't use the word "bully" to label kids. StopBullying.gov. Retrieved from https://www.stopbullying.gov/blog/2013 /10/23/why-we-dont-use-word-bully-label-kids.html

Rieder, B. (2013), Studying Facebook via data extraction: The Netvizz application. *Proceedings of the 5th Annual ACM Web Science Conference.* ACM; 346–355.

Rigby, K. (1996). *Bullying in schools and what to do about it.* Melbourne: Australian Council for Educational Research.

Rigby, K. (1998, October). The relationship between reported health and involvement in bully/victim problems among male and female secondary schoolchildren. *Journal of Health Psychology, 3*(4), 465–476. Retrieved from https:// www.ncbi.nlm.nih.gov/pubmed/22021407

Rigby, K. (2003, October). Consequences of bullying in schools. *Canadian Journal of Psychiatry, 48*(9), 583–591. doi:10.1177/070674370304800904

Rigby, K., & Slee, P. (1999). Suicidal ideation among adolescent school children, involvement in bully-victim problems, and perceived social support. *Suicide & Life-Threatening Behavior, 29*(2), 119–130.

Ringrose, J., Harvey, L., Gill, R., & Livingstone, S. (2013). Teen girls, sexual double standards and "sexting": Gendered value in digital image exchange. *Feminist Theory, 14*(3), 305–323. doi:10.1177/1464700113499853

Ringrose, J., & Rawlings, V. (2015). Posthuman performativity, gender and school bullying: Exploring the material-discursive intra-actions of skirts, hair, sluts, and poofs. *Confero: Essays on Education, Philosophy and Politics, 3*(2), 80–119. Retrieved from http://www.confero.ep.liu.se /issues/2015/v3/i2/150626a/confero15v3i2150626a.pdf

Rivers, I., & Smith. P. K. (1994). Types of bullying behavior and their correlates. *Aggressive Behavior, 20*, 359–368.

Rocque, M., & Duwe, G. (2018). Rampage shootings: An historical, empirical, and theoretical overview. *Current Opinion in Psychology, 19*, 28–33. doi:10.1016/j.copsyc .2017.03.025

Rogers, K. N., Buchanan, C. M., & Winchel, M. E. (2003). Psychological control during early adolescence: Links to adjustment in differing parent/adolescent dyads. *Journal of Early Adolescence, 23*, 349–383.

Rose, A. J., Swenson, L. P., & Waller, E. M. (2004, May). Overt and relational aggression and perceived popularity: Developmental differences in concurrent and prospective relations. *Developmental Psychology, 40*(3), 378–387. Retrieved from https://www.ncbi.nlm.nih.gov/pubmed /15122964

Rozsa, L., Berman, M., & Merle, R. (2018, February). Accused South Florida school shooter confessed to rampage that killed 17 people, police say. *Washington Post*. Retrieved from https://www.washingtonpost.com/news/post-nation

/wp/2018/02/15/florida-school-shooting-suspect-booked
-on-17-counts-of-murder-premeditated/

Sacks, V., & Murphey, D. (2018, February 20). The
prevalence of adverse childhood experiences, nationally,
by state, and by race or ethnicity. Child Trends. Retrieved
from https://www.childtrends.org/publications/prevalence
-adverse-childhood-experiences-nationally-state-race
-ethnicity

Salmivalli, C., Lagerspetz, K., Björkqvist, K., Osterman, K.,
& Kaukiainen, A. (1996). Bullying as a group process:
Participant roles and their relations to social status within
the group. *Aggressive Behavior, 22*, 1–15.

Sanchez, E., Robertson, T., Lewis, C., Rosenbluth, B.,
Bohman, T., & Casey, D. (2001). Preventing bullying
and sexual harassment in elementary schools. *Journal of
Emotional Abuse, 2*(2–3), 157–180. doi:10.1300/J135v
02n02_10

Schacter, H. L., White, S. J., Chang, V. Y., & Juvonen, J.
(2015). "Why me?": Characterological self-blame and
continued victimization in the first year of middle school.
Journal of Clinical Child & Adolescent Psychology, 44(3),
446–455.

Scharrer, E. (2008). Media exposure and sensitivity to
violence in news reports: Evidence of desensitization.
Journalism & Mass Communication Quarterly, 85(2),
291–310.

Schwartz, D., Dodge, K. A., Pettit, G. S., & Bates, J. E.
(1997). The early socialization of aggressive victims
of bullying. *Child Development, 68*(4), 665–675.
doi:10.1111/j.1467-8624.1997.tb04228.x

Servadio, G. (2005). *Renaissance woman*. New York: I. B.
Tauris & Co.

Shore, T. W. (1906). *Origin of the Anglo-Saxon race: A study of the settlement of England and the tribal origin of the Old English people.* London: E. Stock.

Simmons, R. (2011). *Odd girl out: The hidden culture of aggression in girls.* Boston, MA: Mariner Books.

Simon, T. R., Ikeda, R. M., Smith, E. P., Reese, L. R. E., Rabiner, D. L., Miller, S., et al. (2009). The ecological effects of universal and selective violence prevention programs for middle school students: A randomized trial. *Journal of Consulting and Clinical Psychology, 77*(3), 526–542. doi:10.1037/a0014395

Skiba, R. J. (2014). The failure of zero tolerance. *Reclaiming Children and Youth, 22*(4), 27–33.

Skiba, R. J., & Knesting, K. (2001, December). Zero tolerance, zero evidence: An analysis of school disciplinary practice. *New Directions for Student Leadership, 92,* 17–43.

Smith, P. K. (2004, September). Bullying: Recent developments. *Child and Adolescent Mental Health, 9*(3), 98–103. doi:10.1111/j.1475-3588.2004.00089.x

Smith, P. K., & Thompson, D. A. (1991). *Practical approaches to bullying.* London: David Fulton.

StopBullying.gov. (2017, August). Fact sheet: Bullying as an adverse childhood experience (ACE). Retrieved from https://www.stopbullying.gov/sites/default/files/2017-10/bullying-as-an-ace-fact-sheet.pdf

StopBullying.gov. (2019). What is bullying? Retrieved from https://www.stopbullying.gov/what-is-bullying/index.html

Strøm, I. F., Thoresen, S., Wentzel-Larsen, T. Sagatun, A., & Dyb, G. (2014). A prospective study of the potential moderating role of social support in preventing marginalization among individuals exposed to bullying and abuse in junior high school youth. *Adolescence, 43,* 1642–1657.

Sutherland, A. (2006). *The relationship among parental and peer victimization and adolescent maladjustment* (Master's thesis). Queen's University, Kingston, Ontario, Canada, 1–58.

Sutton, J., Smith, P. K., & Swettenham, J. (1999). Bullying and "theory of mind": A critique of the social skills deficit view of antisocial behaviour. *Social Development, 8*(1), 117–127.

Swearer, S. M., & Doll, B. (2001). Bullying in schools: An ecological framework. *Journal of Emotional Abuse, 2*(2–3), 7–23. doi:10.1300/J135v02n02_02

Swearer, S. M., Espelage, D. L., & Napolitano, S. A. (2009, January). *Bullying prevention and intervention: Realistic strategies for schools.* New York: Guilford.

Swearer, S. M., Espelage, D. L., Vaillancourt, T., & Hymel, S. (2010). What can be done about school bullying?: Linking research to educational practice. *Educational Researcher, 39*(1), 38–47. doi:10.3102/0013/0013189X09357622

Swearer, S. M., Song, S. Y., Cary, P. T., Eagle, J. W., & Mickelson, W. T. (2001). Psychosocial correlates in bullying and victimization: The relationship between depression, anxiety, and bully/victim status. *Journal of Emotional Abuse, 2*(2–3), 95–121. doi:10.1300/J135v02n02_07

Swearer Napolitano, S. M. (2008, November 10). Bullying and depression. Retrieved from http://digitalcommons.unl .edu/edpsychpapers/134

Sweeting, H., Young, R., West, P., & Der, G. (2006). Peer victimization and depression in early-mid adolescence: A longitudinal study. *British Journal of Educational Psychology, 76*, 577–594. doi:10.1348/000709905X49890

Taillieu, T. L., & Brownridge, D. A. (2013). Aggressive parental discipline experienced in childhood and internalizing problems in early adulthood. *Journal of Family Violence, 28*, 445–458.

Ttofi, M. M., & Farrington, D. P. (2008, May). Bullying: Short-term and long-term effects, and the importance of defiance theory in explanation and prevention. *Victims & Offenders, 3*(2–3), 289–312. doi:10.1080/15564880802143397

Ttofi, M. M., & Farrington, D. P. (2011). Effectiveness of school-based programs to reduce bullying: A systematic and meta-analytic review. *Journal of Experimental Criminology, 7*(1), 27–56.

Türkmen, D. N., Dokgöz, M. H., Akgöz, S. S., Eren, B. N., Vural, H. P., & Polat, H. O. (2013). Bullying among high school students. *Maedica, 8*(2), 143–152.

Twemlow, S. W., & Fonagy, P. (2005, December). The prevalence of teachers who bully students in schools with differing levels of behavioral problems. *American Journal of Psychiatry, 162*(12), 2387–2388. doi:10.1176/appi.ajp.162.12.2387

Twemlow, S. W., Fonagy, P., Sacco, F. C., & Brethour, J. R. (2006, May). Teachers who bully students: A hidden trauma. *International Journal of Social Psychiatry, 52*(3), 187–198. doi:10.1177/0020764006067234

Twenge, J. M. (2006, April). *The me generation: Why today's young Americans are more confident, assertive, entitled—And more miserable than ever before.* New York: Simon & Schuster.

Twenge, J. M., Gentile, B., DeWall, C. N., Ma, D., Lacefield, K., & Schurtz, D. R. (2010). Birth cohort increases in psychopathology among young Americans, 1938–2007: A cross-temporal meta-analysis of the MMPI. *Clinical Psychology Review, 30*(2), 145–154. doi:10.1016/j.cpr.2009.10.005

Twenge, J. M., Joiner, T. E., Rogers, M. L., & Martin, G. N. (2018). Increases in depressive symptoms, suicide-related outcomes, and suicide rates among U.S. adolescents after 2010 and links to increased new media screen time. *Clinical Psychological Science, 6*(1), 3–17. doi:10.1177/2167702617723376

Vaillancourt, T., & Hymel, S. (2006). Aggression and social status: The moderating roles of sex and peer-valued characteristics. *Aggressive Behavior, 32*(4), 396–408.

Vaillancourt, T., Hymel, S., & McDougall, P. (2003). Bullying is power: Implications for school-based intervention strategies. *Journal of Applied School Psychology, 19*, 157–176. doi:10.1300/J008v19n02_10

Van Cleemput, K., Vandebosch, H., & Pabian, S. (2014). Personal characteristics and contextual factors that determine "helping," "joining in," and "doing nothing" when witnessing cyberbullying. *Aggressive Behavior, 40*(5), 383–396.

Vandebosch, H., & Cleemput, K. V. (2008, August). Defining cyberbullying: A qualitative research into the perceptions of youngsters. *CyberPsychology & Behavior, 11*(4), 499–503.

Vaughn, M. G., Fu, Q., Beaver, K. M., DeLisi, M., Perron, B. E., & Howard, M. O. (2011). Effects of childhood adversity on bullying and cruelty to animals in the United States: Findings from a national sample. *Journal of Interpersonal Violence, 26*(17), 3509–3525. doi:10.1177/0886260511403763

Vega, G., & Comer, D. R. (2005, May). Sticks and stones may break your bones, but words can break your spirit: Bullying in the workplace. *Journal of Business Ethics, 58*(1–3), 101–109. Retrieved from https://link.springer.com/article/10.1007/s10551-005-1422-7

Violence Prevention Works Olweus Bullying Prevention Program. (2007). The world's foremost bullying prevention program. Hazelden Foundation. Retrieved from http://www.violencepreventionworks.org/public/olweus_bullying_prevention_program.page

Waldman, A. E. (2018). Are anti-bullying laws effective? *Cornell Law Review, 103*, 135–144.

Wallace, J. B. (2018, May 4). Review—The teenage social-media trap—Adolescents increasingly measure and manage social success online, and it may be taking a toll on their mental health. *Wall Street Journal*. Retrieved from https://www.wsj.com/articles/the-teenage-social-media-trap-1525444767

Wang, J., Iannotti, R. J., & Luk, J. W. (2012). Patterns of adolescent bullying behaviors: Physical, verbal, exclusion, rumor, and cyber. *Journal of School Psychology, 50*(4), 521–534.

Wang, J., Iannotti, R. J., Luk, J. W., & Nansel, T. R. (2010). Co-occurrence of victimization from five subtypes of bullying: Physical, verbal, social exclusion, spreading rumors, and cyber. *Journal of Pediatric Psychology, 35*, 1103–1112.

Wang, M. T., & Kenny, S. (2014). Parental physical discipline and adolescent adjustment: Bidirectionality and the moderation effects of child ethnicity and parental warmth. *Journal of Abnormal Child Psychology, 42*, 717–730.

Wehrwein, P. (2011, October 20). Astounding increase in antidepressant use by Americans. Retrieved from https://www.health.harvard.edu/blog/astounding-increase-in-antidepressant-use-by-americans-201110203624

Wei, M. (2017). Bullying, incognito: Deliberate social exclusion. Psych Central. Retrieved from https://psychcentral.com/blog/bullying-incognito-deliberate-social-exclusion/

Weinhold, B. K. (2000). Uncovering the hidden causes of bullying and school violence. *Counseling and Human Development, 32*(6), 1.

White, C. (2018, November 14). ACEs teach us why racism is a health equity issue: Dr. Flojaune Cofer (part one). Parenting with ACES: ACES Sciences & Stories. Retrieved from https://www.acesconnection.com/g/Parenting-with-ACEs/blog/aces-teach-us-why-racism-is-a-health-equity-issue-dr-flojaune-cofer-part-one

Whitted, K. S., & Dupper, D. R. (2008, March). Do teachers bully students?: Findings from a survey of students in an alternative education setting. *Education and Urban Society, 40*(3), 329–341. doi:10.1177/0013124507304487

Williams, K. D. (2007). Ostracism. *Annual Review of Psychology, 58*, 425–452. doi:10.1146/annurev.psych.58.110405.085641

Wiseman, R. (2016, July). *Queen bees and wannabes: Helping your daughter survive cliques, gossip, boys, and the new realities of girl world* (3rd ed.). New York: Harmony.

Xie, H., Farmer, T. W., & Cairns, B. D. (2003). Different forms of aggression among inner-city African American children: Gender, configurations, and school social networks. *Journal of School Psychology, 4*(5), 355–375.

Zadro, L., Williams, K. D., & Richardson, R. (2004). How low can you go?: Ostracism by a computer is sufficient to lower self-reported levels of belonging, control, self-esteem, and meaningful existence. *Journal of Experimental Social Psychology, 40*, 560–567. doi:10.1016/j.jesp.2003.11.006

Zhang, Y., Tian, J., von Deneen, K. M., Liu, Y., & Gold, M. S. (2012). Process addictions in 2012: Food, internet and gambling. *Neuropsychiatry, 2*(2), 155–161. doi:10.2217/npy.12.14

Zhao, X. (2011). *Development under stress: The culture of academic competition and adolescent friendship participation in china's secondary school* (Dissertation). Cambridge, MA: Harvard Graduate School of Education. Retrieved from ProQuest Dissertations Publishing.

Zimmer-Gembeck, M. J., Pronk, R. E., Goodwin, B., Mastro, S., & Crick, N. R. (2012). Connected and isolated victims of relational aggression: Associations with peer group status and differences between girls and boys. *Sex Roles, 68*, 363–377. doi:10.1007/s11199-012-0239-y

Zottis, G. A. H., Salum, G. A., Isolan, L. R., Manfro, G. G., & Heldt, E. (2014). Associations between child disciplinary practices and bullying behavior in adolescents. *Journal de Pediatria, 90*, 408–414.

What can be done to support students who are bullied and to protect them from future assaults? How can we help youths who bully others to treat people instead with respect and dignity? School bullying is a complex social problem that requires critical analysis in order to address these questions.

This chapter outlines some problems and controversies, starting with the differences among scholars and experts on how to define bullying. Problems include concerns about whether bullying, like aggression, is innate and the extent to which schools, as social microcosms, mirror systemic social problems. Most important, what are the solutions and the recommendations for prevention and intervention?

Definition(s)

Bullying and Social Conflict

Before she wrote the book *Bullied*, Goldman (2012) wrote a popular article about her experiences with her own six-year-old child, who was being bullied at school. She posed the question: "When is it normal social conflict and when is it bullying?" On the Motherlode blog of the *New York Times* (2014), she wrote, "In normal social conflict, where each kid has relatively equal power, it is best for adults to avoid rescuing too soon. Let the kids try to work it

When school authorities and community leaders actively support GLBTQI+ students with gay-straight alliances, school bullying decreases. (Rick Eglinton/Toronto Star via Getty Images)

out first." If it is bullying, she cautions, adults should intervene immediately: "A power imbalance exists that limits the target's ability to make the cruelty stop" (see chapter 3 herein).

The Health Resources and Services Administration (HRSA n.d.) states, "Bullying is a form of victimization, *not* conflict. It is no more a 'conflict' than are child abuse or domestic violence." Goldman (2014) explains that normal social conflict tends to be over something external—like a third friend or an iPad. Without the external issue, the conflict would disappear. In bullying, a person's internal identity is attacked as with comments such as "you are fat" or "you are stupid" or "you are gay." Since these qualities can't be removed, as one might an external object, people tend to take them personally and feelings get hurt.

Others don't see the distinction between bullying and conflict to be as clear-cut. Writing about bullying in the workplace, Baillien et al. (2008) suggest that bullying *can* develop from escalated conflict, and Hoel et al. (1999) agree, seeing severe bullying as "unresolved conflict" (in Keashly & Nowell 2003). Zapf and Gross (2001) describe bullying as "long-lasting and badly managed conflicts" (499). Einarsen (1999) suggests that one type of bullying hinges on conflict: grievances among two or more parties that involve retaliation. If one or more party emerges as more powerful, another person may be bullied, and therein are the blurry lines between bullying and other types of conflict.

Variations

A consistent definition of bullying is helpful for statistical research, since it makes it more possible for researchers to assess comparable behaviors and create conditions for replicated research, and it makes it easier for school officials to report and respond specifically to these behaviors (Carrera et al. 2011). Even as the U.S. government has settled on a uniform bullying definition, though, multiple definitions are still used by researchers and experts.

Even slight variations in the definition can shift the way behavior is interpreted. Dan Olweus's (Olweus Bullying Prevention Program 2007) definition, for instance, is still considered the standard, with its three components of *intent, repetition,* and *power imbalance.* According to Olweus, bullying occurs "when someone repeatedly and on purpose says or does mean or hurtful things to another person who has a hard time defending himself or herself." For an action to be defined as bullying, Olweus specifies that the perpetrator has hurt the other party intentionally. At this stage in the evolution of the definition, Olweus does not address the injured party's experience.

Paraphrasing the Centers for Disease and Prevention's federal definition, StopBullying.gov (2019) posted a fourth component. In addition to determining *intent*, that the more powerful party purposely hurt the person perceived to be weaker, school officials need to determine that the latter person experienced the behavior negatively, specifically as *unwanted*. It defines bullying as "*unwanted, aggressive* behavior among school aged children that involves a real or perceived power imbalance. The behavior is repeated, or has the potential to be repeated, over time" (italics added).

Attempts to define bullying have also given rise to student protests. Until 2018, the *Oxford English Dictionary* defined a bully as "[a] person who uses strength or influence to harm or intimidate those who are weaker." Supported by the charity the Diana Award, students created the banner #IAMNOTWEAK and pressured Oxford and other dictionary publishers to take the word "weak" out of the definition. The activists explained that the word "weak" unfairly stigmatized bullied students. One leader in the movement said that the majority of bullied students he knows "are some of the strongest and bravest I've met" (BBC 2018, June).

The students won some victories. In 2018, the Google, Collins, Oxford, and Cambridge dictionaries took the word "weak" out of their definitions and offered a new set of meanings that focused on how the people bullying perceive the person they are hurting, rather than the character trait of the person being bullied. Oxford then rewrote the definition as "[a] person who habitually seeks to harm or intimidate those whom they *perceive as vulnerable*" (BBC 2018, June; italics added). Rather than an objectively determined power imbalance, the definition suggests that the power imbalance is based on a perspective.

Subjectivity

Given the four components of the U.S. federal definition of bullying—*intent, repetition, power imbalance*, and *unwantedness* on the part of the person being bullied—schools are charged with determining when behaviors meet these criteria.

What role, then, does a school official's subjectivity play in making this determination? How can schools ascertain whether the person accused of bullying *intended* to harm, whether a *power imbalance* exists among parties, and how many times the behavior is *repeated*? What if a student attacks a student perceived as weaker in front of many other students only once? Would that be bullying (Smith & Ananiadou 2003; Smith 2004; Bansel et al. 2009; Cornell & Bandyopadhyay 2010; Carrera et al. 2011)?

Schools may also misinterpret behaviors and then inadvertently overlook them. Hymel et al. (2010) write that assessing what behaviors qualify as bullying can be tricky: "Physical bullying is often construed as 'horsing around' or 'rough and tumble play'; verbal bullying can be mistaken for playful teasing among friends that can be dismissed if the perpetrator was 'just kidding'" (102).

Citing many other scholars, Felmlee and Faris also conclude that the formal definition of bullying is too limiting (2016: 245):

> Our definition departs from the strict definition of bullying, which requires that harmful behavior be repeated over time and target a less powerful victim (Olweus 1993), and is the subject of some debate (e.g., Langos 2012).

We believe the important aspects of both bullying and cyber aggression are harm and intent, and we have chosen to abandon requirements that bullying be repeated or directed toward a less powerful victim. While repetition increases the anguish of victimization, unrepeated aggression—a single rumor or trip in a crowded cafeteria, for example—can cause substantial trauma (Ybarra et al. 2014). In some cases, moreover, those with less power are able to harm their more influential schoolmates (particularly, but not necessarily, while anonymous). Our conceptualization is consistent with definitions elicited from children and teens themselves, who rarely include power imbalance or repetition in their definitions (Vaillancourt et al. 2008).

Vaillancourt et al. (2008) write that in interviews students' definitions of bullying did not tend to include "the three prominent criteria typically endorsed by researchers: intentionality (1.7%), repetition (6%), and power imbalance (26%)" (2008: 486).

Blurry lines around the definition of bullying also exist when assessing behaviors that might be considered sexual or racial harassment, which Rigby (2007) describes as a kind of bullying in which "the victim is treated badly by a stronger person or group because of his or her membership of a social group" (22). The words "harassment" and "bullying" are often used interchangeably as synonyms. And yet, the legal definition for sexual harassment, according to the U.S. Equal Opportunity Commission, is distinct from the official definition for bullying. The sexual harassment definition prioritizes the experience of the harmed party, and specifies that the harassment includes "unwelcome advances." The definition for bullying focuses primarily on the perpetrators' intentions.

In Stein's articles (Stein et al. 2002; Stein 2003) and in her essay in chapter 3, she writes that categorizing these behaviors as "bullying" does a disservice to the hurt party. Bullying directed at a student because of gender, she writes, is often aggressive, repetitive, and involves a power imbalance, as per the classic bullying definition, but should be categorized instead as "sexual harassment." These issues, Stein writes, may require legal measures, potentially undermined by categorizing the incidents as school bullying.

Intent and Unwanted

Assessing what behaviors are intentional and/or unwanted is also problematic. For intent, the person(s) involved in bullying would likely have to admit their effort to harm or a school must be able to prove their intent. Many youths who bully, though, may lack self-awareness or the willingness to be forthcoming. Often perpetrators suggest, sometimes honestly and other times deceptively, that they were playfully teasing or roughhousing rather than purposely setting out to harm (Meyer 2008).

In teasing and even roughhousing, it can be difficult to determine where the play ends and the hurt beings and at what point the target begins to experience distress in these interactions. What may begin as socially accepted, even affectionate, ways of relating (Swain 1998) may morph into insidious cruelty.

Some forms of common social teasing in schools are formally referred to as "roasting," defined at Urbandictionary.com as being "tactfully mean (snarky) without being mean-spirited in poking fun at someone, teasing, ruthlessly ridiculing, trash talking, and even mocking them." The website cautions that "roasting people that you know is usually a bad idea because people will believe that there is truth in every joke and might laugh in the moment but remember nothing but bitterness."

It may be difficult for both the perpetrator and the person possibly bullied, as well as the school staff assessing the incident, to discern where, when, and if the roasting has become mean-spirited or not and to determine whether an initially friendly dynamic has shifted into a repetitively abusive one.

To make it more complicated, what one youth finds offensive and painful, another might not at all (Rigby 2007).

Rigby writes,

> So, what appears to one person as playful teasing (which may sometimes actually be enjoyed by teaser and teased) can in some circumstances be extremely hurtful. Most children say that they are adversely affected by attempts to bully them. But some say that it doesn't bother them, and although there certainly can be an element of "denial" in this response, there are students who appear unperturbed and unaffected and who deny that it has any real effect. (21)

To make clear that the behaviors are *unwelcome* requires that students are able and willing to refer to themselves as bullied. Youths, though, often don't want to admit that they are being bullied to school officials, or even to themselves. While the student movement was able to get many dictionaries to take the word "weak" out of their definitions, there is still stigma attached to being bullied. Students may feel uncomfortable referring to themselves as bullied, and they also may be unaware that the behavior they experience is, vis à vis the official definition, bullying.

Repeated roasting is common and can be painful for the person who experiences the behavior as bullying, but it is often excluded from the formal definition, even if the behaviors look the same as bullying and cause a student anxiety and fear.

Boys and men who are sexually harassed or victims of dating or domestic violence often won't admit that they are victims of violence for fear of "appearing unmanly" and failing "to live up to masculine ideals" (Rees 2019). In a U.S. national survey, more men were victims of domestic violence than women, and yet they were turned away and ridiculed when they tried to report their experiences to domestic violence hotlines (Hoff 2012). Boys in schools are similarly reluctant to report unwanted bullying, due to the comparable anxiety that they may be teased for not being able to handle the attacks on their own (Klein 2012a).

Students' resistance to admit and report being bullied complicates accurate assessment. Rigby (2007) raises a fifth component, which could help clarify or make defining bullying even more confounding. Rigby accepts the dominant definition, that bullying is *repetitive*, that it involves a *power balance*, that it is *intentionally aggressive*, and that the person being bullied experiences the behavior as *unwanted*. Rigby suggests also, though, that the persons bullying *know* that their actions are causing the other person distress: "The rule is that if the aggressor knows that the action is distressing another and is aware that the victim wants it to stop—and still continues—that is 'bullying'" (21).

Power Imbalance

A power dynamic may also be difficult to assess, especially in bullying that involves relational aggression among seeming friends (Schäfer et al. 2002; Meyer 2008). Bullying includes social exclusion, gossip, silent treatment, and isolation from one's peer group (Olweus 1991). Here, among "friends" or former friends, the power dynamic can shift back and forth. Someone who is popular one day and mercilessly excluding others can be kicked out of their social group and targeted the next (Schäfer et al. 2002).

When one becomes more socially powerful than others, they sometimes recruit supporters and plot the others' social demise. Writing about girls, Simmons (2002) suggests that popularity contests can be devastating. Peers do what they can to socially destroy each other, and "[t]he closer you get to the epicenter of popularity, the more perilous it gets" (218). According to Simmons, "every day can be unpredictable" and "alliances shift with whispers under cover of girlish intimacy and play" (69). Simmons explains further that kids are rarely, if ever, one [bully] or the other [victim]. Social dynamics can turn on a dime. Targets can become self-protecting bullies, and bullies are unseated in startling coups. Besides, a child's peer culture is complex and in constant flux. You may have been on top in fifth grade, but at your new, bigger middle school, you're desperate to be included. Roles rotate and hierarchies shift. There is no single profile of a bully, or a target. Everyone is fair game. (Simmons 2010, October 14)

In cyberspace too, bullying often takes place among students with similar school status. Felmlee and Faris (2016) write that contrary to popular opinions, cyberaggression occurs more frequently among popular youths, not just against students perceived to be on the fringe. Students attack people they were close enough to know how to hurt. It involves "jockeying for status and recognition among relative equals" (16). And too often, what students experience as devastating and escalating social exclusion, school staff may dismiss as normal growing pains (Simmons 2002).

So, while some experts see "normal social conflict" as distinct from "bullying," others write that conflict can fester and become bullying when youths are unable to resolve their differences. Instead of talking with each other respectfully about, for instance, the jealousy over a third friend, one may start spreading rumors. Without skills to constructively resolve conflicts, some students try to get other friends on their side and exclude the other(s) with fluctuating power imbalance or military-type alliances. An issue that started as a "normal social conflict," dismissed by school officials, may leave an excluded youth painfully isolated, hurt, and even despairing. In the film version (2005) of Simmons's book *Odd Girl Out*, the once-popular-turned-socially-excluded protagonist is so distraught that she tries to commit suicide. The film ends with roles reversed again. In a crowded hallway, the bullied girl tells off her former friend and bully.

Repetition

Another controversial aspect of the formal bullying definition involves repetition. How many times should a behavior occur before it is considered bullying? Olweus (1999) recognizes that even one incident may fit the definition of bullying: "Even if a single instance of more serious harassment can be regarded as bullying under certain circumstances, the definition. . . . emphasizes negative actions that are carried out 'repeatedly and over time'" (11). Single abusive incidents may differ from the repetitive incidents, more classically defined as bullying, only quantitatively but not qualitatively.

Rigby (2007) writes, "Many incidents will be misunderstood or misconstrued, because the sequence of events preceding the integrative action will not be known, and bullying essentially involves repeated episodes" (25). Cyberbullying is also excluded from the requirement that the behavior be repetitive mostly because one public attack has the potential for being viewed by hundreds and is by that nature repetitive (Langos 2012). And a highly public bullying incident in the middle of a large high school's cafeteria may meet the same criterion as a widely viewed cyberattack.

Authorities, then, need to take care when categorizing school incidents and refrain from dismissing some incidents as less important if they are assessed as falling outside of their bullying parameter perspective. Youths and adults tend to need help to resolve conflicts, role models to communicate effectively and assertively, and support to navigate the often grave and complex challenges they encounter at school and work.

Problems That Lead to Bullying

To stop bullying and other forms of school violence, schools need to internally address the impact of social problems.

Bullying as Innate

Is bullying an indomitable part of the human condition, or does bullying breed under particular social conditions that can be shifted and overcome?

Some people do suggest that bullying is innate, that the hierarchies and bigotry associated with creating conditions ripe for bullying are a bedrock of most societies, that mass violence is also fundamental, and that since schools are smaller versions of the larger society, school bullying cannot be stopped.

It may be less likely that efforts will be made to prevent bullying if people think it is natural and intractable. After all, bullying has existed for generations. Even in the Bible, Joseph was bullied by his brothers, who, jealous of him, put him in a hole in the ground and left him for dead. Hughes (1890) describes bullying in his book *Tom Brown's School Days*, as do Golding and Epstein (1954) in *Lord of the Flies*.

Yet if violence and bullying are intrinsic, it doesn't mean that the behaviors can't be decreased or eliminated. Theorists writing about human tendencies toward violence also mostly write that society has a responsibility to develop institutional structures to curb those behaviors and help people coexist.

In *Leviathan* (1651), Thomas Hobbes argued that without social constraints, life for people would be "nasty, brutish, and short." In this early historical period, he said that government should exert control over people to prevent a self-interested "war of all against all" and that people need to enter into a form of social contract granting the government absolute sovereignty in exchange for maintaining the peace.

Later theorists proposed a democratic social contract to keep social harmony. Hobbes's assumption that government's purpose is to create stability and prevent chaos prevails, and as small societies, schools have historically adopted this responsibility. The question is, what kind of school society can prevent the social chaos that pervades schools struggling with rampant bullying?

In *Two Treatises of Government*, John Locke (1689) argues that both civil society and government institutions are necessary to resolve conflicts. Jean Jacques Rousseau, Adam Smith, Karl Marx, and many others proposed ideas for how society should be constructed in order for humans to develop their highest potential and to create a peaceful society. Schools today struggle with these fundamental questions. What will help students thrive and coexist in a collaborative community?

Throughout history, social- and education-focused writers have built on one another's work to develop concepts of civilization that incorporate democracy and humane models of justice in order to both control aggressive, violent, and destructive impulses and to help people thrive in safe and supportive spaces. Some suggest that even to the extent that humans are self-interested, strategies that build cooperative relationships are biologically "self-serving." People need positive social ties and collective input to prosper (Wanjek 2017).

Other philosophers, such as Marshall Rosenberg, argue that human nature is nonviolent and that people's greatest need is to contribute compassionately to life (Bazirake & Zimmermann 2018). Practicing gratitude and service to others is used to alleviate depression because, as Rosenberg (2000) states, helping others and "contributing to life" is a primary human need. One set of virtues integral to authentic happiness, as described in positive psychology, includes "love, kindness, and social intelligence" (Seligman 2002); and all of these are important for creating more peaceful schools. These ideas offer hope that schools can create environments that decrease violence, social exclusion, and other forms of bullying by building a more compassionate civilization (Rosenberg 2003; Klein 2012a).

There are also peaceful societies with little violence around the world, which challenges assumptions that humans are primarily self-interested and aggressive. The University of Alabama at Birmingham's Department of Anthropology profiles twenty-five peaceful societies, including the G/wi in central Botswana, southern Africa; some rural Thai communities; and the Ladakhi, in the northern Indian state of Jammu and Kashmir, where communities resolve conflicts via consensus.

Social conditions can aggravate or decrease bullying. An aggressive predisposition may remain dormant in supportive circumstances and become triggered by difficult family (psychological) or problematic school (sociological) environments. A proclivity to be aggressive, fueled by genetics, neurology, psychology, or society, emerges when people feel threatened, and this can be transformed in safe and nurturing school environments, where students are helped to feel peaceful in themselves and with others (Brown & Gerbarg 2012; Brown et al. 2013; Gerbarg & Brown 2015, 2016; Brown & Gerbarg 2017; Porges & Carter 2017; Miller 2018; Gerbarg et al. 2019).

Bigotry

Without concerted efforts schools reproduce societal problems, including bigotry, that triggers more violence. Prejudice is at the root of bullying against the three most targeted groups: LGBTQI+ people; those perceived to be emotionally, cognitively, or physically disabled (Fekkes et al. 2006; Yee 2019); and people targeted because of their weight (Olsen et al. 2014; Bucchianeri et al. 2016; McNicholas & Orpinas 2016). Bullying against lower-income students (Napoletano et al. 2016), race-based bullying (Bucchianeri et al. 2016), and sexual harassment of females and of males perceived to be feminine is also common (Lefkowitz 1997; Klein & Chancer 2000; Messerschmidt 2000; Stein 2003; Connell 2005; Kimmel 2008).

Between 2015 and 2018, hate groups in the United States rose 30 percent, to a record high. According to the FBI, racist and anti-Semitic violence rose by 30 percent between 2015 and 2017 (Southern Poverty Law Center 2019). Populations vulnerable to school bullying mirror the targets of contemporary and historical white nationalist hate crimes.

The Nazi Primer: Official Handbook for Schooling the Hitler Youth (Hitler 1938) expected Nazis to be "perfect physically" and white, "an Aryan" (xxvi), with traditional gender: "The boy must be strong, the girl beautiful" (xx). Hitler Youth propaganda that circulated in schools idealized Nordic people from Germany, England, Denmark, the Netherlands, Sweden, and Norway—people with tall stature, long faces, narrow and straight noses, lean builds, straight light hair, light eyes, and fair skin (Hitler 1938).

In many schools, youths are bullied precisely because they deviate from these Nazi prescriptions. In addition to students who do not have traditional gender and/or sexual expression and students whose bodies are perceived to have too much or too little weight, students are assaulted because they are small or because they have other kinds of ethnic features. *The Nazi Primer* disparaged people who were "short and large-boned" and if their nose was "sunk low" (31).

Nazis used "a Nordic standpoint" to judge others' "bodily structure, and physical beauty" (Hitler & Murphy 1938: 34) and the extent to which they demonstrated "the spirit of domination" (xxxii) as the "the cream of Germany's manhood" (xxvi). Contemporary white supremacist websites, according to Kimmel (2017), also rail against "legions of sissies and weaklings, of flabby, limp-wristed, non-aggressive, non-physical, indecisive, slack-jawed, fearful males who while still heterosexual in theory and practice have not even a vestige of the old macho spirit" (255).

In high-profile school shootings, some of those who actively or reactively bullied explicitly mentioned Hitler, Nazis, and other supremacist defenses. Some were targets of bullying because of their height, weight, and gender expression. In these shootings, they referenced Nazi ideology, perhaps as an effort to declare their own superiority. Examples include Luke Woodham, sixteen, in Mississippi (1997); Eric Harris, seventeen, and Dylan Klebold, eighteen, in Colorado (1999); Jeff Weise, sixteen, in Minnesota (2005); Justin Paul Doucet, fifteen, in Louisiana (2009); and Nikolas Cruz, nineteen, in Florida (2018). Police found white supremacist propaganda associated with Brandon McInerney, fourteen, in California (2008), who targeted and killed a student, according to reports, because he was transgender (Klein 2012b; Rozsa et al. 2018).

Bullying is most often directed at those who deviate from the Nazi prototype and are therefore seen as inferior. These groups of people are also stereotyped and discriminated against in adult society. Those who are overweight are often derisively referred to as "self-indulgent" or "weak-willed" (American Academy of Pediatrics n.d.), and prejudice is virulent against those with disabilities (Yee 2019) and those who are LGBTQI+ (Meyer 2003). Schools mirror these widespread hostilities that fuel vicious bullying against "non-Aryan" students.

Hierarchy

Hierarchies that determine that any people are superior to others risk fueling violent hatred and hostilities. Systemic bullying is embedded in U.S. schools and society, according to Derber and Magrass in *Bully Nation* (2016), where steep pecking orders make it seem that some are better than others. Students who tend to be bullied in schools are the same ones who are discriminated against in the adult economy, including around gender, race, sexuality, class, and ablest hierarchies (13–14). Masculinity-associated values common in aggressive business models are reproduced when school communities idealize popular students who use their power to dominate others (Klein 2012a; Derber & Magrass 2016).

Derber and Magrass (2016) write, "A bully economy is one with significant wealth and power inequality, where the economy is structured to maximize profit or wealth for the rich and force submission by the rest, while at the same time subordinating animals and all of nature to the will of the wealthy. Inequality is endemic to the bully economic system" (26).

Status hierarchies are an expected outcome when pervasive and entrenched adult hierarchies are structured around various forms of inequalities and beliefs that some are more valuable than others. "Upper-class" adults maintain their ranks by behaving unethically toward those perceived to be "lower class," and this behavior creates status differences that predict prejudices from those at the top (Wilkinson 2005; Piff et al. 2012).

In workplaces, more extreme hierarchies also predict high rates of bullying. According to the Workplace Bullying Institute, 35 percent of U.S. workers report being bullied. Many professions acknowledge this problem, noting that these behaviors undermine productivity and morale. Some are studying and implementing strategies to combat the phenomenon (Strandmark & Rahm 2014). Twale and DeLuca (2008) write that in academia in particular, a rigid hierarchy and exercise of superiority incites bullying, humiliation, and other distress. Rocker (2008) recommends methods for managing bullying in the nursing profession, cautioning that when nurses are "nice to a bully," this only "confirms the bully's superior beliefs."

There is systemic subordination and disrespect afforded to care workers in the United States, especially against "nannies" and housekeepers, for instance, on the Upper East Side of Manhattan (Romero 2013; Romero & Pérez 2016). Hostility to and subordination of immigrants also exists across the world (Lee 2005; Esses et al. 2007; Ware 2014). When adult society considers some people to be worth more than others, attitudes of social dominance appear natural. School status hierarchies are then more likely to copy the entrenched adult hierarchies that support these kinds of belief systems.

Income inequality is also associated with school bullying. The more economic inequality in a country, the more bullying (Elgar et al. 2013). Those "at the lower end of the wealth-distribution" tend to be perceived as inferior and are "subjected to harsher conditions at school." The "relative deprivation" of the less affluent students makes them more vulnerable and increases the likelihood that bullying will be accepted (Napoletano et al. 2016: 3443). Income inequality also predicts high interpersonal distrust, racism, firearm assaults, sexual assaults, homicides, incarceration, and other health and social problems (Pickett & Wilkinson 2010; Elgar et al. 2013). Social harassment is exacerbated when student status depends on financially keeping up with fashion trends. Students who can't afford the required status items risk being victimized and excluded (Attree 2006).

When popularity-focused social hierarchies persist, bullying is also higher. Among ninth grade students in four public Brazilian schools, students perceived to be popular, who excelled in physical education and did badly in academics, frequently bullied others. Those thought to be unpopular and low-performing in physical education were bullied. School bullying is frequent in schools that tolerate rigid social hierarchies (Garandeau et al. 2014b; Crochík 2016).

When peers have fixed roles on a social ladder, rather than more egalitarian and accepting relationships, prejudice often develops and can generate violence. Youths perceived to be from high-status groups are more likely to be hostile to lower-status peers (Berger & Dijkstra 2013). Those who bully often consider the students they bully to be inferior because they perceive them to be less popular, athletic, attractive, and/ or insufficiently cisgender, white, wealthy, able, and so on. When students focus on friendships, on the other hand, violence decreases (de Bruyn et al. 2010; Zwaan et al. 2013; Li & Wright 2014).

Beliefs that some beings are superior to others have ancient roots. Lovejoy (1936) traces this to Aristotle's ideas that reasoning abilities make people distinct from nonhuman animals. The Great Chain of Being is described where God is at the top, possessing, among other qualities, life, will, reason, immortality, and omniscience, and humans have only life, will, and reason. Nonhuman animals, considered inferior to people, are thought to have life and will, but no abstract ability to reason.

A parallel hierarchy was used in the United States in the 1940s to rationalize the mass sterilization of those perceived to be less able to reason, or "unfit." The 1927 U.S. Supreme Court case *Buck v. Bell* determined that states may sterilize people who were thought to be "imbeciles," "epileptic," or "feebleminded"

(Black 2003). This hierarchy may play a role in the disrespect toward and unusually high rates of bullying against those perceived to be disabled or mentally ill (McNicholas & Orpinas 2016; Yee 2019), as well as in the legal and culturally accepted position that nonhuman animals are people's commodities (Sanbonmatsu 2011). These ideas and practices have roots in eighteenth-century theories.

Some now infamous naturalists used analogous "Chain of Being" schema to suggest that a hierarchy exists among different races. In the 1700s, Carl Linnaeus in *Systema Naturae* (Linné 1767) wrote that Americans, Europeans, Asians, and Africans are different species. Linnaeus's descriptions of each human type gave rise to ideas that Caucasians are superior to others. Johann Blumenbach's MD thesis "On the Natural Variety of Humankind" (1775) developed a "science" of craniology, placing the Western European Caucasian at the top of civilized beings. Christoph Meiners, a defender of slavery, wrote in 1785 that the most important characteristic of peoples is their "beauty or ugliness," and he suggested that only Caucasians could be beautiful. "Negroes," he said, "approach animals most closely," because they are less able to experience pain, with "no human, barely any animal, feeling" (Gustav: 42). Proslavery activists used these perspectives to advance rights to their "property." Remnants of these ideas still exist in the twenty-first century and play a role in bullying.

The United States can be confusing to youth and adults, as it embraces beliefs that people should be equal but also that people from certain groups are superior, or, to quote Orwell in *Animal Farm* (1945), "some animals are more equal than others." Richard Shweder (1991) wrote about American society, "We do not know how to justify status obligations and hierarchical relationships, but we live them" (108, in Merton 1997).

The meritocracy integral to U.S. economic and social systems and oft considered a model of "equal opportunity for all" affords some people more importance than others. Meritocracy is defined on Dictionary.com as "(1) an *elite group* of people whose progress is based on ability and talent rather than on class privilege or wealth (2) a system in which such persons are rewarded and advanced (3) leadership by able and talented persons" (italics added). The *Collins British Dictionary* suggests even starker supremacy; it defines meritocracy as "*rule* by persons chosen not because of birth or wealth, but for their *superior* talents or intellect" (italics added). Inequalities, reified in a meritocracy, create seeds for bullying, justifying the idea that some people are elite and have a right, for whatever reason, to exercise their power over others.

It is not necessarily birth, wealth, race, or gender that vests power in people here; instead, *elitism* and *superiority* are granted to those with particular talents, intellect, or ability. Those with certain kinds of learning or physical challenges, and people with fewer market-value talents or skills (e.g., care workers), are among those perceived to be inferior and thus often exploited and subordinated.

Meritocracy also assumes an even playing field where people have equal opportunities to develop abilities and potential, even in contexts when it is manifestly not level. In the United States, if someone does not get access to an elite education or high-ranking social and economic position, they may be thought to have character defects or a weak work ethic. Such beliefs mask the systemic social and economic inequalities that create these circumstances, fuel prejudice and supremacy, and contribute to increased violence, bullying, depression, anxiety, and suicidal ideation (Kwate & Meyer 2010; Kahn 2011; Kaplan 2011; Mijs 2016).

These conditions are important to understand, because those who have been bullied and reactively bully back (bully-victims) are often perceived to be inferior. They tend to suffer negative physical and emotional health outcomes, further undermining opportunities to succeed. For instance, the Equalities and Human Rights Commission reports that race-based bullying and harassment are associated with considerable health disparities and are likely responsible for black students receiving lower grades in the United Kingdom (EFE News Service 2011; Rosenthal et al. 2015).

When students are bullied and reactively bully back, or even commit school shootings, authorities often blame their mental instability. Inequalities and supremacy, though, tend to be at the root of these crimes, and as C. Wright Mills (1967) writes, "public issues" are more often at fault than "private troubles."

A society structured around superiority/inferiority and ruler/ruled motivates people to try to be better than others, rather than to be part of a supportive and collaborative community. Youths strive for perfection to obtain scarce seats in colleges, graduate schools, and professional positions—and in some areas, such as New York City, also for spots in competitive preschools and elementary, middle, and high schools.

Since 1989, perfectionism among college students has increased by 33 percent (Curran & Hill 2017). Meritocracy is implicated in the trend for students to compare themselves to others and to be concerned about their social standing. Students suffer status anxiety and are more likely to believe that others will only value them if they are perceived to be perfect on a host of barometers (Levine 2006; Curran & Hill 2017). Among adolescents age thirteen to nineteen, approximately 23 percent show a lifetime prevalence of an anxiety disorder (females 38%; males 26%) (NIMH 2017).

Young people struggling with perfectionism rarely feel good about their accomplishments and tend to be self-critical, frustrated, and anguished. Such students are more likely to feel angry, aggressive, and hostile, since they are not meeting their own expectations and judge themselves harshly. They tend to believe that parents and other authorities expect flawless achievements from them, and this can also trigger anger, hostility, and aggression, both verbal and physical. They may blame others for imposing high, unfair, and unreasonable goals on them and may perceive their environment to be critical and harsh (Chester et al. 2015; Vicent et al. 2017). This rise in perfectionism suggests that more youth will harm themselves. Unleashing their anger and aggression can provide students with a sense of relief, as it can temporarily relieve the discomfort of being angry and upset (Chester et al. 2015).

Many youths feel depressed and anxious about not meeting external-turned-internal expectations around academics. They also become consumed with trying to achieve contemporary body expectations and can develop body dysmorphia and eating disorders (Jelenchick et al. 2013). Appearance-based cyberbullying, such as on Facebook, develops from these body pressures. Girls are most often called "fat," and boys receive comments about "looking or seeming 'gay,'" propelling high rates of anorexia, bulimia, and "bigorexia." Since the advent of social media, eating disorders among adolescent girls have increased by 30 percent. Males are taking muscle-building supplements in record numbers, and increasing numbers of both males and females are turning to plastic surgery (Quart 2003; Berne et al. 2014; Curran & Hill 2017: 11).

The emotional angst that develops from unrealistic body pressures and comparisons on social media is so common that a new diagnosis is called Facebook depression (Jelenchick et al. 2013). Students become consumed with appearance perfectionism, partly to ward off bullying, and this obsession can lead to addiction, depression, impulsive behavior, and increased aggression (Kim et al. 2015).

Abusive hierarchies, extreme inequalities, exploitation, and degradation of those perceived to be inferior, informs, buttresses, and maintains school bullying cultures.

Violent Culture

When societies routinely accept certain forms of violence, school bullying may be expected. Easy access to guns, mass incarceration, animal cruelty, and emotional abuse are some of the systemic violence that penetrates schools and is linked to school bullying.

Easy Access to Guns

"Access to guns is the only cause that appears in every school shooting case, and is a necessary prerequisite for a school shooting," writes Muschert (2007). Following the 2018 shooting in Parkland (2018), in which the shooter, Nikolas Cruz, bought his weapon legally in Florida (Herrera 2018, Feb. 15; Rozsa et al. 2018), students spearheaded a massive gun-control movement, March for Our Lives, widely credited for beginning to reform gun control laws (Witt 2019, Feb. 13).

Compared to the rest of the world, the United States has one of the highest rates of gun deaths—eight times the rate of Canada and twenty-seven times that of Denmark (Aizenman 2017, Oct. 6). Of people killed by firearms among twenty-three high-income countries, 82 percent are from the United States (Grinshteyn & Hemenway 2016).

Mass Incarceration

The "school-to-prison pipeline" refers to the impact of zero-tolerance policies that mandate harsh disciplinary measures for school infractions. Many cases are sent through law enforcement and students can end up in prisons (Cole 2019, May 30).

Between 1979 and 2008, shootings at least partly motivated by rage at schools, including in response to being suspended, accounted for almost 30 percent of 148 shootings (Klein 2012a, 2012b; Skiba 2014).

There was sixteen-year-old Toby Sincino, in 1995, who killed two math teachers before killing himself. He had been picked on by other students and "stuffed into garbage cans and lockers." A week before the shooting, he was suspended for making an obscene gesture. And Eric Hainstock, fifteen, killed his principal in his Wisconsin high school in 2006. Hainstock reported that students were rubbing up again him and calling him gay. They put his head in the toilet and threw him in bushes. He was serving an in-school suspension with a disciplinary warning for having tobacco at school (Klein 2012b).

The still-systemic school zero-tolerance policies often fail to address underlying issues that fuel bullying. While this trend is beginning to shift, schools still rarely use the restorative practices that can help students make amends, repair relationships, redress harms, and make different choices. Dostoyevsky (1862) famously said in *The House of the Dead* (1862) that "the degree of civilization in a society can be judged by entering its prisons." The same may be said of schools.

The United States has one of the highest prison recidivism rates in the world. According to a Bureau of Justice Statistics report (2014), when U.S. prisoners serve their sentences, 76.6 percent of them are rearrested within five years. The United States has 5 percent of the world's population, incarcerates 25 percent of the world's prisoners, and executes far more people per year than any other democracy (Loevy 2015). The United States uses solitary confinement for many years at a time, including for minor offenses, even as the United Nations expert on torture reported that more than fifteen days at a time can be considered torture and cause permanent psychological damage (UN News 2011).

The American Civil Liberties Union (2019) refers to U.S. prisons as "cruel, inhuman, and degrading" and lists concerns about overcrowding, violence, sexual abuse, and other grave risks to prisoner health and safety. Mistreatment based on race, sex, gender, identity, or disability remains common. When prisoners return to civilian life, they often have little if any work skills or support systems and are disenfranchised. Many stay homeless.

In Norway, in contrast, when prisoners are released, they are more likely to stay out; the recidivism rate is 20 percent. Nils Öberg, director general of Sweden's prison and probation service, reported, "Our role is not to punish. The punishment is that they are with us." Prisons in Scandinavian countries focus on rehabilitation and use restorative justice to repair the harm caused by the crime instead of punishing people (Kjolberg 2016).

Their correctional officers serve both rehabilitative and security roles, helping prisoners reenter civilian life with new social and work skills. The practice is meant to help the prisoner *and* the officer, so that the officer is not damaged by being immersed only in punitive functions. The perspective is that when prisoners return to society, they have a right to the same entitlements as other citizens: free health, prenatal, child, education, and elder care (Kjolberg 2016). Norway and other Scandinavian countries with similar programs also had among the least amount of bullying in a study of forty countries (Harel-Fisch et al. 2009).

Restorative justice is widely considered the most effective way to reduce recidivism. On StopBullying.gov, restorative justice is recommended to curb bullying. Zero-tolerance policies are widely seen to have had a negative impact on U.S. schools and students since they were implemented in the 1990s, although a shift toward some restorative justice, while nascent, has begun (Fronius et al. 2019).

Animal Cruelty

Abuse of nonhuman animals is also linked to bullying and school shootings. Adolescents with the highest rates of physical bullying tend to be involved in multiple acts of animal abuse and have the lowest sensitivity to animals (Henry & Sanders 2007; Sanders et al. 2013). Witnessing animal abuse is associated with bullying, suggesting that the culture of animal cruelty in agriculture and in the production of clothing and shoes negatively affects efforts to curb school violence. Developing empathy in bullying prevention programs is also recommended for reducing animal abuse (Gullone & Robertson 2008).

Animal abuse is linked to school shootings, serial murder, domestic violence, and child abuse. In a 2015 report, the FBI's National Incident-Based Reporting System stated that starting January 1, 2016, animal cruelty "without just cause" would be considered a Class A felony offense. It includes four types of abuses: gross neglect, intentional abuse and torture, organized abuse (dog and cock fighting), and sexual abuse (FBI 2015, January). However, it still permits comparable violence and torture on nonhuman animals made into food, coats, and cosmetics.

Those who bully often use animal references to dehumanize students they target (Davis 2011). When targets are bullied because they are from an historically exploited or oppressed group, they are often called names of nonhuman animals as a means of objectifying them and claiming superiority. "Rats, vermin, and cockroaches," for instance, were names used about African American slaves, Jews during the holocaust, and in warfare between the Hutus and Tutsis in Rwanda (Sanbonmatsu 2011; Waytz & Epley 2012).

To put down their targets, those who bully often call other youths names of nonhuman animals, such as "pig" to call someone dirty or disgusting, "chicken" to say scared, "mouse" for timid, "snail" for slow, and "slug" for lazy and loathsome. Those who bully often call girls a separate set of animal names including "b—h" (female dog) for aggressive, "dog" for ugly, and "cow" for fat and slow.

Legitimized hierarchies persist in mainstream agriculture, where humans kill over fifty billion nonhuman animals each year for food, including cows, pigs, goats, sheep, rabbits, turkeys, chickens, and their babies—calves, lamb, and chicks. In spite of overwhelming evidence that nonhuman animals are sentient, empathetic, intelligent, and experience joy and zest for life, the law still considers nonhuman animals as people's objects (Lin 2019).

Films and books, such as *Food Inc.* (2009), *Live and Let Live* (2013), *Earthlings* (2005), and *The Witness* (2000), expose the meat, poultry, fish, egg, and dairy industries that factory farm, keeping nonhuman animals imprisoned in unsafe, inhumane, and unsanitary conditions, routinizing their torture. Nonhuman animals are sent alive through death machines and skinned while writhing in order to provide humans with food, leather, and fur.

The cultural acceptance of torment and degradation toward nonhuman animals can be linked to histories of dehumanizing violence against humans as well as systemic school bullying.

Emotional Abuse

Emotional abuse is also associated with bullying and other school violence. While other adverse childhood experiences (ACEs), are also linked to bullying, emotional abuse can seem invisible to perpetrators, victims, and witnesses.

Even as psychological aggression is considered to be as damaging to children as corporal punishment, it remains largely unnoticed in a society that rarely recognizes screaming as assault (Sutherland 2006; Wang & Kenny 2014). Authoritarian parenting and teaching is associated with emotional abuse (Georgiou et al. 2013; Martínez et al. 2019). Victims tend to feel badly about themselves and to suffer from anxiety, depression, suicidal ideation, suicide, and increases in anger and aggression (Goldsmith & Freyd 2005; Sutherland 2006). These symptoms, as discussed in chapter 1, are also associated with being more likely to be bullied and to bully others.

Emotional abuse doesn't leave physical scars and often takes place in private places that others can't see. Many teens also endure emotionally abusive dating violence. Sometimes victims believe that the hurts are inflicted because the abuser loves them. Victims of emotional abuse are at risk for becoming abusive, depressed, anxious, and suicidal (Visualz 2008). When psychological aggression is considered normal in families and schools, verbal and related bullying is similarly sanctioned.

Normal or Deviant?

Social problems including bigotry, accepted and entrenched hierarchies, and systemic and normalized violence fuel school bullying and should be addressed in school efforts to prevent and stop it. Given how pervasive these behaviors are in adult society, another question concerns whether bullying is deviant or an expected social outcome. Does bullying develop from emotional problems, from deviant morality, or as a normal reaction to a society that condones inequality and violence?

When youths bully and hurt others because they have been emotionally or physically abused themselves (Kaltiala-Heino et al. 1999; Swearer et al. 2001; Ivarsson et al. 2005; Crawford & Wright 2007; Ellenbogen 2008; Hodgdon 2009; Copeland et al. 2013), it may be because they identify with their abusers and then participate in the same *deviant* behavior. Bullying can become a way to feel powerful instead of helpless (Patterson & Reid 1975; Gerbarg, personal communication 2018, Sept. 18).

Students who bully and bully-victims are also more likely to be morally disengaged and perceived to be deviant. Those who perpetuate "aggressive, antisocial, and criminal acts," writes Obermann (2011, November), tend to find ways to rationalize their immoral behavior (133). Many of the school shooters, for instance, self-described victims turned bullies, believed they were entitled to commit retribution, including murdering those who tormented them or did nothing to help them (NCAVC 1999–2002; Klein 2012a, 2012b).

At the same time, bullying may be a *normal*, anticipated consequence in a society steeped in inequality, hierarchy, systemic violence, and other values that communicate that aggression and dominating others is necessary for and even anticipated in competitive academic and workplace environments (Messerschmidt 2000; Connell 2005; Kimmel 2008; Pickett & Wilkinson 2010; Kaplan 2011; Klein 2012a; Elgar et al. 2013; Mijs 2016).

There may also be a relationship between the perceived deviance that triggers bullying and the social contexts that make bullying a normal outcome of an unequal and violent society. Parents and caregivers may be more likely to yell at or otherwise treat their children in destructive and abusive ways (perpetuating the bully-victim cycle) if they are anxious as a result of being excluded from fair competition in the adult workforce or because they are stressed members of cutthroat work environments. Others are overwhelmed and struggling without affordable child or elderly care, extended family, or community support. They also may be parenting while dealing with their own or loved ones' social isolation, depression, and anxiety, as is suggested by high rates of these conditions (McPherson et al. 2006; Twenge et al. 2010, 2018).

Laws: In the United States, there is no federal law prohibiting bullying, suggesting that bullying is legal, although now every state has some form of anti-bullying policy. In many European countries, bullying is prohibited at the national level. In a 1998 U.S. Supreme Court decision, Justice Antonia Scalia wrote for the unanimous court that the law "does not prohibit all verbal or physical harassment in the workplace" (*Oncale v. Sundowner*, 523 U.S. 75: 1998).

Harassment in the workplace is defined by the U.S. Equal Opportunity Employment Commission as "unwelcome conduct that is based on race, color, religion, sex (including pregnancy), national origin, age (40 or older), disability or genetic information." If harassment or bullying is not directed against a protected class, it may be permitted. As such, in many competitive business sites, people are expected to do what they can to "get to the top." Bullying may be used as a *normal* method for acquiring success.

While bullying in workplaces is often overlooked, many schools are taking a harder line. In 2013, the U.S. Department of Education sent a letter to school districts regarding the high rates of bullying targeted at special education students: "Bullying of any student by another student, for any reason, cannot be tolerated in our schools. Bullying is no longer dismissed as an ordinary part of growing up, and every effort should be made to structure environments and provide supports to students and staff so that bullying does not occur" (Darden 2015: 77).

Character: Some still suggest that some forms of bullying can build character and should be seen as relatively normal—an attitude typified by the adage "what doesn't kill you makes you stronger." For instance, in a 2011 post, Guldberg, author of

Reclaiming Childhood (2009), wrote that "without a doubt some children can and do come out of difficult situations stronger and more resilient" and she is concerned that the "anti-bullying movement" may prevent students from managing on their own and building confidence.

Emily Bazelon, author of *Sticks and Stones* (2013), recommends a balance between circumstances that require intervention and ones where it might be better to let children work it out themselves. She writes, "Doing this right means recognizing that there is truth in the old sticks-and-stones chant: most kids *do* bounce back from cruelty at the hands of other kids. They'll remember being bullied or being a bully, they'll also learn something useful if painful." Bazelon refers to Massachusetts bullying prevention psychologist Elizabeth Englander, who said that parents should not always run to their children's defense because dealing with bullying behaviors gives them practice to cope with the adult world. Englander explained, that's "why mother nature has promoted the existence of run-of-the-mill social cruelty between children" (11).

Aggression: Bullying may also be a normal reaction in hyper-competitive societies and difficult to redress when the same behaviors are socially rewarded. Today's high rates of perfectionism and depression are associated with unstable self-esteem, a sense of self that dramatically shifts in response to external achievements and others' perceptions. Unstable self-esteem is also associated with depression and predicts anger arousal and hostility (Kernis et al. 1989, 1998). This instability can embolden would-be bullies, as masculinity pressures, competitive businesses, and academia often promote and encourage aggression and the dominating behaviors associated with popularity and high status. When students are given social support, status, and power for abusing and dominating others, they also tend to be most resistant to anti-bullying programs (Garandeau et al. 2014a: 44).

Although the evidence-based 2009 Finnish anti-bullying program KiVa significantly reduces overall bullying, it is least

effective in decreasing bullying among youths considered popular. Through an intensive curriculum integrating prevention,
intervention, and monitoring, the program leads to decreases
in bullying by those of "medium or low popular status but
not for highly popular bullies." Researchers expressed concern
that this powerful program is "less effective at reducing bullying among perpetrators enjoying high social power in the peer
group . . . and that popular bullies may be the most resistant to
anti-bullying intervention" (Garandeau et al. 2014a: 44). A society that rewards dominating behaviors essentially prescribes
school bullying.

The KiVa finding is of particular concern, in that popular
male bullies often encourage one another to commit socially
normative heterosexist and homophobic bullying. Sexual violence has been historically justified, creating opportunities for
young men to commit violence at social events and to advocate it in dating advice, by justifying physical abuse toward a
partner (Messerschmidt 2000; Connell 2005; Kimmel 2008;
Basile et al. 2009; Klein 2012a). Similarly, marital rape in
the United States was not criminalized in all fifty states until
1993.

Masculinity expectations: The standards that normalize
masculinity-fueled bullying are depicted regularly in films.
Dixon describes in *Straight* how a typical man in cinema is
attracted to only heterosexual women of comparable socioeconomic class and proves himself through "his fists" and "ardor"
for the heroine (2003: 49). Dixon writes that men in cinema
have to "compete in violent sports as heroes. [They] must have
deep voices, must not be interested in art, cooking, music, sew-
ing or reading, all seen as traditionally feminine pursuits. [They
must] make aggressive and suggestive comments about and/
or to women, who are expected to view this attention as both
expected and desired."

Females are similarly straight-jacketed. According to Dixon,
"Straight women aren't supposed to be bold or seductive (unless in a porn or noir film in which case they will be punished

for their sexual aggression). . . . Only 'bad' straight girls and women embrace their sexuality; 'good' straight women repress their carnal desires" (8–9). Dixon writes that the "pernicious hold of these racist, colonialist, and sexist stereotypes, has become, if anything, more rigidly encoded today" (49–50). These prescriptions in popular movies can inform the school bullying targeted at males perceived to seem "feminine" and females considered "too sexual."

In his chapter "Homes Fit for Homos," Cook (2011) writes that "modern concepts of manhood have alienated men from each other." In the 1950s and 1960s, "the binary heterosexual-homosexual understanding of sexuality became more entrenched," with cultural anxiety and a wider backlash rising in the 1980s (304). The hostility to the feminine keeps males from accepting and appreciating the more vulnerable (feminine) aspects of being human and fuels violence against females (as iconic representations of the feminine) and men perceived to be gay or feminine. The contemporary anxiety also spawns self-hatred and self-harm. Male youths and adults deny who they are, fallible and sensitive persons, in order to be socially accepted (Klein 2012a).

These expectations that spur bullying are features of contemporary gender expectations. "Loving, intimate friendships" among men were normal among elite families in the 1700s and were "a common feature of the social landscape at the turn of the nineteenth century," writes Rotundo in *American Manhood*. In the 1800s, middle-class boys dressed in clothing and with hairstyles resembling girls (1990: 7). There was also an "open intimacy" between men, and "romantic male friendships" were common (292). Young college men often slept in the same bed, as they did with their brothers in their childhood, and they enjoyed warm and affectionate relationships, including holding hands and draping their arms around one another. Cook notes that "in the absence of a deep cultural anxiety about homosexuality, men did not have to worry about the meaning of those moments of contact" (85). Male friendships had a similar intensity as that between men and women—with a gentle vulnerability that is often tragically teased and bashed today.

Bullying may then be a *deviant* behavior in that it is mostly condemned and not tolerated in schools. At the same time, bullying develops from all-to-normal contemporary conditions, including systemic hierarchy, bigotry, and expectations rooted in hyper-individualism, cutthroat economic competition, and violence-associated hyper-masculinity.

Whether bullying is primarily buttressed by socially sanctioned violence, constitutes antisocial deviant behavior, or develops as a normal aspect of the human condition, most research and highly regarded writings from foundational philosophers and theorists suggest that by shifting social environments, by building "civilization," and by implementing positive prevention and intervention strategies, such violence decreases.

Prevention

What can schools do to prevent school bullying from taking place? How can schools respond in ways that create safe spaces where school members can reach across their differences and treat each other with more kindness and less pain than people often do in the larger society?

Schools can be a reprieve from harsh social environments. Doing nothing different means that schools reproduce external problems, attitudes, and behaviors. School violence is "anti-civilizational." It obstructs student learning, for perpetrators, victims, and witnesses. Instead, schools can become a safe "civilization," where students and staff build caring, compassionate, accepting, and egalitarian relationships and community (Crochík 2016).

School culture and climate can create a feeling of safety and support, where teachers are aware of their students' needs, intervene in social disputes and bullying incidents, and help students stand up for one another. To create compassionate schools, school staff need support to develop collegial bonds with one another while simultaneously helping to build positive student relationships (Lee & Song 2012).

A whole-school approach is considered ideal for preventing bullying. As much as possible, everyone, from the security officers to each administrator, should be recruited to work together to create a positive school climate. Parents and community members can help decrease bullying by engaging proactively with the school. Parent trainings and meetings are among the most effective strategies for decreasing bullying. Conversely, blaming schools or parents for high rates of bullying is unhelpful. It is the responsibility of everyone (administrators, teachers, parents, students, community members, and even local businesses) to be part of the solution (Olsen et al. 2014; Evans & Smokowski 2016). The Centers for Disease Control (CDC 2009a, 2009b) states that "family support" and "strong school connectedness" are "protective factors" that reduce risks for bullying others and also for suicide-related behaviors.

Implementing prevention methods in early childhood education helps students grow up with more positive and caring attitudes for one another. They thrive with help to develop empathy and communication skills and with support and guidance for resolving disputes (Rigby 2003). The Centers for Disease Control and Prevention (CDC 2009a, 2009b) recommends helping youths feel more connected to school. Even small gestures can make a difference, and the CDC suggests that people "[g]reet them by name every day. Ask them how they are doing. Encourage their extracurricular interests and involvement. A strong sense of connectedness to caring, responsible adults at school can provide invaluable support to youths who may be struggling socially and/or emotionally."

The StopBullying.gov fact sheet "Bullying as a Childhood Adverse Experience" (2017, August) discusses four empathy-building approaches used in schools to prevent bullying: first, social-emotional learning; second, trauma-sensitive schools; third, mindfulness; and fourth, talking circles. Other recommendations from anti-bullying resources include "boosting self-esteem," helping "bystanders become upstanders," and "promoting equality."

Social-Emotional Learning (SEL)

Social-emotional learning is defined by the Collaborative for Academic, Social, and Emotional Learning (CASEL) website as "the process through which children and adults acquire and effectively apply the knowledge, attitudes, and skills necessary to understand and manage emotions, set and achieve positive goals, feel and show empathy for others, establish and maintain positive relationships, and make responsible decisions" (2019).

StopBullying.gov states that SEL

> teaches children at a young age how to name and recognize their feelings and build skills to manage emotions. This approach provides children the opportunity to work together, understand each other, take responsibility, and to resolve disagreements peacefully. By understanding each other personally, children are less likely to bully or do other unkind acts to each other. If bullying does occur, SEL approaches can be helpful to name what is happening, identify the feelings behind the actions, and to resolve.

Marshall Rosenberg created nonviolent communication (NVC), a language based on skills endemic to social-emotional learning. In many of his books, including *Nonviolent Communication: A Language of Life* (2003), he writes that at every moment, everything we do is to meet a universal human need. People across the planet have the same needs (although we may have different needs at different times). Helping people to identify their feelings and needs and to guess the feelings and needs of others builds self-empathy and empathy for others—and can dissipate anger and aggression.

NVC has four components: learning to *observe* without judging or evaluating (e.g., a "missing" ball, rather than a "stolen" ball); identifying *feelings* (e.g., "I feel sad," instead of "I feel like you always upset me"); connecting to *needs* (e.g., "I have a need for respect, compassion, and connection," rather than "I need you to stop interrupting me"); and making *requests* instead of demands (e.g., "I wonder if you would be open to taking turns speaking. I can let you know when I'm done, and you could let me know when you are," instead of "You just have to stop talking and listen sometimes"). Rosenberg writes that judgment is an expression of an unmet need. When people blame themselves or others, they are less likely to find constructive strategies that effectively get their needs met, and they are more likely to stay upset in ways that can foster anger, aggression, and depression.

Many bullying prevention programs use nonviolent communication to teach social-emotional skills, such as Peace in Schools, the Relationship Foundation, and Creating Compassionate Communities, profiled in chapters 3 and 4. Families and schools can learn NVC by playing empathy-building games, such as Empathy Poker (a game that uses "feeling" and "need" cards sold by Grok the World, or available for free from Peggy Smith's Open Communication resources link) and the No-Fault Zone game from No-Fault Zone.

Family programs that foster empathy and social-emotional learning often use the group workshop kits from Faber/Mazlish Workshops. The materials were created by Adele Faber and Elaine Mazlish to help parents collaboratively lead a group that teaches the skills from their books *How to Talk So Kids Will Listen & Listen So Kids Will Talk* (1982) and *Siblings without Rivalry* (1988).

Schools can provide rooms for caregivers to run these groups, make the space available at times that are sensitive to working parents' diverse needs, and provide telephone-based parent programs. The CDC (2009a, 2009b) also found that children are more likely to thrive with "social networks" outside their families, when families receive excellent "parent education," and when there are present, "caring adults outside the family who can serve as role models or mentors." It is also important to help students "boost their self-esteem."

Boost Self-Esteem

Parents and schools can help young people develop the healthy self-esteem and self-worth that aid social-emotional learning, which can help with bullying, since depression and self-blame are risk factors for being bullied (Kochenderfer-Ladd & Wardrop 2001; Sweeting et al. 2006; Reijntjes et al. 2010; Copeland et al. 2013; Schacter & Juvonen 2015). Youths can be taught early that if others disrespect them, it is a reflection of that person's challenges and difficulties rather than anything about themselves.

Adults can refer often to young people's positive qualities, especially when speaking with other people within earshot of the youths. It is also suggested that adults help students reflect on ways they have inspired others and discuss obstacles that they have overcome. Youths sometimes need to be reminded that parents appreciate them for who they are. When youths know they are loved and accepted, they are more able to cope with criticisms and setbacks (Faber & Mazlish 1982; Voors 2000; Levine 2006).

Students don't benefit from being told that they are "smart" or "wonderful," according to many experts. Telling people *what* they are doesn't contribute to building a stable self-esteem. They may instead become "addicted" to external evaluations and then willing to behave in ways that are likely to attract the positive labels (Rosenberg 2003; Dweck 2007), including sometimes bullying and dominating others. Faber and Mazlish (1982) suggest that caregivers describe behaviors that might represent courage or kindness so that youths can see the relationship between their actions and the qualities they are demonstrating.

Families and schools can help students respond constructively to setbacks. Hyper-assessment-focused schools and society can inadvertently teach youths that they are not smart or talented or worthwhile if they get a bad grade, lose a tournament, or get rejected. To build stable self-esteem, students can be helped to view failure as an aspect of learning. They can get information on how best to fulfill their potential and to recognize that hard work, rather than fixed traits (e.g., intelligence or athletic talent), will help them achieve the goals that are important to them (Dweck 2007).

Mental Health America (2019) encourages parents to teach children how to be assertive, including expressing their feelings clearly, saying no when they feel uncomfortable or pressured, standing up for themselves without fighting, and walking away in dangerous situations. Parents can help children and teens build friendships by coordinating positive activities, extending invitations, and taking them to a friend's place, a movie, or a sports event. When young people develop outside interests, they tend to feel creatively engaged and more positive about themselves. It helps to remind them that their school is not the whole world and that there are kind and respectful people to bond with elsewhere. They may also meet new peers and adults who can become part of their support system (Voors 2000; Stella 2007; Carpenter 2009; Alexander 2016).

Efforts to create positive and affirming cultures for youths make it difficult for bullying to fester, even when students contend with emotionally challenging circumstances at home or elsewhere.

Trauma-Sensitive Schools

Trauma makes it more likely that students' fight-or-flight responses are overstimulated, which puts them more at risk for being aggressive, hostile, depressed, anxious, and prone to bullying or being bullied. Being involved in bullying can be traumatic, inciting a vicious cycle of unhealthy aggressive and passive behaviors (Gerbarg & Brown 2016; Porges & Carter 2017; StopBullying.gov 2017, August).

According to StopBullying.gov (2017, August), the trauma-sensitive school movement, like the whole-school approach,

> ensures that all school staff—from the principal to the janitor—understands the nature and impact of trauma. A student's behavior can be a sign that they have been exposed to trauma. This approach recognizes the trauma, responds with compassion and intervention, and avoids certain responses that do more harm than good (such as isolation and suspension).

Adverse childhood experiences often occur as a result of caregivers' abuse over time, and their impact can manifest in school behavior issues. Trauma-sensitive schools understand the impact of ACEs and support students accordingly. Helping students build resilience and coping skills decreases their impulse to engage in difficult behaviors.

Because trauma is so common, most students can benefit from trauma-sensitive-focused schools. ACEs affect 50 percent of the U.S. population. A little less than half of all U.S. children have experienced at least one ACE, especially divorce, separation of a parent or guardian, and economic hardship, which are followed in frequency by alcohol and drug abuse, witnessing neighborhood violence, and living with a family member with a mental illness. "One in ten youths have experienced three or more ACEs . . . sixty-one percent of black non-Hispanic children and fifty-one percent of Hispanic children have experienced at least one ACE, compared with forty percent of white non-Hispanic children and twenty-three percent of Asian non-Hispanic children" (Sacks & Murphey 2018).

Experiencing ACEs can trigger mental health issues and substance abuse and can make it more difficult for people to respond in productive ways to daily stressors (American Academy of Pediatrics 2014). Almost everyone, student and adult, is affected by systemic social conditions associated with increased anxiety, depression, and social isolation (Levine 2006;

McPherson et al. 2006), and this is especially so for people from vulnerable populations (Slack et al. 2017).

Less visible trauma is also transmitted from one generation to the next. Such trauma affects "parenting in a negative way and perpetuates a continuing exposure to ACEs across generations" (American Academy of Pediatrics 2014). Many different peoples still suffer from the impact of trauma generations after their families experienced severe exploitation and oppression (Nagata 1991; Brave Heart & DeBruyn 1998; Felsen 1998; Kupelian et al. 1998; Klain & Pavić 2002; DeGruy 2005; Evans-Campbell 2008; Kahane-Nissembaum 2011; Perreira & Ornelas 2013; Graff 2014).

Children with trauma are often misdiagnosed with learning disabilities and severe behavior problems when they could instead thrive from trauma-sensitive holistic interventions (Plumb et al. 2016). Schools benefit when school-based mental-health professionals and teachers receive training in the evidence-based model of trauma-sensitive schooling. James Redford, the son of actor Robert Redford, documented a trauma-sensitive school, Lincoln Alternative High School in Walla Walla, Wisconsin, in a film called *Paper Tiger* (Brainstorm Media 2016). The title refers to the idea that traumatized youth often feel so easily threatened that they have the same response to a paper tiger as they might to a real tiger; any stimuli that they experience as threatening can set them off. The metaphor helps explain why many students become aggressive, and even bully others, with seemingly little provocation. A minor or imagined threat can powerfully impact a person who is traumatized.

According to the documentary, this trauma-sensitive school offered their students unconditional acceptance and even love. Students overwhelmed by trauma, who had dropped out or been kicked out of previous schools, thrived in this environment and developed strong bonds with students, teachers, and administrators, and many went off to college with scholarships. The documentary emphasized that a relationship with even one caring adult can make a difference in youths' lives.

Trauma-sensitive schools take different forms, often incorporating a model of restorative discipline. Humanities Preparatory Academy (Prep) in New York City was started by teachers from a large school in the same building that struggled with student violence, including gangs. Prep is a small, community-focused school, where students have a voice in creating school policy, participate and lead all-school discussions that affect their lives, and build caring and supportive relationships with one another and their teachers.

The school uses a model of discipline that includes the Fairness Committee, to which students can take teachers, teachers can take students, or students can take other students. The committee consists of members of the community, including students and teachers, who are committed to helping the parties involved come to an understanding and resolution of the problem. The grievant explains their concerns in relationship to one of the school's core values. If a student cuts a class, a teacher might express concern about "Respect for the Intellect" (Hantzopoulos 2008, 2013).

Students call teachers by their first name and speak about feeling cared about and supported. Even though the Prep population comes predominantly from the larger, more bully-ridden school, there is almost no violence at Prep and few suspensions. The student body tends to be economically and racially diverse (Hantzopoulos 2008, 2013). One student explained, "A lot of what I've learned here is just be nicer and be more outspoken and, you know, don't be so shy. . . . I do think twice before I wanna get mad at someone or I wanna, you know, use physical violence against them, and I guess that's a value that I've obtained while being at Prep" (Hantzopoulos 2008).

Another important activity for preventing bullying is learning and practicing mindfulness.

Meditation

According to StopBullying.gov (2017, August), "Many schools are seeing the benefits of teaching mindfulness to youths—or the skill to become aware of thoughts, emotions, and behavior. Mindfulness is usually goal oriented and guided by teachers. Mindfulness can be a useful skill for students who are inclined to act out or who have bullied in the past, because it helps them identify negative feelings before acting on them."

Trauma has a detrimental effect on the brain, especially in young people (Plumb et al. 2016). Children who endure ACEs and are then repeatedly punished in harsh school environments when they act out on their pain generally have underlying imbalances in their autonomic nervous systems. Without a supportive and compassionate social environment, they are more likely to be triggered by perceived threats that people who have not experienced trauma might not even notice.

Gerbarg (personal oral communication 2019, Sept. 18) suggests that youths who have experienced abuse and other adverse events need help to balance their autonomic nervous systems. In order to correct the imbalance found in children who engage in bullying, Gerbarg says that it is necessary to improve the function of both parts of the autonomic system, sympathetic and parasympathetic. While antianxiety and antidepressant medication can help dampen the excess activity of the sympathetic system (fight or flight), they do not activate the underactive parasympathetic system (soothing and bonding).

Students can benefit from practices that heal and rewire their autonomic nervous systems. When schools help them balance the parasympathetic and sympathetic parts of their brain through focused breath work, meditation, and movement, students can experience more internal peace and empathy, and violence decreases. Integrative psychiatrists Dr. Richard Brown and Dr. Patricia Gerbarg created a program called Breath-Body-Mind, profiled in chapter 4, which they teach in schools. Based on ancient healing practices, it is designed to help students balance their autonomic nervous system and thereby improve their ability to self-regulate emotions and behaviors (Gerbarg & Brown 2016; Porges & Carter 2017).

More conventional talking "top-down" therapeutic approaches aid students with aggression issues using cognitive and behavioral modification. These methods, according to Gerbarg, attempt to engage youths' thinking processes to help them regulate their emotional and behavior responses to stimuli they find upsetting. This approach can be helpful, but "bottom-up" practices that balance the autonomic system by using the body's internal neural communication pathways are critical to helping students accomplish these goals (Brown & Gerbarg 2012; Brown et al. 2013; Gerbarg & Brown 2015, 2016; Brown & Gerbarg 2017; Porges & Carter 2017; Miller 2018; Gerbarg et al. 2019).

When students learn meditative breathing and movement, they are less likely to bully or behave aggressively in other ways (fight), resist coming to school (avoidance), run away (flight) or become paralyzed with fear (freeze). These practices can help students more easily shift from acting on defensive patterns to choosing more positive social and emotional responses and behaviors. Changing breathing patterns affects the messages being carried from the respiratory system to the brain and influences perceptions, emotions, and behaviors.

Mind-body methods rapidly balance the autonomic system by quieting the agitated sympathetic branch, activating the calming parasympathetic branch, and increasing the flexibility of the brain to respond more appropriately. Students are then more able to communicate, feel empathy and compassion, bond, and cooperate. Rather than attacking themselves with self-blame, hurting people, or running away, students develop capacities for connecting more compassionately with themselves and others (Gerbarg & Brown 2015; Brown & Gerbarg 2017; Porges & Carter 2017; Gerbarg et al. 2019).

Schools have begun to implement many different forms of mindfulness programs in order to help students strengthen abilities to regulate their emotions, develop internal peace and balance, build their focus and attention, and make more thoughtful behavior choices. Another program profiled in chapter 4 is Peace in Schools, created by Caverly Morgan. She studied mindfulness for eight years in a Zen monastic setting and teaches an intensive, full-credit course to help students feel interconnected with one another and communicate from a place of compassion. Professor Cristina Zaccarini integrates mindfulness in one of the college history courses she teaches about these practices.

When students are in a more peaceful place internally and externally, they are also more able to make positive contributions. School staff and parents can then more easily help youths become proactive influences when bullying takes place, and cognitive approaches can also become more effective. When students want to help each other in response to bullying or other hurtful behaviors, school members can help "bystanders" to bullying become constructive "upstanders."

Prevent "Bystanders" and Develop "Upstanders"

If witnesses to bullying intervene, the behaviors stop within ten seconds, 57 percent of the time (Hawkins et al. 2001). Yet, in 85 percent of bullying situations, bystanders encourage or allow the bullying to persist (Padgett & Notar 2013). Simply removing the audience (and the implicit peer acceptance) can reduce or stop bullying. One way to help bystanders become upstanders is to teach empathy and prosocial behavior. To change a bullying school climate, the primary target should be witnesses, write Garandeau et al. (2014b).

If you ask them, most youths would say that they are opposed to bullying, even if they do nothing to stop the behavior when they see it and even if they encourage the behavior. By helping children to develop empathy and a commitment to their community and by encouraging everyone to intervene if they see hurtful behavior, parents and schools can help youths see the inconsistencies between their beliefs and their actions (Garandeau et al. 2014a).

The Child Mind Institute suggests that the most effective way to prevent and combat bullying is through peer support and intervention. When young people are recruited to notice and try to resolve conflicts in peer mediation and restorative justice programs, they are more invested in a peaceful school environment. For instance, KiVa, which has been recognized as a successful research-based Blueprints for Healthy Development anti-bullying program, has a strong emphasis on influencing onlookers to support the people being bullied rather than to encourage the people bullying. Schools are expected to continuously challenge peers to provide support for targeted classmates (Garandeau et al. 2014a).

The Education Development Center states that parents should help children become upstanders. Adults can let young people know that they will support students if they try to help and can inspire students by talking about courageous people who have made a real-life difference in their own experiences. Give examples of ways to be helpful, such as discouraging the person bullying, defending the person being bullied, redirecting the focus away from the bullying situation, rallying support from peers to stand up against the bullying, or reporting the bullying to an adult.

Students can also make it clear to others that they won't be involved in bullying. They can refuse to stand by and watch or to encourage hurtful behavior. They can consciously avoid harassing, teasing, or spreading gossip about others. They can also do random acts of kindness. Mentoring Minds, a national K–12 publisher, also suggests helping students hold on to their own power. They can refuse to empower bullies by giving them the attention or popularity they seek. Since desire for acceptance often triggers bullying, schools can help students to actively decrease the social rewards (Reijntjes et al. 2013).

Mental Health America recommends that parents and teachers talk to students about the difference between "telling" and "tattling." Tattling is telling an adult in order to get someone in trouble. Telling is sharing the information with an adult to help someone in trouble. Schools can provide ways for students to report incidents or concerns to adults anonymously so that they don't have to fear retribution.

Student Activism

Students across the nation have empowered themselves to speak out against the most severe form of bullying ravishing schools: school shootings. Demanding tighter gun control laws, the students who survived the shooting in Parkland, Florida, where seventeen people were killed, created a movement they called March for Our Lives. The youths made powerful speeches and organized hundreds of thousands of people across the nation (Holpuch & Owen 2018).

Students are standing up for the change they want to see in the world. For example, environmental activist Greta Thunberg, age sixteen, delivered an emotional speech to European leaders about climate change and initiated a school strike for climate change movement that surged globally. If schools empower students to strengthen their voice and passion for change, these youths can become the leaders who end school bullying.

They can also be trained to be facilitators in circle discussions. Schools use circle discussions to help students and school staff bond with one another and to self-reflect so that students are more likely to feel appreciative and respectful and to want to help each other.

Circle Discussions

A circle discussion is used to draw out open discussion, build understanding, and help bring about justice. Restorative justice organizations, such as the Morningside Center for Teaching Social Responsibility profiled in chapter 4, train school staff on how to facilitate justice-focused circles. A discussion might begin with a prompt for each student to answer, such as "say something nice to the person sitting next to you" or "name something you look forward to this week."

The StopBullying.gov website (2017, August) states, "Guided by community-building questions, children and youth in the class or group are asked to participate, but can decline if they do not want to participate. If bullying occurs, circle discussions can bring the group together to focus on supportive, collaborative, and healthy actions." These circles help participants—including teachers and sometimes parents if they are involved—bond and see past external differences in order to recognize one another's vulnerabilities and humanity.

Follestad and Wroldsen (2019) write in *Using Restorative Circles in Schools*, "When students know each other well there is less chance of inappropriate or aggressive behavior and bullying" in school, outside, and on social media (41). In circles, all people are equal, have a chance to speak without receiving negative comments, and have an important voice. Anyone can initiate a circle including to get to know one another; build and reflect on their class culture; disagree about something; work together as a team; discuss something difficult; or learn from one another.

Circle discussions are based on collaborative education and support. The model was developed from educators including John Dewey (1916) and Pablo Friere (1968). The teacher is involved in both learning and teaching, and works with students to create a strong and connected class culture based on respect and dignity. Circle discussions prevent bullying by helping students to feel secure, appreciated, and heard in their school and in their classroom (Follestad & Wroldsen 2019).

These talks can be used to increase sensitivity to groups who experience prejudice—including about homosexuality, disabilities, and race. Students and school staff are able to let go of their stereotypes when they see the pain such thinking causes their classmates. Experiencing the connection and openness together makes it difficult to continue objectifying one another (Mirsky 2014). A circle can also address the stigma around mental illnesses, which are too often used as insults rather than approached with the sensitivity and care people sometimes reserve for those suffering with physical illnesses. Bullying against students with these kinds of challenges can be brutal (Yee 2019).

Circles can build compassion for those who are depressed; have anxiety and panic disorders; struggle with eating disorders—anorexia, bulimia, binge eating; have borderline personality disorders; or have bipolar disorder or schizophrenia. Students are more likely to seek help and get support if they know that they won't be judged by their peers for their difficulties. Often these kinds of illnesses develop from various kinds of trauma, including physical, sexual, and emotional abuse (CDC ACEs Study 2002; Goldsmith & Freyd 2005; Sutherland 2006). Teasing students for having a mental illness is comparable to taunting someone because they survived childhood abuse.

Following the December 2012 deadly shooting of first graders in Newton, Connecticut, President Barack Obama called on schools to identify students who suffer with mental illnesses and to get them help. It is time to "bring mental illness out of the shadows," he said. More than 75 percent of mental illnesses emerge in school-aged children, but only half of the children receive the help they need. Untreated mental illness disorders can lead to more social isolation at school, poor academic performance, and even suicide and violence (Adams 2013).

Some school shootings may be avoided if students with mental illnesses are helped and supported rather than feared and bullied. Otherwise, troubled students who may already be on edge and, easily triggered, could find that peer abuse about their problems is the "last straw" (Gerbarg & Brown 2016; Porges & Carter 2017). While many experts blame school shootings on mental illness (e.g., Cullen 2009), it is often the bullying of students with these difficulties that sets them off—another reason why it is vital to build sensitivity and support for people who have such overwhelming challenges (Klein 2012a).

Circle discussions, then, can both build sensitivity and also help students regulate their emotions so that they are less likely to act on feelings like overwhelming anger or fear. Being emotional, in schools and elsewhere, is often frowned upon and experienced as weak or embarrassing. Helping youths identify and express their feelings in a circle is a safe way to build empathy for self and others.

Several scholars also recommend that school efforts focus on expanding masculinity expectations to include empathy, vulnerability, and compassion in order to prevent heterosexist bullying behaviors and other forms of violence. When addressing sexual assault, gay-bashing, and gender-based aggression, interventions that punish students often fail to effectively address the harm. In many cases, after being punished, male students may feel more bent on committing violence in order to reinstate a perceived affront to their masculinity. School staff and students often even condone the cultural practices that manifest in gender- and sex-based assault. They may judge females' sexuality and support masculine-associated dominating behaviors. These perspectives are damaging and still common and are unlikely to change unless schools work together to self-reflect and shift these biases (Messerschmidt 2000; Connell 2005; Kimmel 2008; Klein 2012a; Ringrose & Rawlings 2015).

Circles can create space for boys and men to experience a full range of emotions and attitudes, not just the narrow expectations that allow little more than anger (Pollack 1999). Many schools that have implemented restorative justice programs engage in daily circles (Follestad & Wroldsen 2019). Once students feel safe and empowered in these circles, harmful masculinity expectations and other hurtful gender norms can be discussed, including teen pregnancy prevention, dating violence, and sexual assault (Messerschmidt 2000; Connell 2005; Kimmel 2008; Klein 2012a; personal oral communication, Rowe-Small 2019, June 24). Circle work aids in prevention efforts to create social equality, which is integral for building safe schools.

Promoting Equality

School hierarchies undermine academic and social functioning, and high inequality and severe hierarchies increase bullying. Schools can prevent bullying from developing by creating a shared balance of power in the classroom. Achieving equality in social relationships requires that schools make strong and conscious efforts to create supportive and egalitarian relationships (Garandeau et al. 2014b; Crochík 2016).

Teachers can directly affect the social dynamics in their classrooms by being sensitive to classroom friendship and victimization patterns and by using responsive teaching strategies. They can create positive shifts in students' bonding with one another and in their motivation to treat each other with kindness and respect (Gest & Rodkin 2011). Classrooms are also friendlier, more collegial and less divided by social cliques and popularity contests when teachers utilize small student-group discussions and thoughtfully manage seating charts.

Helping students build friendships outside excluding social cliques can make a difference (e.g., assigning bus partners and mixing up group discussion participants). Shifting hierarchies toward more collaborative relationships creates positive social dynamics and the potential for higher levels of instructional support (Garandeau et al. 2014b). Schools also tend to have less bullying when students and teachers trust each other and students feel they are respected and that rules are fair (Olsen et al. 2014).

Creating school policies that foster dignity and respect for the most targeted groups of bullied youths—LGBTQI+ students; those susceptible to weight-based bullying; and mentally, physically, or cognitively challenged students—also decreases violence. Pages on StopBullying.gov about LGBTQI+ youth and bullying and youth with special health needs recommend that schools create intentional peer support, build staff sensitivity, and raise LGBTQI+ awareness.

Bullying often involves cross harassment. When students are perceived to be over- or underweight, they are at greater risk for other bigoted assaults, including around their race, gender, sex, and class. Schools can support body-positive cultures, raise awareness about the impact of weight-related comments and also encourage teachers and students to speak up and curb teasing when they observe it (Bucchianeri et al. 2013).

Empathy-building prevention efforts should make bullying less likely. If bullying does occur, empathy-focused interventions tend to be most effective.

Interventions

Bullying and conflict are often considered distinct problems warranting wholly different interventions (Goldman 2012; HRSA n.d.). The HRSA, for instance, states that bullying is victimization, like child abuse or domestic violence, not conflict and warns against using peer mediation to address it:

> Mediating a bullying incident may send inappropriate messages to the students who are involved (such as, "You are both partly right and partly wrong," or "We need to work out this conflict between you"). The appropriate message to the child who is bullied should be, "No one deserves to be bullied, and we are going to do everything we can to stop it." The message for children who bully should be, "Your behavior is inappropriate and must be stopped." (HRSA n.d.)

StopBullying.gov (2017, August) states, "Peer mediation or conflict resolution are not recommended to deal with bullying." However, according to other scholars, bullying often develops from unresolved conflict—especially relational aggression, when a badly handled conflict can morph into popularity and social exclusion wars such that power dynamics shift cruelly and dramatically from day to day (Einarsen 1999; Hoel et al. 1999; Zapf & Gross 2001; Simmons 2002; Keashly & Nowell 2003; Baillien et al. 2008; Wiseman 2016).

Many youths and adults have difficulty resolving their conflicts without guidance, instruction, and role modeling. If adults intervene in even minor disputes by helping parties hear and express feelings and concerns, students are more likely to resolve their immediate conflict, and they are also better equipped to resolve future conflicts that could explode into bullying. Some scholars encourage schools to help students learn how to resolve conflicts early and intervene quickly, for instance through conflict resolution programs, as a way to avoid bullying (Levine & Tamburrino 2014).

While perspectives differ on what is considered "normal social conflict" and what is "bullying," experts and scholars widely recommend whole-school empathy-focused interventions and restorative justice.

Whole-School Approach

As in prevention, whole-school empathy-focused interventions recruit school staff, families, students, and community members to work together to stop bullying and other antisocial behaviors, including helping people to understand different perspectives and to care about their feelings and needs. School staff and families are also most effective if they are understanding and empathetic to all parties. This does not mean condoning the bullying; instead, whole-school approaches focus on behaviors rather than people in order to maximize the possibilities for transformation and change. Help the person being bullied and the person involved in bullying (Eisenberg & Miller 1988; Espelage et al. 2018).

For Those Who Bully Others

When teachers yell at, belittle, and put down students with whom they have difficulties, according to one study, the behavior gets much worse. The school inadvertently intensifies the aggressive behavior instead of mitigating it (Hepburn 1997), much like the parent who yells at a child who is misbehaving and thereby increases, rather than decreases, the objectionable behavior (Wang & Kenny 2014).

People who bully may have issues at home, or they may feel this is the only way they can be accepted by their peers. They might feel vulnerable and want undivided peer attention because they are shielding themselves from feeling overwhelmingly empty and needy. By helping those who bully understand how their behavior affects themselves, others, families, and their school, these youths may be able to give themselves and others the needed empathy and compassion that helps stop the behaviors.

When adults speak to youths involved in bullying privately, there is a greater likelihood that the child will respect and appreciate the guidance. Rosenberg (2003) writes that students can be helped to find strategies that "are more wonderful and less costly" to meet their needs. For instance, hurting others to gain peer acceptance doesn't tend to help students meet their needs for connection and can cause cycles of discord for everyone involved.

Circle discussions and nonviolent communication, on the other hand, can more effectively and directly help students meet needs "to see and be seen," "to hear and be heard," "to know and be known," and to connect in meaningful ways with others.

Schools often inadvertently aggravate bullying in their efforts to quell it. When individual students are blamed for a school's bullying problem, the school may miss the larger issues that exacerbate bullying. Perceiving the person as having a fixed aggressive personality trait or an inability to relate interpersonally can prevent school members from constructively reflecting on how to create a more supportive environment, stop the behaviors, and even become a lifesaving buffer.

For Students Being Bullied

Schools and families can be more sensitive to some of the signs that a youth may be bullied. These youths may show signs of depression, including sadness, isolating themselves, difficulty concentrating, and having difficulty sleeping. They might refuse to go to school or come up with excuses to stay home. Youths often want to know that adults are available, even if they are not ready to talk about their challenges. A parent might try to take a walk with their child, go on a car trip, or sit together and talk about less charged subjects. Youths, like adults, are sometimes more comfortable opening up after they have established a level of comfort and rapport talking about other things (Voors 2000; Stella 2007; Carpenter 2009; Alexander 2016).

Parents, caregivers, and teachers can encourage young people to stand up for themselves and advocate on their own behalf. StopBullying.gov recommends that students who are bullied "look at the kid bullying you and tell him to stop in a calm, clear voice. . . . If speaking up seems too hard or not safe, walk away and stay away. Don't fight back. Find an adult to stop the bullying on the spot." Schools and families can make sure that targeted students have supportive allies at school and elsewhere.

Intervene Quickly

If adults see hurtful behavior taking place, they can be positive role models by taking immediate action to stop the behavior. By remaining silent, they may tacitly encourage it or make it worse.

It is important for adults to emphasize to all involved that the bullying a youth experiences is not that youth's fault. No one should expect or want the youth to change to fit their peers' expectations or demands, including about their weight, clothing, or interests, nor to be ashamed of their race, ethnicity, gender identity, disability, or economic status.

Speaking to the parents or caregivers of the children involved is sensitive. When parents and caregivers believe their children are being bullied or when their children are being accused of bullying, it can recall their own childhood pain or trauma. It can be difficult to focus on resolving the situation for the youths involved rather than trying to persuade the other parent that their child behaved badly. A strong anti-bullying school program can help families communicate constructively and work together to end the problem behaviors. This is one of the most difficult types of intervention, and often contraindicated due to parents' inability to stay calm and focused on the problem, rather than blaming the students involved (Voors 2000; Stella 2007; Carpenter 2009; Alexander 2016).

Create an Action Plan

If bullying is in early stages, problem-solve, suggests the International Center for Assault Prevention Bullying Prevention Program (2017). Some student workshops engage youths in role-play and encourage students to brainstorm successful strategies. The New York City Children's Theater, profiled in chapter 4, leads these kinds of workshops.

When bullying occurs, caregivers and school staff members can sit with the youth and list every idea that each can think of to help the student being bullied. The list can include excellent, ordinary, and ridiculous suggestions—every idea gets listed. For example:

- Tell the person(s) bullying to stop.
- Practice/role-play how to speak firmly and confidently to the person(s) bullying.
- Ask for a restorative justice process.
- Have parents speak calmly and compassionately to the caregiver of the person bullying.
- Change classrooms.
- Change schools.
- Spend lunchtime in another area of the school.
- Come home from school with a different mode of transportation.
- Seek revenge on the person bullying.

- Send the bully to the moon.
- Seek advice from a trusted grandparent or family friend.
- Find a more trustworthy group of friends (if there is social exclusion involved).
- Join an extracurricular activity in order to make new supportive friends.

The adult and youth then discuss the list and cross out anything impossible like "Send the bully to the moon," anything destructive like "Seek revenge on the bully" (this generally leads to the conflict escalating and more hurt to the youths involved), and anything else that the adult or the youth do not want to do.

Since bullied youths often feel out of control already, this process can help them regain agency, and build self-esteem and confidence. An action plan should play to the youths and adults' strengths and can be shared with other concerned adults in the young person's life so that they feel bolstered by a strong support system. The result of the brainstorm is Plan A. If Plan A is not effective, the brainstorming process can be revisited to create a Plan B.

Document the Behavior

While responses that emphasize compassion and communication are most effective in dealing with bullying behaviors, they do not work in every case. As a precaution, school staff and families should also immediately start to document the hurtful behaviors as soon as they begin. Adults and youths can try implementing action plans A, B, and even C, but if the behavior persists or becomes dangerous, legal measures may be necessary to protect the person being bullied. Schools and families should write in detail every bullying incident, including the time, date, and place it occurred; the way the child responded and the person to whom the child or parent reported the incident.

Intervene in Cyberbullying

StopBullying.gov suggests that parents and schools talk to everyone involved in a cyberbullying incident in order to find out what is happening, how it started, and who is involved. Parents and schools should keep a record of what is occurring and where it is taking place, including taking screenshots of harmful posts. Students who are dealing with cyberbullying should save messages even if they appear minor, as hurtful interactions may escalate. Cyberbullying should be reported both to the school and to the app or social media platforms where it occurred. The offensive content should be removed. If there are physical threats, a potential crime, or illegal behavior, it can be reported to the police.

Peers and trusted adults can rally together to publicly try to end cyberbullying attacks. Public intervention includes encouraging other peers to post affirming comments about the bullied person in order to shift the online conversation in a positive direction. Parents and teachers can sensitively speak to both the child being bullied and the child bullying, if the latter is known. The more a community works together, the more effective the intervention. Young people should talk to a trusted adult—whether a parent, a school counselor, a teacher, or all three. Students should refrain from writing negative posts back to the bully, as this can escalate the situation and implicate the person being bullied in the offense.

If possible, cyberbullying and face-to-face bullying can be addressed in school in positive restorative processes. Outmoded zero-tolerance policies often make things worse. Many policymakers, experts, and scholars recommend shifting their emphasis away from zero-tolerance policies at the federal, state, and district level (Welsh & Little 2018). Zero-tolerance school-discipline policies mandate typically severe, punitive, and exclusionary (suspension and expulsion) responses for certain types of misbehavior, even if seemingly minor, and regardless of the rationale or context in which it took place.

Zero-Tolerance Policies

Suspensions and expulsions are complicated by the fact that, for instance, U.S. students are guaranteed a "free and appropriate education," and yet students who are suspended and then return to school without constructive intervention tend to repeat the same offenses and are suspended again, often missing extensive amounts of school. Students also tend to escalate the misbehavior if they believe that the rules are unfairly applied. They may come to see the confrontational discipline as a contest that students want to win (Skiba & Knesting 2001).

Many states (eighteen, as of this writing) provide a means for victims to seek legal redress and send those accused of bullying through the criminal justice system. Nine of these states mandate that schools report bullying incidents to the police. New Jersey has what many consider the toughest anti-bullying law in the nation. The New Jersey Anti-Bullying Bill of Rights requires that students found guilty of bullying must be expelled or suspended. It forces administrators and employees to report bullying incidents, whether or not they occur in school. Anyone who fails to make such a report can face disciplinary action and may even lose their license. Under many of the state policies, if enforced, students accused of bullying will spend significant time in jail (Garby 2013).

These "get tough" discipline tactics are still a facet of anti-bullying policies in approximately 75 percent of U.S. schools. The American Psychological Association's (APA) Zero Tolerance Task Force found that several laws authorize harsh punitive school consequences, such as long-term suspension, expulsion, and transfer to alternative school settings. The APA stated its concerns about the high demand for zero-tolerance policies for bullying and the extensive criticism about these policies, which, they wrote, tend not to "address the needs of students who bully and could have a chilling effect on reporting by children and adults" (Cornell & Limber 2016).

These policies were also studied extensively in research titled "Zero Tolerance, Zero Evidence." When schools mete out harsh punishments for minor infractions, they can undermine morale and devastate students' lives (Skiba & Knesting 2001; Bleakley & Bleakley 2018).

Zero-tolerance policies tend to increase suspension rates without decreasing problem behaviors. The harsh discipline is also disproportionately used against black students when compared with the same infractions committed by white students. It also contributes to the school-to-prison pipeline, whereby students who get suspended are significantly more likely to drop out of school and end up in prison (Curtis 2014; Berlowitz et al. 2017; Curran 2019). Zero-tolerance discipline often contributes to behavior escalation, and then legal responses are often pursued.

Legal Responses

Bullying is illegal in most European countries, but in the United States, with its federal system, the legal context is more complex. U.S. federal law requires that schools that receive federal funding must intervene in discrimination against persons in a protected class. School bullying, then, violates federal law only if students are targeted due to race, color, religion, sex, disability, familial status, and national origin. Meanwhile, all fifty states now have some form of anti-bullying legislation.

When bullying and harassment against a person(s) from a protected class overlap, a civil rights issue may be present and federally funded schools are obligated to resolve the situation. If the school fails to help, it falls under the purview of the U.S. Department of Education's Office of Civil Rights and the U.S. Department of Justice's Civil Rights Division (Stein et al. 2002; Stein 2003).

While Title IX prohibits sex-based bullying in schools that receive federal funding (against someone because of their gender), it does not prohibit discrimination based on sexual orientation.

Title IX can only protect students, including students perceived to be LGBTQI+, from sex-based harassment—an unfortunate loophole, as LGBTQI+ students are bullied most often because of their sexual orientation and are also among the students most frequently bullied (Spidel 2014; Yee 2019).

There continues to be legal controversies on the extent to which cyberbullying falls under the jurisdiction of public schools. How can a public school, a government actor, legislate speech restrictions in cyberspace (outside or at least distinct from the school's physical space) given the First Amendment? One answer is that cyberattacks—including defamation, threats, intentional infliction of emotional distress, technological sabotage, and bias-motivated abuse—are civil rights violations that are not protected under the First Amendment, since they create a hostile learning and work environment (Citron 2009).

Many, but not all, states mandate that schools respond to face-to-face bullying, even if it is done off school property, as long as the perpetrator or the youths being bullied are community members. New Jersey gives schools permission to punish students who bully or cyberbully off campus.

Cyberbullying laws that involve sexting are still in their infancy and can escalate situations quickly if the legal route is pursued. The Canadian government passed Bill C-13 (2014), the Protecting Canadians from Online Crime Act, which prohibits the posting of nonconsensual, sexually explicit images or participating in harassing or annoying behavior conducted via electronic communication. Concerns were raised about the likelihood of nondisclosure and confusing youths. It was also a concern that too many young people could be processed through the criminal justice system because of this law (Olthof et al. 2011; Coburn et al. 2015).

U.S. states have been slow to create laws that deal appropriately with sexting issues, both legally and within school districts. Students caught sexting in the United States can be charged for the federal crime of producing and distributing child pornography. A first-time offender may face fines and a minimum of fifteen to thirty years in prison (Citizens Guide to U.S. Federal Law on Child Pornography 2017). Youths as young as five years old have been charged with felonies, and students have been placed on sex offender registries, even when their actions were not motivated by coercion, material gain, or malice (Primack 2018).

Alternatively, the ACEs StopBullying.gov fact sheet (2017, August) posts details about using restorative justice practices, as many schools are beginning to do, where teachers and other school staff can be trained to facilitate constructive justice alternatives to respond effectively to bullying.

Restorative Justice

Restorative justice is sometimes used for students accused of bullying (or other problems) to take accountability for their actions, repair harm, and rebuild relationships and for students who have been hurt to have the opportunity to tell the accused how the behavior affected them and what they want the other party to do to make repairs. Other students involved can also speak about how the behavior impacted them and what they think might make the situation better, and the accused can speak on their own behalf and try to explain their actions. Schools that involve students in the process of self-reflection and active participation tend to be successful at reducing bullying.

As stopbullying.org (2017, August) notes,

> Restorative Justice programs focus on restoring the relationships and repairing harm. Schools are also using restorative justice as a way to bring all parties together to repair the harm that was done.
>
> Like circle discussions, restorative justice moves away from individual punishment to community learning. This approach can be very helpful for children and youth to understand bullying from the perspective of the

person being bullied, the person bullying another, and the witnesses.

With punishment, even if a particular misbehavior stops, there is little to suggest that the behavior will change in the future, and the punitive measure doesn't tend to help the students who were bullied. Instead, punishment often perpetuates the bully-victim cycle, where bullied students may become bullies in order to regain lost status (Marx & Kettrey 2016). Mullet (2014) writes that restorative justice is a constructive model of school discipline that can also teach prosocial behavior, motivate healthier decision-making, and stop behavior that is hurtful.

Restorative justice is an empathy-based philosophy that is also becoming more common in juvenile justice initiatives, framed around the harm done to relationships. Practitioners find opportunities to rebuild the relationships negatively affected by misbehavior and to create opportunities for restitution. The process is meant to heal injured relationships and to address the feelings and needs of affected persons. At the same time, accountability is gained through self-reflection and a collaborative decision-making process between the harmer and the harmed. The perspective in restorative justice is that "[n]o problem is too difficult once it is recognized as a common task" (Marx & Kettrey 2016: 158).

When schools use restorative justice to address bullying, people tend to become more compassionate and concerned about one another. Wachtel (2012) writes,

When bullying occurs, it's addressed in face-to-face restorative circles, bringing together everyone affected by the incident: students, teachers, and potentially parents. In the circle's safe environment, all participants speak candidly about how they are impacted and receive understanding and support.

> Unlike punishment, the circle confronts bullies with the emotional consequences of their behavior and offers them an opportunity to make amends and provide assurances that their harmful behavior will stop. (31)

When restorative justice is effective, it is not coercive. Students who hurt others make amends. The harmed party benefits, and the harmer emerges with more self-respect and respect from others for working hard to repair the relationships. The harmer develops more respect and compassion for the person they hurt. A strong restorative justice process reintegrates the harmer into the community. Everyone in the community works together to restore trust and build healthier decision-making abilities with the person who harmed. This supports the developing identity of that child or adolescent and reinforces prosocial behaviors, rather than the more conventional shaming or shunning that often invites retaliation (Marx & Kettrey 2016).

The process of getting the harmed and the harmer in a circle to discuss ways for the harmer to make amends "de-escalates anger, encourages reconciliation and empowers healthy decision making in the future," write Marx and Kettrey (2016: 162). Not all children are comfortable with this process, and some schools offer a choice: the punitive route or the opportunity to make amends through a restorative circle. Some say the process is too time-consuming. Because relationships are restored, though, and revenge and other harmful acting-out behaviors are avoided, time can be saved.

Other critics suggest that it is too easy. However, Marx and Kettrey (2016) write that restorative practices tend to involve "hard work and thrives on the principles of obligation, empathy, dignity, and making things right. Wrongdoers do not 'get away' with anything. They recognize their obligations and commit to restore, reconcile, and make restitution, which are real consequences of their actions" (161).

The harmer tends not to be stigmatized or resented, and the positive will generated allows for a fresh slate and the ability to shift the dynamics between the students. While holding those who bully accountable, the restorative practices avoid labeling children "bullies" and "victims." Restorative justice only works, though, if facilitators are effectively trained. The process is powerful; when done correctly, it affirms the worth of the youths involved, while still recognizing that many school bullies have been abused or bullied themselves. The experience empowers students to take responsibility for resolving their own conflicts (Van der Valk 2013).

In many states, students accused of bullying may not be involved in a restorative justice circle until one-on-one discussions take place with that person and talks with family members are involved. New York City Department of Education (NYC-DOE) policies, for instance, require students involved in bullying to first write statements about what happened. School administrators then make an assessment and decision about how the situation will be handled. When students are suspended, and if appropriate, the school can move forward with a restorative justice circle after the students return to school. In some circumstances family members are expected to participate in the circle. Other times those who bullied others might not be involved in the circle at all. Trained school staff make educated judgments about the best ways to deal with each situation (personal oral communication, Rowe-Small 2019, June 24). According to the Stopbullying.gov website, many state policies now include restorative justice as an intervention option.

When restorative justice is used for adult crimes in countries that prioritize this process, everyone involved is included. The Restorative Justice Council (2016) explains,

> Restorative justice gives victims the chance to meet or communicate with their offender to explain the real impact of the crime—it empowers victims by giving them a voice. It also holds offenders to account for what they have done and helps them to take responsibility and make

amends. Restorative justice often involves a conference, where a victim meets their offender face to face.

With excellent restorative practice training, school staff can address a wide range of challenges. The Morningside Center for Teaching Social Responsibility, a school restorative justice training program, explains on their website:

> Restorative practices can offer a positive alternative to the punitive forms of discipline that can lead to the disproportionately harsh discipline of students of color. They enable both young people and adults to:
> - Strengthen their sense of connection with each other, creating a kind and productive classroom and school
> - Bolster their social and emotional skills and their cultural and racial awareness
> - Develop skills to resolve conflicts and problem-solve, and repair harm in restorative ways rather than impose punishment

A Morningside facilitator explained on the website that in one of her circles, several students shared about being bullied in a previous school and said that the teachers there who knew about the psychological and physical aggression hadn't intervened. These students felt so frustrated about no one helping that they decided to "take matters into their own hands. For the sake of self-preservation, they had turned to what they were familiar with: violence. So, violence begot more violence." Another student in the circle said that after he heard these stories, he realized he had been a bully himself. He would "laugh at other kids who had been teased," and he "would pile on and do his own teasing." Now he realized "the *scars* his behavior might have left." He showed remorse as he spoke about the harm he realized he inflicted (van Woerkom 2016).

These kinds of open, honest, and vulnerable discussions are typical in restorative circles. Another effective restorative-justice intervention occurred in the Kosciuszko Middle School, located in a culturally diverse area of Hamtramck, Michigan. The school was plagued with bullying until restorative practices helped students recognize their common humanity. A fifteen-year-old Bengali student at the school said, "In circles, everyone gets to know each other. You can say anything that comes into your head, from your heart. I felt shame at other schools. I feel good here. I never saw a school before where there was no bullying" (Wachtel 2012: 31).

References

Adams, J. M. (2013, June 3). President Obama calls on teachers to help identify mental health disorders in students. EdSource. Retrieved from https://edsource.org/2013/president-obama-calls-on-teachers-to-help-identify-mental-health-disorders-seek-help-for-students/32959

Aizenman, N. (2017, October 6). Gun violence: How the U.S. compares with other countries, NPR, "Goats and Soda Stories of Life in a Changing World." Retrieved from https://www.npr.org/sections/goatsandsoda/2017/10/06/555861898/gun-violence-how-the-u-s-compares-to-other-countries

Alexander, J. (2016). *Bullying: Practical and easy-follow-advice for parents*. New York: Pavilion Books.

American Academy of Pediatrics. (2014). Adverse childhood experiences and the lifelong consequences of trauma. Retrieved from https://www.aap.org/en-us/Documents/ttb_aces_consequences.pdf

American Academy of Pediatrics. (n.d.). Childhood obesity: Common misconceptions. Retrieved from https://www.healthychildren.org/English/health-issues/conditions/obesity/Pages/Childhood-Obesity-Common-Misconceptions.aspx

American Civil Liberties Union. (2019). Cruel, inhuman, and degrading conditions. Retrieved from https://www.aclu .org/issues/prisoners-rights/cruel-inhuman-and-degrading -conditions

Attree, P. (2006, February). The social costs of child poverty: A systematic review of the qualitative evidence. *Children & Society, 20*(1), 54–66. doi:10.1002/CHI.854

Baillien, E., Neyens, I., De Witte, H., & De Cuyper, N. (2008, December). A qualitative study on the development of workplace bullying: Towards a three way model. *Journal of Community & Applied Social Psychology, 19*(1), 1–16. doi:10.1002/casp.977

Bansel, P., Davies, B., Laws, C., & Linnell, S. (2009). Bullies, bullying and power in the contexts of schooling. *British Journal of Sociology of Education, 30*(1), 59–69.

Basile, K. C., Espelage, D. L., Rivers, I., McMahon, M., & Simon, T. R. (2009, September–October). The theoretical and empirical links between bullying behavior and male sexual violence perpetration. *Aggression and Violent Behavior, 14*(5), 336–347. doi:10.1016/j.avb.2009.06.001

Bazelon, E. (2013). *Sticks and stones: Defeating the culture of bullying and rediscovering the power of character and empathy*. New York: Random House.

Bazirake, J. B., & Zimmermann, G. (2018, May). Peace profile: Marshall Rosenberg. *Peace Review: A Journal of Social Justice, 30*(2), 246–253. doi:10.1080/10402659.201 8.1458970

BBC. (2018, June). Bullying now means something different. CBBC Newsround. Retrieved from https://www.bbc.co.uk /newsround/44355541

Berger, C., & Dijkstra, J. K. (2013, August). Competition, envy, or snobbism?: How popularity and friendships shape antipathy networks of adolescents. *Journal of Research on Adolescence, 23*(3), 586–595. doi:10.1111/jora.12048

Berlowitz, M. J., Frye, R., & Jette, K. M. (2017, March). Bullying and zero-tolerance policies: The school to prison pipeline. *Multicultural Learning and Teaching, 12*(1), 7–25. Retrieved from https://eric.ed.gov/?id=EJ1133316

Berne, S., Frisen, A., & Kling, J. (2014). Appearance-related cyberbullying: A qualitative investigation of characteristics, content, reasons, and effects. *Body Image, 11*(4), 527–533.

Black, E. (2003, September). The horrifying American roots of Nazi eugenics. Retrieved from https://historynewsnet work.org/article/1796

Bleakley, P., & Bleakley, C. (2018, May). School resource officers, "zero tolerance" and the enforcement of compliance in the American education system. *Interchange, 49*(2), 247–261. doi:10.1007/s10780-018-9326-5

Brainstorm Media. (2016, September 2). *Paper Tigers* trailer. Retrieved from https://www.youtube.com/watch?v=KdDr _nZOIXc

Brave Heart, M., & DeBruyn, L. (1998). The American Indian holocaust: Healing historical unresolved grief. *American Indian and Alaska Native Mental Health Research, 8,* 60–82.

Brown, R. P., & Gerbarg, P. L. (2012, June). *The healing power of the breath: Simple techniques to reduce stress and anxiety, enhance concentration, and balance your emotions.* Boston, MA: Shambhala.

Brown, R. P., & Gerbarg, P. L. (2017). Breathing techniques in psychiatric treatment. In P. L. Gerbarg, R. P. Brown, & P. R. Muskin (Eds.), *Complementary and integrative treatments in psychiatric practice* (pp. 241–250). Washington, DC: American Psychiatric Association.

Brown, R. P., Gerbarg, P. L., & Muench, F. (2013). Breathing practices for treatment of psychiatric and stress-related medical conditions. In P. R. Muskin, P. L. Gerbarg, &

R. P. Brown (Eds.), *Complementary and integrative therapies for psychiatric disorders*. Philadelphia, PA: Elsevier.

Bucchianeri, M. M., Eisenberg, M. E., & Neumark-Sztainer, D. (2013, July). Weightism, racism, classism, and sexism: Shared forms of harassment in adolescents. *Journal of Adolescent Health, 53*(1), 47–53.

Bucchianeri, M. M., Gower, A. L., McMorris, B. J., & Eisenberg, M. E. (2016, August). Youth experiences with multiple types of prejudice-based harassment. *Journal of Adolescence, 51*, 68–75. Retrieved from https://www.ncbi .nlm.nih.gov/pubmed/27310725

Bureau of Justice Statistics. (2014). Recidivism of prisoners released in 30 states in 2005: Patterns from 2005 to 2010. Retrieved from https://www.bjs.gov/index.cfm?ty=pbdetail &iid=4986

Carpenter, D. (2009). *The everything parent's guide to dealing with bullies: From playground teasing to cyberbullying, all you need to ensure your child's safety and happiness*. Avon, MA: An Everything Series Book.

Carrera, M., Depalma, R., & Lameiras, M. (2011). Toward a more comprehensive understanding of bullying in school settings. *Educational Psychology Review, 23*(4), 479–499. doi:10.1007/s10648-011-9171-x

Centers for Disease Control and Prevention. (2009a). School connectedness: Strategies for increasing protective factors among youth. Atlanta, GA: U.S. Department of Health and Human Services. Retrieved from https://www.cdc.gov /healthyyouth/protective/pdf/connectedness.pdf

Centers for Disease Control and Prevention. (2009b). Fostering school connectedness: Improving student health and academic achievement. Atlanta, GA: U.S. Department of Health and Human Services. Retrieved from https:// www.cdc.gov/healthyyouth/protective/pdf/connectedness _administrators.pdf

Chester, D. S., Merwin, L. M., & DeWall, C. N. (2015, September–October). Maladaptive perfectionism linked to aggression and self-harm: Emotion regulation as a mechanism. *Aggressive Behavior, 41*(5), 443–454. Retrieved from https://www.ncbi.nlm.nih.gov/pubmed/26918433

Citizen's Guide to U.S. Federal Law on Child Pornography. (2017, December). Retrieved from https://www.justice .gov/criminal-ceos/citizens-guide-us-federal-law-child -pornography

Citron, D. K. (2009, December). Law's expressive value in combating cyber gender harassment. *Michigan Law Review, 108*(3), 373–415.

Coburn, P. I., Connolly, D. A., & Roesch, R. (2015, October). Cyberbullying: Is federal criminal legislation the solution? *Canadian Journal of Criminology & Criminal Justice, 57*(4), 566–579.

Cole, N. L. (2019, May 30). Understanding the school-to-prison pipeline, ThoughtCo. Retrieved from https://www .thoughtco.com/school-to-prison-pipeline-4136170

Collaborative for Academic, Social, and Emotional Learning. (2019). What Is SEL? Retrieved from https://casel.org/what -is-sel/

Connell, R. W. (2005). *Masculinities.* Oakland: University of California Press.

Cook, M. (2011). Homes fit for homos: Joe Orton, masculinity and the domesticated queer. In J. H. Arnold & S. Brady (Eds.), *What is masculinity? Historical dynamics from antiquity to the contemporary world* (pp. 303–322). Basingstoke, UK: Palgrave.

Copeland, W. E., Wolke, D., Angold, A., & Costello, E. J. (2013). Adult psychiatric outcomes of bullying and being bullied by peers in childhood and adolescence. *JAMA Psychiatry, 70*(4), 419–426. doi:10.1001/jamapsychiatry .2013.504

Cornell, D. G., & Bandyopadhyay, S. (2010). The assessment of bullying. In S. R. Jimerson, S. M. Swearer, & D. L. Espelage (Eds.), *Handbook of bullying in schools: An international perspective* (pp. 265–276). New York: Routledge.

Cornell, D. G., & Limber, S. P. (2016, February). Do U.S. laws go far enough to prevent bullying at school? *American Psychological Association, 47*(2). Retrieved from https://www.apa.org/monitor/2016/02/ce-corner

Crawford, E., & Wright, M. O. (2007). The impact of childhood psychological maltreatment on interpersonal schemas and subsequent experiences of relationship aggression. *Journal of Emotional Abuse, 7*(2), 93–116. Retrieved from https://psycnet.apa.org/record/2008-01102-006

Crochík, J. L. (2016). Hierarchy, violence and bullying among students of public middle schools. *Paidéia (Ribeirão Preto), 26*(65), 307–315. Retrieved from http://www.scielo.br/scielo.php?script=sci_arttext

Cullen, D. (2009). *Columbine.* New York: Twelve.

Curran, F. C. (2019, March). The law, policy, and portrayal of zero tolerance school discipline: Examining prevalence and characteristics across levels of governance and school districts. *Educational Policy, 33*(2), 319–349. doi:10.1177/0895904817691840

Curran, T., & Hill, A. P. (2017). Perfectionism is increasing over time: A meta-analysis of birth cohort differences from 1989 to 2016. *Psychological Bulletin.* doi:10.1037/bul000

Curtis, A. J. (2014). Tracing the school-to-prison pipeline from zero-tolerance policies to juvenile justice dispositions. *Georgetown Law Journal, 102*(4), 1251–1277. Retrieved from https://georgetownlawjournal.org/articles/86/tracing-school-to-prison-pipeline-from

Darden, E. C. (2015, March). ED law: Courts join crackdown on school bullies. *Phi Delta Kappan, 96*(7), 76–77. doi:10.1177/0031721715579048

Davis, K. (2011). Procrustean solutions to animal identity and welfare problems. In J. Sanbonmatsu (Ed.), *Critical theory and animal liberation* (pp. 35–54). Landham, MD: Rowman and Littlefield.

de Bruyn, E. H., Cillessen, A. H. N., & Wissink, I. B. (2010). Associations of peer acceptance and perceived popularity with bullying and victimization in early adolescence. *Journal of Early Adolescence, 30*, 543–566. doi:10.1177/0272431609340517

DeGruy, J. (2005). *Post traumatic slave syndrome: America's legacy of enduring injury and healing.* Milwaukie, OR: Uptone Press.

Derber, C., & Magrass, Y. R. (2016). *Bully nation: How the American establishment creates a bullying society.* Lawrence: University Press of Kansas.

Dewey, J. (1916). *Democracy and education: An introduction to the philosophy of education.* New York: Free Press.

Dixon, W. W. (2003). *Straight: Constructions of heterosexuality in the cinema.* New York: SUNY Press.

Dostoevsky, F. (1862). *The House of the dead.* Translated by David McDuff. New York: Penguin Classics (published 1985). ISBN 9780140444568.

Dweck, C. S. (2007). *Mindset: The new psychology of success.* New York: Random House.

EFE News Service. (2011). School bullying has bigger effect on Latino, black students. *Latin American Herald Tribune.* Retrieved from http://laht.com/article.asp?ArticleId=419045&CategoryId=12395

Einarsen, S. (1999). The nature and causes of bullying at work. *International Journal of Manpower, 20*, 16–31.

Eisenberg, N., & Miller, P. A. (1988, May). The relation of empathy to aggressive and externalizing/antisocial behavior. *Psychological Bulletin, 103*(3), 324–344.

Elgar, F. J., Pickett, K. E., Pickett, W., Craig, W., Molcho, M., Hurrelmann, K., & Lenzi, M. (2013, April). School bullying, homicide and income inequality: A cross-national pooled time series analysis. *International Journal of Public Health, 58*(2), 237–245. Retrieved from https://www.ncbi .nlm.nih.gov/pubmed/22714137

Ellenbogen, S. (2008). *From physical abuse victim to aggressor: Exploring the relationship,* Montreal, Quebec: Gill Library and Collections. Masters in Social Work thesis. Retrieved from ProQuest Central; ProQuest Dissertations & Theses Global. (Order No. NR66294.)

Espelage, D. L., Hong, J. S., Him, D. H., & Nan, L. (2018). Empathy, attitude towards bullying, theory-of-mind, and non-physical forms of bully perpetration and victimization among U.S. middle school students. *Child Youth Care Forum, 47,* 45–60. doi:10.1007/s10566-017-9416-z

Esses, V. M., Dietz, J., Bennett-Abuayyash, C., & Joshi, C. (2007). Prejudice in the workplace: The role of bias against visible minorities in the devaluation of immigrants' foreign-acquired qualifications and credentials. *Canadian Issues, Spring,* 114–118.

Evans, C., & Smokowski, P. (2016, August). Theoretical explanations for bullying in school: How ecological processes propagate perpetration and victimization. *Child & Adolescent Social Work Journal, 33*(4), 365–375.

Evans-Campbell, T. (2008, March). Historical trauma in American Indian/Native Alaska communities. *Journal of Interpersonal Violence, 23*(3), 316–338. Retrieved from https://www.ncbi.nlm.nih.gov/pubmed/18245571

Faber, A., & Mazlish, E. (1982). *How to talk so kids will listen & listen so kids will talk.* New York: Avon.

Faber, A., & Mazlish, E. (1988). *Siblings without rivalry: How to help your children live together so you can live too.* New York: Avon.

Federal Bureau of Investigation. (2015, January). UCR program quarterly. Retrieved from https://ucr.fbi.gov/ucr -program-quarterly/ucr-quarterly-january-2015

Fekkes, M., Pijpers, F. I., Fredriks, A. M., Vogels, T., & Verloove-Vanhorick, S. P. (2006, May). Do bullied children get ill, or do ill children get bullied? A prospective cohort study on the relationship between bullying and health-related symptoms. *Pediatrics, 117*(5), 1568–1574. Retrieved from https://www.ncbi.nlm.nih.gov/pubmed /16651310

Felmlee, D., & Faris, R. (2016). Toxic ties: Networks of friendship, dating, and cyber victimization. *Social Psychology Quarterly, 79*(3), 243–262. doi:10.1177 /0190272516656585

Felsen, I. (1998). Transgenerational transmission of effects of the Holocaust. In Y. Danieli (Ed.), *International handbook of multigenerational legacies of trauma* (pp. 43–68). New York: Plenum.

Follestad, B., & Wroldsen, N. (2019). *Using restorative circles in schools: How to build strong learning communities and foster student wellbeing.* London: Jessica Kingsley.

Friere, P. (1968). *Pedagogy of the oppressed.* New York: Seabury.

Fronius, T., Darling-Hammond, S., Persson, H., Guckenburg, S., Hurley, N., & Petrosino, A. (2019, March). Restorative justice in U.S. schools: An updated research review. West Ed Justice & Prevention Center. Retrieved from https:// www.wested.org/wp-content/uploads/2019/04/resource -restorative-justice-in-u-s-schools-an-updated-research -review.pdf

Garandeau, C. F., Lee, I. A., & Salmivalli, C. (2014a). Differential effects of the KiVa anti-bullying program on popular and unpopular bullies. *Journal of Applied Developmental Psychology, 35*(1), 44–50. Retrieved from https://www.deepdyve.com/lp/elsevier/differential-effects -of-the-kiva-anti-bullying-program-on-popular-and -5iJHFJOLoa

Garandeau, C. F., Lee, I. A., & Salmivalli, C. (2014b). Inequality matters: Classroom status hierarchy and adolescents' bullying. *Journal of Youth Adolescence, 43*, 1123–1133. doi:10.1007/s10964-013-0040-4

Garby, L. (2013, summer). Direct bullying: Criminal act or mimicking what has been learned? *Education, 133*(4), 448–450.

Georgiou, S. N., Fousiani, K., Michaelides, M., & Stavrinides, P. (2013). Cultural value orientation and authoritarian parenting as parameters of bullying and victimization at school. *International Journal of Psychology, 48*(1), 69–78.

Gerbarg, P. (2018, September 18). Assistant clinical professor in psychiatry New York Medical College, personal oral communication, New York.

Gerbarg, P. L., & Brown, R. P. (2015). Yoga and neuronal pathways to enhance stress response, emotion regulation, bonding, and spirituality. In E. G. Horovitz & S. Elgelid (Eds.), *Yoga therapy: Theory and practice* (pp. 49–64). New York: Routledge.

Gerbarg, P. L., & Brown, R. P. (2016, November). Neurobiology and neurophysiology of breath practices in psychiatric care. *Psychiatric Times, 33*(11), 22–25. Retrieved from https://www.psychiatrictimes.com/special-reports /neurobiology-and-neurophysiology-breath-practices -psychiatric-care

Gerbarg, P. L., Brown, R. P., Streeter, C. C., Katzman, M., & Vermani, M. (2019). Breath practices for survivor and caregiver stress, depression, and post-traumatic stress disorder: Connection, co-regulation, compassion. *OBM Integrative and Complementary Medicine.*

Gest, S. D., & Rodkin, P. C. (2011). Teaching practices and elementary classroom peer ecologies. *Journal of Applied Developmental Psychology, 32*(5), 288–296. doi:10.1016/j. appdev.2011.02.004

Golding, W., & Epstein, E. L. (1954). *Lord of the flies.* New York: Perigee.

Goldman, C. (2012). *Bullied: What every parent, teacher, and kid needs to know about ending the cycle of fear.* New York: HarperCollins.

Goldman, C. (2014, October). How do I know what's bullying and what's normal conflict? *New York Times.* Retrieved from https://parenting.blogs.nytimes.com/2014 /10/10/how-do-i-know-whats-bullying-and-whats-normal -conflict/

Goldsmith, R. E., & Freyd, J. J. (2005, April). Awareness for emotional abuse. *Journal of Emotional Abuse, 5*(1), 95–123.

Graff, G. (2014). The intergenerational trauma of slavery and its aftermath. *Journal of Psychohistory, 41*(3), 181–197.

Grinshteyn, E., & Hemenway, D. (2016). Violent death rates: The US compared with other high-income OECD countries, 2010. *The American Journal of Medicine, 129*(3), 266.

Guldberg, H. (2009, February). *Reclaiming childhood: Freedom and play in an age of fear.* Abingdon, England: Routledge.

Guldberg, H. (2011, November). Anti-bullying campaigns: Doing more harm than good? Retrieved from http://www .heleneguldberg.co.uk/index.php/site/article/109/

Gullone, E., & Robertson, N. (2008, July). The relationship between bullying and animal abuse behaviors in adolescents: The importance of witnessing animal abuse.

Journal of Applied Developmental Psychology, 29(5), 371–379. Retrieved from https://www.sciencedirect.com/science/article/pii/S0193397308000518

Hantzopoulos, M. (2008, May 16). *Sizing up small: An ethnographic case study of a critical small high school in New York City* (Dissertation). Teachers College, Columbia University

Hantzopoulos, M. (2013). The fairness committee: Restorative justice in a small urban public high school. *Prevention Researcher, 20*(1), 7–10.

Harel-Fisch, Y., Walsh, S. D., Fogel-Grinvald, H., Dostaler, S., Hetland, J., Simons-Morton, B., & Pickett, W. (2009). A cross-national profile of bullying and victimization among adolescents in 40 countries. *International Journal of Public Health, 54,* 216–224.

Hawkins, D. L., Pepler, D. J., & Craig, W. M. (2001). Naturalistic observations of peer interventions in bullying. *Social Development, 10*(4), 512–527.

Health Resources and Services Administration. (n.d.). Misdirections in bullying prevention and intervention. Retrieved from https://www.cde.state.co.us/mtss/misdirectionsinbullyingprevention

Henry, B., & Sanders, C. (2007). Bullying and animal abuse: Is there a connection? *Society and Animals, 15*(2), 107–126. Retrieved from https://www.animalsandsociety.org/wp-content/uploads/2016/04/henry.pdf

Hepburn, A. (1997, January). Teachers and secondary school bullying: A postmodern discourse analysis. *Discourse & Society, 8*(1), 27–48. doi:10.1177/0957926597008001003

Herrera, C. (2018, February 15). Gun shop owners distraught over firearm sold to teen now held in school massacre. *Miami Herald.* Retrieved from https://www.miamiherald.com/news/local/community/broward/article200434884.html

Hitler, A. (1938). *The Nazi primer: Official handbook for schooling the Hitler Youth* (H. L. Childs, Trans.). New York: Harper & Brothers.

Hobbes, T. (1651). *Leviathan*. U.S.: Pacific Publishing Studio, 2010.

Hodgdon, H. B. (2009). *Child maltreatment and aggression: The mediating role of moral disengagement, emotion regulation, and emotional callousness among juvenile offenders*. Temple University Graduate Board for Doctor in Philosophy. Retrieved from ProQuest Central; ProQuest Dissertations & Theses Global. (Order No. 3371980.)

Hoel, H., Rayner, C., & Cooper, C. (1999). Workplace bullying. *International Review of Industrial and Organizational Psychology, 14,* 195–230.

Hoff, B. H. (2012). US national survey: More men than women victims of intimate partner violence. *Journal of Aggression, Conflict and Peace Research, 4*(3), 155–163. Retrieved from https://psycnet.apa.org/record/2012-17749 -004

Holpuch, A., & Owen, P. (2018, March 24). March for Our Lives: Hundreds of thousands demand end to gun violence-as it happened. *Guardian*. Retrieved from https:// www.theguardian.com/us-news/live/2018/mar/24/march -for-our-lives-protest-gun-violence-washington

Hughes, T., 1833–1896. (1890). *Tom Brown's School Days*. New York: Y. Crowell.

Hymel, S., Schonert-Reichl, K. A., Bonanno, R. A., Vaillancourt, T., & Henderson, N. R. (2010). Bullying and morality: Understanding how good kids can act badly. In S. R. Jimerson, S. M. Swearer, & D. L. Espelage (Eds.), *International handbook of school bullying: An international perspective* (pp. 1010–118). New York: Routledge.

International Center for Assault Prevention. (2017). CAP's bullying prevention guide: A project of the NJ Department of Children and Families. Retrieved from https://njcap.org/wp-content/uploads/2017/09/CBPP-Adult-packet-english-2017.pdf

Ivarsson, T., Broberg, A. G., Arvidsson, T., & Gillberg, C. (2005). Bullying in adolescence: Psychiatric problems in victims and bullies as measured by the Youth Self Report (YSR) and the Depression Self-Rating Scale (DSRS). *Nordic Journal of Psychiatry, 59*(5), 365–373. Retrieved from https://www.ncbi.nlm.nih.gov/pubmed/16757465

Jahoda, G. (2018). Towards scientific racism. In T. D. Gupta, C. E. James, C. Andersen, G. Galabuzi, & R. C. A. Maaka (Eds.), *Race and racialization: Essential readings* (2nd ed., pp. 38–51). Toronto, Ontario: Canadian Scholars.

Jelenchick, L., & Eickhoff, J. C., & Moreno, M. (2013). "Facebook depression?": Social networking site use and depression in older adolescents. *Journal of Adolescent Health, 52*(1), 128–30. doi:10.1016/j.jadohealth.2012.05.008

Kahane-Nissembaum, M. (2011). Exploring intergenerational trauma in third generation holocaust survivors. *Penn Social Policy & Practice*, Philadelphia, PA: University of Pennsylvania, *Doctorate in Social Work (DSW) Dissertations, 16*, 1–81. Retrieved from https://repository.upenn.edu/edissertations_sp2/16

Kahn, S. R. (2011). *Privilege: The making of an adolescent elite at St. Paul's School.* Princeton, NJ: Princeton University Press.

Kaltiala-Heino, R., Rimpela, M., Marttunen, M., Rimpela, A., & Rantanen, P. (1999, August). Bullying, depression, and suicidal ideation in Finnish adolescents: School survey. *British Medical Journal, 319*(7206), 348–351. Retrieved from https://www.bmj.com/content/319/7206/348.full

Kaplan, H. R. (2011, April). Racial inequality and "meritocracy": A closer look. Racism Review. Retrieved

from http://www.racismreview.com/blog/2011/04/22/racial
-inequality-and-meritocracy-a-closer-look/

Keashly, L., Nowell, B. L., Einarsen, S., Hoel, H., Zapf,
D., & Cooper, C. (2011). Conflict, conflict resolution,
and bullying. *Bullying and harassment in the workplace:
Developments in theory, research, and practice, 2* (pp. 423–
445). Boca Raton, FL: CRC Press.

Kernis, M. H., Grannemann, B. D., & Barclay, L. C. (1989).
Stability and level of self-esteem as predictors of anger
arousal and hostility. *Journal of Personality and Social
Psychology, 56*(6), 1013–1022. Retrieved from https://www
.ncbi.nlm.nih.gov/pubmed/2746456

Kernis, M. H., Whisenhunt, C. R., Waschull, S. B.,
Greenier, K. D., Berry, A. J., Herlocker, C. E., &
Anderson, C. A. (1998, June). Multiple facets of self-
esteem and their relations to depressive symptoms.
Personality and Social Psychology Bulletin, 24(6), 657–668.
doi:10.1177/0146167298246009

Kim, M., Kim, H., Kim, K., Ju, S., Choi, J., & Yu, M. (2015,
October). Smartphone addiction: (Focused depression,
aggression and impulsion) among college students.
Indian Journal of Science and Technology, 8(25), 706–716.
Retrieved from http://www.indjst.org/index.php/indjst
/article/view/80215, doi: 10.17485/ijst/2015/v8i25/80215

Kimmel, M. (2008). *Guyland: The perilous world where boys
become men.* New York: HarperCollins.

Kimmel, M. (2017). *Angry white men: American masculinity at
the end of the era* (Revised ed.). New York: National Books.

Kjolberg, T. (2016, May). Prison life in Scandinavia.
Daily Scandinavian. Retrieved from https://www
.dailyscandinavian.com/prison-life-in-scandinavia/

Klain, E., & Pavić, L. (2002). Psychotrauma and
reconciliation. *Croatian Medical Journal, 43*(2), 126–137.
Retrieved from https://www.ncbi.nlm.nih.gov/pubmed
/11885036

Klein, J. (2012a). *The bully society: School shootings and the crisis of bullying in America's schools.* New York: NYU Press.

Klein, J. (2012b). *For educators: The bully society: School shootings and the crisis of bullying in America's schools.* New York: NYU Press. Retrieved from https://nyupress.org/resources/for-educators/ or jessieklein.com

Klein, J., & Chancer, L. S. (2000). Masculinity matters: The role of gender in high-profile school violence cases. In S. U. Spina (Ed.), *Smoke and mirrors: The hidden context of violence in schools and society* (pp. 129–162). New York: Rowman and Littlefield.

Kochenderfer-Ladd, B., & Wardrop, J. L. (2001). Chronicity and instability of children's peer victimization experiences as predictors of loneliness and social satisfaction trajectories. *Child Development, 72*(1), 134–151. doi:10.1111/1467-8624.00270

Kupelian, D., Kalayjian, A., & Kassabian, A. (1998). The Turkish genocide of the Armenians: Continuing effects on survivors and their families eight decades after massive trauma. In Y. Danieli (Ed.), *International handbook of multigenerational legacies of trauma* (pp. 191–210). New York: Plenum.

Kwate, N., & Meyer, I. H. (2010, October). The myth of meritocracy and African American health. *Journal of Public Health, 100*(10), 1831–1834. Retrieved from https://www.ncbi.nlm.nih.gov/pmc/articles/PMC2936997/

Langos, C. (2012, June). Cyberbullying: The challenge to define. *Cyberpsychology, Behavior, and Social Networking, 15*(6), 285–289.

Lee, C. H., & Song, J. (2012). Functions of parental involvement and effects of school climate on bullying behaviors among South Korean middle school students. *Journal of Interpersonal Violence, 27,* 2437–2464.

Lee, S. J. (2005). *Up against whiteness: Race, school, and immigrant youth.* New York: Teachers College Press.

Lefkowitz, B. (1997). *Our guys: The Glen Ridge rape and the secret life of the perfect suburb*. Berkeley: University of California Press.

Levine, E., & Tamburrino, M. (2014, July). Bullying among young children: Strategies for prevention. *Early Childhood Education Journal, 42*(4), 271–278. Retrieved from https://link.springer.com/article/10.1007/s10643-013-0600-y

Levine, M. (2006). *The price of privilege: How parental pressure and material advantage are creating a generation of disconnected and unhappy kids*. New York: HarperCollins.

Li, Y., & Wright, M. F. (2014, January). Adolescents' social status goals: Relationships to social status insecurity, aggression, and prosocial behavior. *Journal of Youth Adolescence, 43*(1), 146–160. Retrieved from https://link.springer.com/article/10.1007/s10964-013-9939-z

Lin, D. (2019, May 24). The argument for animal rights: How are those rights different from human rights? ThoughtCo. Retrieved from https://www.thoughtco.com/why-should-animals-have-rights-127603

Linné, C. V., 1707–1778. (1767). *Caroli linné, equitis aur. de stella polari: Systema naturae, per regna tria naturae, secundum classes, ordines, genera, species, cum characteribus, differentiis, synonymis locis (decima tertia ed.)*. Vindobonae: Typis Ioannis Thomae nob. de Trattnern.

Locke, J. (1689). *Two treatises on civil government*. London: George Routledge and Sons.

Loevy, D. (2015, December). How does US justice stack up? An international comparison. Retrieved from https://loevy.com/blog/how-does-us-justice-stack-up-an-international-comparison/

Lovejoy, A. O. (1936). *The great chain of being: A study of the history of an idea*. Cambridge, MA: Harvard University Press.

Martínez, I., Murgui, S., Garcia, F., & Garcia, O. F. (2019). Parenting in the digital era: Protective and risk parenting styles for traditional bullying and cyberbullying victimization. *Computers in Human Behavior, 90*, 84–92.

Marx, R. A., & Kettrey, H. H. (2016, May). Gay-straight alliances are associated with lower levels of school-based victimization of LGBTQ+ youth: A systematic review and meta-analysis. *Journal of Youth & Adolescence, 45*(7), 1269–1282.

McNicholas, C. I., & Orpinas, P. (2016, September). Prevalence of bullying victimisation among students with disabilities in the United States. *Injury Prevention, 22*(Suppl. 2), A1–A397.

McPherson, M., Smith-Lovin, L., & Vrashears, M. E. (2006, June). Social isolation in America: Changes in core discussion networks over two decades. *American Sociological Review, 71*(3), 353–375.

Mental Health America. (2019). Bullying tips for parents. Retrieved from https://www.mentalhealthamerica.net /bullying-tips-parents

Merten, D. E. (1997). The meaning of meanness: Popularity, competition, and conflict among junior high school girls. *Sociology of Education, 70*(3), 175–191.

Messerschmidt, J. W. (2000). *Nine lives: Adolescent masculinities, the body, and violence.* New York: Westview.

Meyer, E. J. (2008). Gendered harassment in secondary schools: Understanding teachers' (non)interventions. *Gender and Education, 20*(6), 555–570.

Meyer, I. H. (2003). Prejudice, social stress, and mental health in lesbian, gay, and bisexual populations: Conceptual issues and research evidence. *Psychological Bulletin, 129*(5), 674–697. doi:10.1037/0033-2909.129.5.674

Mijs, J. J. B. (2016, March). The unfulfillable promise of meritocracy: Three lessons and their implications for justice in education. *Social Justice Research, 29*(1), 14–34.

Retrieved from https://link.springer.com/article/10.1007/s11211-014-0228-0

Miller, J. G. (2018). Physiological mechanisms of prosociality. *Current Opinion in Psychology, 20,* 50–54.

Mills, C. W. (1967). *The sociological imagination.* London and New York: Oxford University Press.

Mirsky, L. (2014, June). The power of the circle. *Educational Leadership, 71*(9), 51–55. Retrieved from http://www.ascd.org/publications/educational-leadership/summer14/vol71/num09/The-Power-of-the-Circle.aspx

The Morningside Center for Teaching Social Responsibility. New York. https://www.morningsidecenter.org/about

Mullet, J. H. (2014, July). Restorative discipline: From getting even to getting well. *Children & Schools, 36*(3), 157–162. Retrieved from https://academic.oup.com/cs/article-abstract/36/3/157/2754025

Muschert, G. W. (2007). Research in school shootings. *Sociology Compass, 1,* 60–80. doi:10.1111/j.1751-9020.2007.00008.x

Nagata, D. K. (1991). Transgenerational impact of the Japanese-American internment: Clinical issues in working with children of former internees. *Psychotherapy: Theory, Research, Practice, Training, 28*(1), 121–128.

Napoletano, A., Elgar, F. J., Saul, G., Dirks, M., & Craig, W. (2016). The view from the bottom: Relative deprivation and bullying victimization in Canadian adolescents. *Journal of Interpersonal Violence, 31*(20), 3443–3463. doi:10.1177/0886260515585528

The National Center for Analysis of Violent Crime. (1999–2002). The school shooter: A quick reference guide. Federal Bureau of Investigation. Retrieved from https://www.hsdl.org/?abstract&

National Institute of Mental Health. (2017). Any anxiety disorder. Mental Health Information. Retrieved from

https://www.nimh.nih.gov/health/statistics/any-anxiety
-disorder.shtml

Obermann, M. (2011, November). Moral disengagement
in self-reported and peer-nominated school bullying.
Aggressive Behavior, 37(2), 133–144. doi:10.1002/ab.20378

Olsen, E. O., Kann, L., Vivolo-Kantor, A., Kinchen, S., &
McManus, T. (2014, September). School violence and
bullying among sexual minority high school students,
2009–2011. *Journal Adolescent Health, 55*(3), 432–438.

Olthof, T., Goossens, F. A., Vermande, M. M., Aleva, E. A., &
van der Meulen, M. (2011). Bullying as strategic behavior:
Relations with desired and acquired dominance in the peer
group. *Journal of School Psychology, 49*, 339–359.

Olweus Bullying Prevention Program. (2007). What is
bullying? Hazelden Foundation. Retrieved from https://
www.bssd.net/cms/lib/MO01910299/Centricity/Domain
/2951/OlweusFactS_What_Is_Bullying.pdf

Olweus, D. (1991). Bully/victim problems among
schoolchildren: Basic facts and effects of a school based
intervention program. In D. J. Pepler & K. H. Rubin
(Eds.), *The development and treatment of childhood aggression*
(pp. 411–448). Hillsdale, NJ: Lawrence Erlbaum
Associates.

Olweus, D. (1993). *Bullying at school: What we know and
what we can do.* Hoboken, NJ: Wiley-Blackwell.

Olweus, D. (1999). Bullying in Norway. In P. K. Smith,
Y. Morita, J. Junger-Tas, D. Olweus, R. Catalano, &
P. Slee (Eds.), *The nature of school bullying: A cross-national
perspective* (pp. 28–48). London and New York: Routledge.

Orwell, G. (1945). *Animal farm: A fairy story.* London: Secker
and Warburg.

Padgett, S., & Notar, C. E. (2013). Bystanders are the key
to stopping bullying. *Universal Journal of Educational
Research, 1*(2), 33–41.

Patterson, G. R., & Reid, J. B. (1975). *A social learning approach to family intervention: Families with aggressive children*. Eugene, OR: Castalia Publishing Company.

Perreira, K. M., & Ornelas, I. (2013). Painful passages: Traumatic experiences and post-traumatic stress among U.S. immigrant, Latino adolescents, and their primary caregivers. *International Migration Review, 47*(4), 976–1005.

Pickett, K., & Wilkinson, R. (2010, November). *The spirit level: Why equality is better for everyone* (Kindle ed.). East Rutherford, NJ: Penguin.

Piff, P. K., Stancato, D. M., Côté, S., Mendoza-Denton, R., & Keltner, D. (2012, March). Higher social class predicts increased unethical behavior. *Proceedings of the National Academy of Sciences of the United States of America, 109*(11), 4086–4091. Retrieved from https://www.pnas.org/content /109/11/4086

Plumb, J. L., Bush, K. A., & Kersevich, S. E. (2016, spring). Trauma-sensitive schools: An evidence-based approach. *School Social Work Journal, 40*(2), 37–61. Retrieved from http://www.communityschools.org/assets/1/AssetManager /TSS.pdf

Pollack, W. S. (1999, April). *Real boys: Rescuing our sons from the myths of boyhood*. New York: Henry Holt & Company.

Porges, S. W., & Carter, C. S. (2017). Polyvagal theory and the social engagement system: Neurophysiological bridge between connectedness and health. In P. L. Gerbarg, R. P. Brown, & P. R. Muskin (Eds.), *Complementary and integrative treatments in psychiatric practice* (pp. 221–240). Washington, DC: American Psychiatric Association.

Primack, A. J. (2018). Youth sexting and the First Amendment: Rhetoric and child pornography doctrine in the age of translation. *New Media & Society, 20*(8), 2917–2933.

Quart, A. (2003). *Branded: The buying and selling of teenagers.* Cambridge, MA: Perseus.

Rees, J. (2019, March). Male domestic abuse victims "suffering in silence." *BBC News.* Retrieved from https://www.bbc.com/news/uk-wales-47252756

Reijntjes, A., Thomaes, S., Bushman, B. J., Boelen, P. A., Bram Orobio de Castro, & Telch, M. J. (2010). The outcast-lash-out effect in youth: Alienation increases aggression following peer rejection. *Psychological Science, 21*(10), 1394–1398. doi:10.1177/0956797610381509

Reijntjes, A., Vermande, M., Olthof, T., Goossens, F. A., van de Schoot, R., & Aleva, L., & van der Meulen, M. (2013). Costs and benefits of bullying in the context of the peer group: A three wave longitudinal analysis. *Journal of Abnormal Child Psychology, 41*, 1217–1229.

Restorative Justice Council. (2016). Promoting quality restorative practice for everyone: What is restorative justice? Retrieved from https://restorativejustice.org.uk/do-you-need-restorative-justice

Rigby, K. (2003, October). Consequences of bullying in schools. *Canadian Journal of Psychiatry, 48*(9), 583–591. doi:10.1177/070674370304800904

Rigby, K. (2007). *Bullying in schools: And what to do about it.* Camberwell, Victoria, Australia: ACER Press.

Ringrose, J., & Rawlings, V. (2015). Posthuman performativity, gender and school bullying: Exploring the material-discursive intra-actions of skirts, hair, sluts, and poofs. *Confero: Essays on Education, Philosophy and Politics, 3*(2), 80–119. Retrieved from http://www.confero.ep.liu.se/issues/2015/v3/i2/150626a/confero15v3i2150626a.pdf

Rocker, C. (2008, August). Addressing nurse-to-nurse bullying to promote nurse retention. *Online Journal of Issues in Nursing, 13*(3). Retrieved from http://ojin

.nursingworld.org/MainMenuCategories/ANAMarketplace
/ANAPeriodicals/OJIN/TableofContents/vol132008
/No3Sept08/ArticlePreviousTopic/NursetoNurseBullying
.html

Romero, M. (2013, April). Nanny diaries and other stories:
Immigrant women's labor in the social reproduction of
American families. *Revista De Estudios Sociales, 45*(45),
186–197. Retrieved from https://www.researchgate.net
/publication/262515330_Nanny_Diaries_and_Other
_Stories_Immigrant_Women's_Labor_in_the_Social
_Reproduction_of_American_Families

Romero, M., & Pérez, N. (2016). Conceptualizing the
foundation of inequalities in care work. *American
Behavioral Scientist, 60*(2), 172–188. doi:10.1177/00027
64215607572

Rosenberg, M. B. (2000). *Giraffe fuel for life.* Corona, CA:
Corona 2000 Recording Series, Center for Nonviolent
Communication.

Rosenberg, M. B. (2003, September). *Nonviolent
communication: A language of life.* Encinitas, CA: Puddle
Dancer.

Rosenthal, L., Earnshaw, V. A., Carroll-Scott, A., Henderson,
K. E., Peters, S. M., McCaslin, C., & Ickovics, J. R. (2015).
Weight- and race-based bullying: Health associations
among urban adolescents. *Journal of Health Psychology,
20*(4), 401–412. doi:10.1177/1359105313502567

Rotundo, A. E. (1990). *American manhood: Transformations in
masculinity from the revolution to the modern era.* Chicago:
University of Chicago Press.

Rowe Small, N. (2019, June 24). University Neighborhood
Middle School counselor, personal oral communication,
New York.

Rozsa, L., Berman, M., & Merle, R. (2018, February).
Accused south Florida school shooter confessed to rampage

that killed 17 people, police say. *Washington Post*. Retrieved from https://www.washingtonpost.com/news/post-nation/wp/2018/02/15/florida-school-shooting-suspect-booked-on-17-counts-of-murder-premeditated/

Sacks, V., & Murphey, D. (2018, February 20). The prevalence of adverse childhood experiences, nationally, by state, and by race or ethnicity. Child Trends. Retrieved from https://www.childtrends.org/publications/prevalence-adverse-childhood-experiences-nationally-state-race-ethnicity

Sanbonmatsu, J. (2011, January). *Critical theory and animal liberation*. Lanham, MD: Rowman & Littlefield.

Sanders, C. E., Henry, B. C., Giuliani, C. N., & Dimmer, L. N. (2013). Bullies, victims, and animal abusers: Do they exhibit similar behavioral difficulties? *Society & Animals, 21*(3), 225–239. Retrieved from https://www.animalsandsociety.org/human-animal-studies/society-and-animals-journal/articles-on-children/bullies-victims-and-animal-abusers-do-they-exhibit-similar-behavioral-difficulties/

Schacter, H. L., & Juvonen, J. (2015). The effects of school-level victimization on self-blame: Evidence for contextualized social cognitions. *Developmental Psychology, 51*(6), 841–847. doi:10.1037/dev0000016

Schäfer, M., Werner, N. E., & Crick, N. R. (2002). A comparison of two approaches to the study of negative peer treatment: General victimization and bully/victim problems among German schoolchildren. *British Journal of Developmental Psychology, 20*, 281–306. doi:10.1348/026151002166451

Seligman, M. E. P. (2002, August). *Authentic happiness: Using the new positive psychology to realize your potential for lasting fulfillment*. New York: Simon and Schuster.

Simmons, R. (2002). *Odd girl out: The hidden culture of aggression in girls*. Boston, MA: Mariner Books.

Simmons, R. (2010, October). The nine most common myths about bullying. *Newsweek.* Retrieved from https://www.newsweek.com/nine-most-common-myths-about-bullying-74185

Skiba, R. J. (2014). The failure of zero tolerance. *Reclaiming Children and Youth, 22*(4), 27–33.

Skiba, R. J., & Knesting, K. (2001, December). Zero tolerance, zero evidence: An analysis of school disciplinary practice. *New Directions for Student Leadership, 92,* 17–43.

Slack, K. S., Font, S. A., & Jones, J. (2017). The complex interplay of adverse childhood experiences, race, and income. *Health & Social Work, 42*(1), e24–e31. doi:10.1093/hsw/hlw059

Smith, P. K. (2004, September). Bullying: Recent developments. *Child and Adolescent Mental Health, 9*(3), 98–103. doi:10.1111/j.1475-3588.2004.00089.x

Smith, P. K., & Ananiadou, K. (2003). The nature of school bullying and the effectiveness of school-based interventions. *Journal of Applied Psychoanalytic Studies, 5,* 189–209.

Southern Poverty Law Center. (2019, February). Hate groups reach record high. Retrieved from https://www.splcenter.org/news/2019/02/19/hate-groups-reach-record-high

Spidel, G. L. (2014, April). Gender expression: A qualitative study of the reflections of recent LGBT high school graduates' experiences. Retrieved from https://digitallibrary.sdsu.edu/islandora/object/sdsu%3A2950

Stein, N. D. (2003). Bullying or sexual harassment?: The missing discourse of rights in an era of zero tolerance. *Arizona Law Review, 45*(3), 783–799. Retrieved from http://arizonalawreview.org/pdf/45-3/45arizlrev783.pdf

Stein, N. D., Tolman, D., Porche, M., & Spencer, R. (2002). Gender safety: A new concept for schools. *Journal of School Violence, 1*(2), 35–49. doi:10.1300/J202v01n02_03

Stella, N. C. (2007, June). *How parents can help stop bullying.* Peterborough, England: Upfront Publishing.

StopBullying.gov. (2017, August). Fact sheet: Bullying as an adverse childhood experience (ACE). Retrieved from https://www.stopbullying.gov/sites/default/files/2017-10/bullying-as-an-ace-fact-sheet.pdf

StopBullying.gov. (2019). What is bullying? Retrieved from https://www.stopbullying.gov/what-is-bullying/index.html

Strandmark, M., & Rahm, G. (2014). Development, implementation and evaluation of a process to prevent and combat workplace bullying. *Scandinavian Journal of Public Health, 42*(15), 66–73. doi:10.1177/1403494814549494

Sutherland, A. (2006). *The relationship among parental and peer victimization and adolescent maladjustment* (Master's thesis). Queen's University, Kingston, Ontario, Canada, 1–58.

Swain, J. (1998). What does bullying really mean? *Educational Research, 40*(3), 358–364.

Swearer, S. M., Song, S. Y., Cary, P. T., Eagle, J. W., & Mickelson, W. T. (2001). Psychosocial correlates in bullying and victimization: The relationship between depression, anxiety, and bully/victim status. In R. A. Geffner, M. Loring, & C. Young (Eds.), *Bullying behavior: Current issues, research, and interventions* (pp. 95–121). Binghamton, NY: Haworth Maltreatment & Trauma Press.

Sweeting, H., Young, R., West, P., & Der, G. (2006). Peer victimization and depression in early-mid adolescence: A longitudinal study. *The British Journal of Educational Psychology, 76*(Pt. 3), 577–594. doi:10.1348/000709905X49890

Twale, D. J., & De Luca, B. M. (2008, February). *Faculty incivility: The rise of the academic bully culture and what to do about it.* San Francisco, CA: Jossey-Bass.

Twenge, J. M., Gentile, B., DeWall, C. N., Ma, D., Lacefield, K., & Schurtz, D. R. (2010). Birth cohort increases in psychopathology among young Americans, 1938–2007: A cross-temporal meta-analysis of the MMPI. *Clinical Psychology Review, 30*(2), 145–154. doi:10.1016/j. cpr.2009.10.005

Twenge, J. M., Joiner, T. E., Rogers, M. L., & Martin, G. N. (2018). Increases in depressive symptoms, suicide-related outcomes, and suicide rates among U.S. adolescents after 2010 and links to increased new media screen time. *Clinical Psychological Science, 6*(1), 3–17.

UN News. (2011, October). Solitary confinement should be banned in most cases, UN expert says. Retrieved from https://news.un.org/en/story/2011/10/392012-solitary -confinement-should-be-banned-most-cases-un-expert-says

Vaillancourt, T., McDougall, P., Hymel, S., Krygsman, A., Miller, J., Stiver, K., & Davis, C. (2008, November). Bullying: Are researchers and children/youth talking about the same thing? *International Journal of Behavioral Development, 32*(6), 486–495. doi:10.1177/01650254 08095553

Van der Valk, A. (2013, fall). There are no bullies: Just children who bully and you can help them. *Teaching Tolerance, 45*, 38–41. Retrieved from https://www.tolerance .org/magazine/fall-2013/there-are-no-bullies

Van Woerkom, M. (2016). In the circle everyone is needed. Morningside Center for Teaching Social Responsibility. Retrieved from https://www.morningsidecenter.org/stories -voices/circle-everyone-needed

Vicent, M., Inglés, C. J., Sanmartín, R., Gonzálvez, C., & García-Fernández, J. M. (2017). Perfectionism and aggression: Identifying risk profiles in children. *Personality and Individual Differences, 112*, 106–112. doi:10.1016/j. paid.2017.02.061

Visualz (2008). Teen safety: Dating and relationships. Retrieved from https://adelphi.kanopy.com/video/teen -safety-dating-relationships

Voors, W. (2000, September). *The parent's book about bullying: Changing the course of your child's life.* Center City, MN: Hazelden.

Wachtel, T. (2012, June). Social bonding is key to limiting bullying. *Education Week, 31*(33), 31. Retrieved from https://www.edweek.org/ew/articles/2012/06/06/33letter-2 .h31.html

Wang, M. T., & Kenny, S. (2014). Parental physical discipline and adolescent adjustment: Bidirectionality and the moderation effects of child ethnicity and parental warmth. *Journal of Abnormal Child Psychology, 42*(5), 717–730. Retrieved from https://www.ncbi.nlm.nih.gov/pubmed /24384596

Wanjek, C. (2017, November). How your brain wiring drives social interactions. Live Science. Retrieved from https:// www.livescience.com/60937-social-brain-wiring.html

Ware, L. (2014). Color-blind racism in France: Bias against ethnic minority immigrants. *Washington University Journal of Law & Policy, 46*, 185–244.

Waytz, A., & Epley, N. (2012, January). Social connection enables dehumanization. *Journal of Experimental Social Psychology, 48*(1), 70–76. doi:10.1016/j.jesp.2011.07.012

Welsh, R. O., & Little, S. (2018). Caste and control in schools: A systematic review of the pathways, rates and correlates of exclusion due to school discipline. *Children and Youth Services Review, 94*(C), 315–339. Retrieved from https://ideas.repec.org/a/eee/cysrev/v94y2018icp315-339 .html

Wilkinson, R. G. (2005). *The impact of inequality: How to make sick societies healthier.* New York: New Press.

Wiseman, R. (2016, July). *Queen bees and wannabes: Helping your daughter survive cliques, gossip, boys, and the new realities of girl world* (3rd ed.). New York: Harmony.

Witt, E. (2019, February 13). From Parkland to Sunrise: A year of extraordinary youth activism. *The New Yorker.* Retrieved from https://www.newyorker.com/news/news-desk/from-parkland-to-sunrise-a-year-of-extraordinary-youth-activism

Ybarra, M. L., Espelage, D. L., & Mitchell, K. J. (2014, August). Differentiating youth who are bullied from other victims of peer-aggression: The importance of differential power and repetition. *Journal of Adolescent Health, 55*(2), 293–300. Retrieved from https://www.ncbi.nlm.nih.gov/pubmed/24726463

Yee, S. (2019). Where prejudice, disability and "disabilism" meet. Disability Rights Education and Defense Fund. Retrieved from https://dredf.org/news/publications/disability-rights-law-and-policy/where-prejudice-disability-and-disabilism-meet/

Zapf, D., & Gross, C. (2001). Conflict escalation and coping with workplace bullying: A replication and extension. *European Journal of Work and Organizational Psychology, 10*, 497–522.

Zwaan, M., Dijkstra, J. K., & Veenstra, R. (2013, February). Status hierarchy, attractiveness hierarchy, and sex ratio: Three contextual factors explaining the status-aggression link among adolescents. *International Journal of Behavioral Development, 37*(3), 211–221. doi:10.1177/0165025412471018

Written by academics, experts, program leaders, and people personally affected by bullying, including a student, these essays contribute different perspectives on bullying. Issues addressed include cyberbullying, sexual harassment, and looksism; prevention via mindfulness, empathy, kindness, restorative justice, and going offline; and bullycide awareness.

Bullying and Looksism
Lynn S. Chancer

In the last twenty years, bullying, as it affects young people in particular, has come to the forefront of educators' and parents' concerns. But have things sufficiently changed? Certainly, cultural awareness has altered. Educators, parents, the media, and the broader public are more cognizant than ever about the seriousness and unacceptability of bullying and its consequences. Social movements about gender, sexuality, and LGBTQI+ rights have highlighted hate speech and crimes. In the United States, young people are arguably more aware than ever about the ongoing problems of sexism and sexual assault, as well as about the diversity of people's sexual preferences.

But I wonder whether what I have elsewhere called "looksism" has changed and, if not, how its ongoing perpetuation

Empathy and community-building decrease school bullying, especially when school staff help students connect with one another across racial, socioeconomic, and other differences. (Lightfieldstudiosprod/Dreamstime.com)

relates to bullying. For instance, do people say offensive things to others—online or offline—about their height, their weight, or other aspects of their bodies, such as whether or not they are good-looking by conventional standards?

I suggest here that judgmental standards related to gender, racial, and class-based personal appearance are taken-for-granted social common sense and that, unless we question, the strong sway of such looks-based judgments, an important cultural soil on which bullying often feeds, particularly among young people, is left intact. On the other hand, arguing with the influence of looksism may create cultural shifts with the potential to diminish some types of looksism and related bullying.

In a book on feminist debates, *Reconcilable Differences: Confronting Beauty, Pornography and the Future of Feminism*, I define the term "looksism" in reference to long-standing cultural and institutionalized practices of judging people on the basis of looks. These standards have been discriminatory; for example, looksism has been tied to sexism insofar as women have been judged by appearance-based standards of conventional prettiness more than men. As Simone de Beauvoir understood and elaborates in her classic *The Second Sex*, these standards affected women's ability to attract partners on whom they have sometimes historically depended for economic as well as social approval and support.

But as Susan Bordo argues with great clarity in *Unbearable Weight*, looksism goes deeper than this, as people have been evaluated disproportionately on the basis of their outer appearance in other contexts too. For instance, racial classification systems of looks have overvalued light skin within social hierarchies that have merged sexism and racialization; likewise, women of Asian descent have sometimes sought cosmetic surgery to "westernize" their eyelids because of the dominance of these ethnic/racial standards of beauty. Standards of looks and appearance also intermesh with class biases when women are judged by their "better" and "lesser" fashions and apparel.

How does this relate to the social problem of bullying, especially as it affects young people? Is there empirical evidence for the assertion that looksism, if indirectly connected with bullying, has not lessened? One example can be gleaned through the phenomenon of anorexia, which remains a problem for too many young women and men.

Dieting and fear of "fatness" seems more of a social pressure than ever, where different forms of social insecurity and concerns about how one will rank up on numerous criteria seem at least as worrisome as in previous generations. Young people across races, ethnicities, and classes may be afraid of experiencing bullying about how they look. Even the perception that one *could* be bullied may contribute to the social problem in question insofar as people worry: Am I too fat (or skinny)? Am I too tall (or short)? Does my chin sag, or are my breasts too large or too small?

If a connection between looksism and bullying seems persuasive—even if difficult to prove in a positivistic sense of social science—then it is worth trying to change the former. But how? Is there an alternative to a society where looksism on the basis of gender, class, sexualities, and/or race and ethnicity may be a firmly, if subtle and relatively overlooked, form of cultural discrimination? I believe an alternative to looksism exists and can be placed in greater social circulation. What would this alternative be?

I contend that we need an alternative to the dominant understanding of attraction as well as the sources of sexual and human affinities and beauty. Presently, it is thought that attraction is based on appearance. I believe, though, that attraction develops from a complex combination of factors including a person's energy, intelligence, sense of humor (or lack thereof), kindness (or meanness); this attraction incorporates but is not reducible to matters of looks. As I contend in *Reconcilable Differences*, a social and sociological theory of attraction needs to be developed such that people recognize the diversity of people's complex, multidimensional, and actual feelings for one another. People's attraction to one another is far more heterogeneous than homogeneous, contrary to what advertisers would have us believe are essential "truths."

If bullying, in at least some of its manifestations, rests on making fun of and deriding others' looks (whether too heavy or too thin, too tall or too short, older or youthful, or on skin or hair or eye color), to the extent that we can debunk the myths of looksism, we can remove one of the biases that sometimes underlies this social problem, particularly in the United States. It is a dimension of bullying worth exploring and beginning to overcome.

Lynn S. Chancer is professor of sociology at Hunter College and the executive officer of the PhD program in sociology at the Graduate Center. She is the author of books including Sadomasochism in Everyday Life, High Profile Crimes, Reconcilable Differences: Confronting Beauty, Pornography and the Future of Feminism, *and* After the Rise and Stall of American Feminism: Taking Back a Revolution, *as well as articles concerning gender, race, class, social movements, and American culture.*

How to Overcome Bullying
Carrie Goldman

When my oldest daughter entered the first grade, she eagerly headed to school each morning, open and enthusiastic about the day ahead. By October, she had lost her smile and hung her head.

"I don't want to go to school tomorrow," she cried one night as I helped her get ready for bed.

"Why? What is wrong?" I asked.

With much cajoling, she finally explained that a boy in her class was calling her Piggy and making fun of her size and that some of the other kids had joined in the name-calling. Our lovely girl will probably never be petite, but she is healthy and active. I felt heartsick about the taunting, and I wondered about the best way to help our seven-year-old.

I started by calling her teacher and quickly learned what moms and dads around the country are experiencing: managing bullying is one of the top concerns of parents and teachers today. From the earliest days of toddler interactions through the postcollege years, we worry about how our kids are faring socially. Do they have a good group of friends? Are they being treated with respect?

The very word "bullying" sets off emotional reactions in our communities, and the stigma around bullying is significant enough that many school administrators mistakenly react by blaming the victim in many forms of social conflict, lest it be thought that their school has a "bullying problem."

The broader conversation needs to be shifted away from fear and toward solutions. The first step in finding a solution is to agree on a shared definition for bullying. Social pain is subjective; one child may brush off the unkind behaviors of her peers, while another child can be devastated by the same circumstances. Thus, it is important to have a common language for defining what bullying is and, equally as important, for defining what bullying is not.

This is why everyone—parents, teachers, and kids—can benefit from understanding the difference between normal social conflict and bullying. Confusing the two has a problematic impact on how we help our kids. In normal social conflict, where each kid has relatively equal power and voice, it is best for adults to hang back and let the kids come up with their own solutions, only stepping in to provide guidance and assistance as necessary. We should not rush in to fix normal social conflict.

In true bullying, however, it is often necessary for adults to intervene more actively, because the target is being victimized, and victimization has long-term negative effects. A power imbalance exists that limits the bullied person's ability to make the cruel behaviors stop. Telling a kid to stop the bullying on his or her own may be asking the impossible. So how do we know if a child is facing bullying or normal social conflict?

Bullying has three conditions, and all three must exist for a situation to be defined as bullying. Bullying exists when there is *repetitive, unwanted aggression* that occurs in the context of a *power imbalance*." Let's look more closely at the three conditions.

Repetitive

If another child shuns your kid one day during lunch and your child is upset, this is not yet bullying. If it happens over and over, then you have a problem. In my daughter's case, she was being called Piggy day after day.

Unwanted Aggression

If another child teases your child and your child is not laughing along, then this is unwanted aggression. The most common defense that aggressive kids use is to proclaim, "I was just kidding," when called out on their poor behavior. The best way for your child to respond is to say, "Kidding means both people are having fun or laughing. Now that you know I'm not having fun, you won't do that again, if you really were just kidding."

If the taunts continue and the aggressor again uses the "just kidding" excuse, your child can reply, "You get a one-time free pass with the 'just kidding' excuse. I explained to you yesterday that I wasn't laughing along with you when you called me Piggy. I know you understood me, so the fact that you are doing this again means you are intending to cause pain. This isn't teasing; it's taunting. It's not okay."

Parents and teachers should also learn to use this simple response to the "just kidding" defense. It is particularly useful when speaking to the parents of kids who act like bullies, because the parents may be dismissive of your concerns and insist that their child was just kidding.

Power Imbalance

Bullying always occurs in the context of a power imbalance. It is a bigger kid against a smaller kid, multiple kids against a single kid (as was happening with the kids calling my daughter Piggy), an older kid against a younger kid, a more popular kid against a less popular kid, or any other form of power imbalance. If there is no power imbalance, the situation is more likely to be a social conflict than a bullying dynamic.

When all the conditions of bullying have been met (repetition, unwantedness, power imbalance), a fourth condition usually develops: fear. The target begins to fear the place where the bullying occurs. This is exactly what happened with my daughter, who cried that she wanted to stay home from school.

Whereas normal social conflict tends to have an *external focus*, bullying generally has an *internal focus*. For example, social conflict may be about an outside item (i.e., two kids fighting over an iPad) or an outside relationship (i.e., two girls fighting over a boy they both like). If you were to hypothetically remove the thing causing the conflict, the conflict would disappear. *Take away the toy that the kids are fighting over, and the conflict ends. Have the sought-after boy start dating a third girl at another school, and the conflict is likely to end.*

In bullying, however, we often see an attack on someone's internal identity (e.g., kids taunting a peer for being overweight or gay or in special education). Your appearance or your learning abilities are a core part of you and cannot be removed. The target is left feeling personally attacked and emotionally upset.

Signs Your Child Might Be a Target of Bullying

- Reluctance to go to the place where the bullying is occurring
- Anxiousness, fearfulness, hypervigilance
- Disturbances in sleep
- Onset of anorexia, bulimia, or binge eating
- Excessive crying or sadness

- Cutting or other forms of self-harm
- Sudden change in friendship groups
- No invitations to play, attend parties, or be part of group outings

Steps to Take If Your Child Is Being Bullied

Most important, do not blame your child for what is happening. Even if your child is a provocative target—meaning that the child has social quirks or tends to be different from the other kids—he or she does not deserve to be bullied.

The following are steps you can take in this case:

- Reassure your child that this is not his or her fault and that no one should be treated this way.
- Document the bullying. (i.e., take a screenshot of cyberbullying activities, photograph bruises or ruined property, write down accounts of exclusion or verbal taunting).
- Ask for school administrators to describe the school's anti-bullying policy.
- Show the school that you have a record of the activity and ask for action.
- Seek counseling for your child.
- Look for places outside of school where your child can form friendships, such as clubs, sports teams, theater groups, and art classes.

Steps to Take If Your Child Is Doing the Bullying

Often, it is painful to acknowledge that our own child is being unkind. It is best for your child if you acknowledge the issue. You can help your child by doing the following:

- Tell your child that the unkind behaviors are unacceptable, but also be sure to reassure your child that you love him or her.

- Seek counseling for your child and your family to deal with the underlying issues causing the aggression.
- Encourage your child to make reparations for the harm he or she has caused, first and foremost by teaching him or her to consider how the targeted child feels (assuming the bullied youth is open to further interaction).
- Reach out to the family of the targeted child and offer a sincere apology.
- Ask the school to help you teach empathy and emotional intelligence to your child.
- Set consequences for continued mistreatment of peers, such as the loss of screen time.

Steps to Take If Your Child Is a Bystander

- Encourage your child to reach out to the target and offer empathy. Even a kind text message makes a huge difference.
- Have your child make a written account of the bullying. Evidence is critical.
- Have your child report the bullying to the school.
- Remind your child not to join in the bullying.

The only way we can stop bullying is to address the roles of all three parties: the aggressors, the targets, and the bystanders. Chances are high that your child has been in at least one of the three roles, if not more, and he or she can use your support and guidance.

In the case of my little girl, her teacher responded immediately to the Piggy situation and spoke to the ringleader. The taunting stopped. The same teasing recurred a year later, though, in another class, and once again, the school addressed it right away. I was grateful for their support.

Carrie Goldman is the award-winning author of Bullied: What Every Parent, Teacher, and Kid Needs to Know about Ending the Cycle of Fear. *She travels around the country educating companies, schools, and community groups about bullying prevention, intervention, and reconciliation.*

Hate Speech, Bullying, and Social Media: Teaching Empathy to Our Kids
Devorah Heitner

Young people are increasingly exposed to videos and speeches that target immigrants and other marginalized communities, blaming them for America's troubles (perceived or actual), and creating and perpetuating hateful stereotypes and violent rhetoric. Social media often makes things worse.

Alternatively, social media can help us repair communities and record these kinds of incidents, and this raises new questions for educators.

For example, referring to building a wall between the United States and Mexico to keep out illegal immigrants, a video was made of students in Royal Oaks, Michigan, shouting "Build a wall" at vulnerable students in a crowded cafeteria. Over two million people viewed the video within a day of the incident. Parents in the community described targeted students as "stricken," some of whom ran out of the room crying (Dickson & Williams 2016).

The chanting middle school students were frozen in time making those statements. One student decided to report the video. This was a brave and ethical choice that the student said produced "evidence." It is often difficult if not impossible, though, to remove the offensive media. Platforms such as YouTube make such viral sharing possible and hard to control.

We Need to Examine Our Motivations for Sharing

When children surround their peers and yell "Build a wall," we need to do more than simply discipline the perpetrators and more than just tell them to "stop it." How do we help students deal with such situations if they see hate speech and images? What if our children are the ones performing the abuse?

After the 2016 elections, another image was circulated of two high school young men wearing handmade "Build That Wall" T-shirts in Moline, Illinois. Many of the Moline students' peers saw the pictures online. Some students defended the men in the photograph. Others criticized them on social media. In one of the Facebook groups where I first saw the picture, some adults recommended public shaming. One adult commented on the photo: "Make sure they never get a job" (Walsh 2016).

As adults, we should examine our motivations for sharing an image like this, especially when we recognize the subjects. We need to address the behavior, but we should be cautious about the ways that social media can amplify these images and hurt the reputations of both the perpetrators and those they intend to harm.

In 1957, at the height of southern desegregation, a white girl named Hazel Bryan was photographed shouting at an African American girl, Elizabeth Eckford, while the first African American students made their way through an angry white mob to integrate Little Rock Central High School. These young African Americans students became known as the "Little Rock Nine" and were widely seen on TV and in newspapers during the civil rights movement. Their lives were altered by the abuse they endured and by becoming famous. Bryan also experienced the amplification of her image in a life-altering way when a photograph of her shouting at Eckford became an icon for racism in this country (Margolick 2011).

Today, kids can take a "selfie" wearing an offensive shirt or a racist Halloween costume, or doing any number of other hurtful actions, and then circulate the image independently on the internet. While the impact of a single picture may not come to define their lives in the same way that Bryan's life was shaped by that one photograph, we need to be aware that even photographs that are self-produced by young people can archive one potentially awful moment in their development.

Understanding Is Not Condoning

School leaders should not dismiss hateful lashing out with a "kids being kids" catch phrase; we need to be compassionate and curious. If we shame students who take these actions, or punish them without asking difficult and uncomfortable questions about their motivations, we may inadvertently plant seeds for more hate. We need to engage young people in conversations and try to understand their actions. This doesn't mean that we accept and condone their behavior. We should implement immediate measures to keep schools safe and protect those who are targeted. We also need to see "visible edges" as a canary in the coal mine—a window into the hearts of those creating hate speech and the beginning of an exchange to seek a more compassionate dialogue.

Maple Grove, Minnesota, is one of many communities where racist graffiti was scrawled on a wall in the days following the Trump presidential victory and shared on social media. The school let students know that the graffiti was unacceptable, and administrators launched an investigation. Other students responded by organizing a school-wide campaign to "counter the hate speech with love." They planned discussion groups, created unity posters, and shared positive messages on social media like "Thank you to everyone who helped spread love and positivity this morning #crimsonfamily" (Olson 2016).

Even so, a few days later, local news reported that an image was shared with Maple Grove police in which a dead deer was hung from a tree, in a form that evoked the lynching of African American people. The picture was posted with a comment, "[I]f only these deer were n—ers." A Maple Grove student was pictured, but the news source did not know if the girl was the creator of the racist image. In addition to the threat of violence, the inclusion of a recognizable student raises questions about rapid circulation of images that might wrongly implicate and create a new victim (Walsh 2016).

We must get to the root of where kids are coming from when they create this kind of image. We need to teach our students when an image is something they should share with us, and we need to help our students resist the urge to forward problematic posts to social media. In Maple Grove and Royal Oak, administrators continued the conversation with significant input from the community.

Yet the fact that Maple Grove, Royal Oak, and many other communities have seen subsequent incidents is an important reminder that we can't simply take an "incident" approach to these issues. These are ominous indicators that a climate of hate speech is not going away as quickly or easily as we might wish.

Working with parents and educators on digital citizenship gives me hope right now. Schools are teaching their students to interact in kind ways online, because it's the right thing to do, and also so that students can become mindful about how to create a positive and even admirable digital footprint.

Creating Dialogue in Schools

When advising parents of young children on how to talk about scary or tragic events, Fred McFeely Rogers, the creator and host of the famous PBS television show *Mr. Rogers' Neighborhood*, says to coach kids to "look for the helpers." I suggest we look specifically to the educators.

For instance, the superintendent of my local high school wrote a letter to students immediately after the 2016 presidential election to encourage our youth to support one another and to assert that their school is a sanctuary from hate. He commented, "We embrace one another's race and ethnicity. We embrace one another's family background, heritage, language and culture. We embrace one another's religion and your right to your own personal customs and beliefs. We embrace your sexual orientation and your gender identity. We embrace your special needs. We embrace you and value you as individual human beings. Never forget: you belong here at ETHS—each and every one of you" (Stevens 2016).

In their efforts to form a positive climate, schools should also support proactive student-initiated actions like this one in

Duluth, where a Muslim student asked her female classmates to wear a hijab one day (the head covering worn in public by some Muslim women) in solidarity with Muslim students who are targeted with prejudice and discriminatory actions, sometimes prohibited from wearing hijabs in their schools. Actions like these can create a positive school climate and should be widely supported (Kruse 2016).

When images and video documenting discriminatory behavior or hateful speech circulate in a community, young people need proactive guidance and support from educators. These conversations are difficult and often painful. Targeted groups need to be made safe, and the burden of these conversations should not fall on them. I would urge educators to open these discussions and reference real-world examples that have happened in their own communities. It helps to hear what parents, educators, and other students have to say.

If we simply drive the conversation underground by trying to shut it down, we lose an opportunity to help our youth understand each other's point of view. A media circus doesn't create a more positive climate, although media can draw attention to a situation and that can sometimes generate a solution. We must be cautious about the way we understand video footage, photographs, and social media posts in order to avoid fanning the flames of intolerance, and to prevent young people from being in a position where they are cemented on social media in a negative role without the opportunity to change. Educators and parents have to step in and mentor kids, ask hard questions, and be as proactive as possible in creating dialogues that promote empathy.

References

Dickson, J. D., & Williams, C. C. (2016, November 10). Royal Oak Middle School students chant "build that wall." *Detroit News*.

Kruse, J. (2016, November 16). Dozens of Duluth East students wear a hijab to support Muslim classmates. WDIO.

Margolick, D. (2011, October 11). The stranger-than-fiction history of the civil rights era's most famous photograph. *Slate*.

Olson, R. (2016, November 10). Maple Grove students fight racist graffiti with unity, love. KMSP.

Stevens, H. (2016, November 14). Why Evanston superintendent's post-election morning announcement went viral. Chicagotribune.com.

Walsh, P. (2016, November 14). Snapchat pic of dead deer, the n-word has attention of Maple Grove police. *Star Tribune*.

Devorah Heitner, PhD, founded Raising Digital Natives to serve as a resource for schools and organizations wishing to cultivate a culture of responsible digital citizenship. She is the author of Screenwise: Helping Kids Thrive (and Survive) in Their Digital World *(Bibliomotion, 2016) and she is the co-author of the* curriculum: Connecting Wisely: Social Emotional Insights and Skills for Plugged-in Kids.

Seven Ways to Wire for Resilience
Tamara Holt

Each day we encounter conflict. Some are small and instant, like missing the bus or bumping an elbow. Some are enormous, like losing a loved one, or ongoing, like having an alcoholic family member. We are surrounded by them. Each of these conflicts, as well as big positive changes like moving homes, are *stress*. Piles of homework, teasing or bullying by others—each stressor saps mental or emotional energy. Usually you can casually carry the load, but when too many or very intense stressors pile up in your brain, you start to feel *distress*.

How do you know you are in distress? Maybe you lash out at a friend or you isolate yourself. Maybe you can't sleep or you binge unhealthily on food or other substances. Maybe it's harder for you to focus on work or calm your inner feelings of anxiety.

The way to prevent or bounce back from distress is *resilience*, the brain's protection from external obstacles, stressors, and other environmental threats.

As life changes, from day to day and over time, your stressors and resilience fluctuate and evolve. The way to get your brain to work at its best—make good decisions and easily finish tasks—is to be sure that your brain's resilience outweighs its stress. It's a balancing act.

The word "resilience" started being used in the 1990s, when University of Minnesota psychology researcher Norman Garmezy looked into why some children struggled in life, while others flourished even in equally challenging environments. Since then, psychology, social science, and neuroscience researchers have been trying to pinpoint what makes some people more resilient. Is it something about who they are? Is it something they do? Something they learn? Can anyone build resilience?

Here's what we know. The brain is a complex system of structures and billions of connections that change in response to experience and training. Some say, "what wires together fires together," meaning that when the brain repeats a pattern—a thought, an exercise, an idea—that pattern gets stronger.

Usually, our brain chooses patterns unconsciously, without telling us. But it turns out that with practice, we *can* take control. Resilience is the ability to choose what path the brain is going to take or not take at each moment in time. It is easier to choose well-traveled routes, so it's best to have strong, healthy pathways to choose from in times of stress and distress.

Resilience can be built—wired and rewired. Here are a few tools that may work for you.

Develop a Daily Practice

The first step to resilience is building *attention*, your ability to focus your brain. Scientific studies have revealed that mindfulness techniques—meditation practices that focus awareness on the present moment—have incredible power to do just that.

University of Miami researcher Dr. Amishi Jha studies mindfulness practice and its effects on cognitive resilience in athletes, students, and the military. She has found that for subjects who had experienced mindfulness training, attention remains stable under stress. For those who haven't been trained, attention decreases. It takes only four weeks for significant changes.

A simple mindfulness practice can strengthen your attention skills and stop your mind from wandering. With continued practice, mindfulness training has been shown to reduce anxiety, protect from depression, and improve working memory. It can also make it easier to wire anything else.

Try this: Sit quietly and pay attention to some aspect of your breath—the movement of your belly or the feeling at the tip of your nose—working up to ten to fifteen minutes per day. You could also try a body scan exercise in which you focus on each body part in turn—head to toe—noticing any sensations you discover. When your mind wanders, bring it back. One free phone app to help is Insight Timer.

Take a Break from Stress

Developing mindfulness skills will give you the fundamentals for focusing your mind. Next, you need to practice using those skills in moments of stress.

A Harvard study on happiness tracked fifteen thousand people of all ages using an iPhone app. When researchers checked in on the subjects, they found that those who were focused on the present moment were happier that those whose minds were wandering to other thoughts.

Each time you successfully *detach* your mind from the stress on the outside (or your negative experience of it) and bring it back to your present experiences, you are both teaching your brain to detach and strengthening your ability to do so. There is no truer present experience than the mindful practice of returning to the breath.

Try this: If you are in distress but not in immediate danger, try taking a minibreak. For a minute or two or even just a few seconds, pretend it isn't there. If you have a mindfulness practice, you can take a minimeditation and focus on your breath or a body part. Or you can try sniffing essential oils with closed eyes and taking deep, long breaths. Lavender oil can be calming.

Reframe Worries as Wishes

When you worry, you are strengthening the pathway of a negative outcome, making that dark thought, such as "I will never finish" or "nobody likes me," more automatic and natural for your brain.

Psychologist George Bonanno, who heads the Loss, Trauma, and Emotion Lab at Columbia University Teachers College, studies how people thrive in the face of loss and potentially traumatic events. Bonanno notes that as real as the stressors may be, we can exaggerate stressors easily in our own minds, making our experience of them worse.

Why not meditate on the best possible outcome instead of the worst? The practice of *reframing* can be a powerful way to build resilience.

Try this: Take the biggest worry and turn it into a wish. Don't wish for your greatest fears not to happen. Instead, wish for the biggest, most positive, most hopeful outcome. Rather than "I wish those girls would stop picking on me," you could wish, "I wish to be surrounded by supportive, kind, loving friends."

Practice Gratitude

Remarkably, there have been scores of studies showing that *gratitude*, even outside the context of religion, is consistently associated with greater happiness and self-esteem, strong relationships, and better ability to deal with adversity. According to University of California researcher Dr. Robert A. Emmons, author of *Thanks! How Practicing Gratitude Can Make You Happier*, gratitude has the power to transform lives.

Try this: Each day, first thing in the morning or just before you go to bed, make a list of the things you are grateful for. Even if your days are filled with unhappy events and undeserved assaults, you can dig deep and find small blessings. Maybe they are simple, like "I can see" or "I have a bed to sleep in," or more specific, such as "I talked to a friend today" or "I had a good visit with my counselor."

Know You Have Control

One attribute of people who have strong resilience is their sense that they are in control of their own fate, rather than that they are a victim of their situation.

Studies with intimate-partner-violence survivors, spinal-cord-injury patients, and college students have all demonstrated that perceiving what researchers call an "internal locus of control" positively correlates with resilience. One example of this is recognizing that your effort, attitude, or preparation has an impact on how well or how badly you do on an exam.

Certainly, it is hard to feel powerful when you're targeted by others. Having a sense of control is not about denying what is happening to you. Instead, it is a way of recognizing all the ways you're able to change the situations in your own life, in general, and over time.

Try this: For each of three items on your gratitude list, identify what actions you took to make them happen. You may be surprised at the role you play in the good things that happen in your life. For the gratitude examples above:

1. "I talked to a new friend today" *because* "I smiled at her."

2. "I had a good visit with my counselor" *because* "I asked for help."

3. "I can see" *because* "I am careful with my body."

4. "I have a bed to sleep in" *because* "I live peacefully (enough) with my family."

Don't Wire Other People's Stories

If people call you names or make accusations, you not have to believe them. And, without doubt, you don't have to repeat them. Each time you pay attention to an idea, you are strengthening it; you are wiring it more firmly in your brain.

Instead, wire positive qualities, abilities, and characteristics so that you always have a resilient sense of self to return to.

According to Meg Jay, PhD, author of *Supernormal: The Untold Story of Adversity and Resilience*, resilient people "talk about themselves as fighters." They focus on "how was I strong, how was I courageous, how has my life arced toward goodness and away from the bad things that have happened."

Try this: For each of the items on your gratitude list for which you have identified your actions, find a quality or strength of yours that the action represents. (These are personal to you. Someone else might take the same action from a different strength.) Each day, you will add to your list of positive qualities. Repeat them to yourself to remind yourself who you are.

For the examples above:

1. "I smiled at her" *because* "I am friendly."

2. "I asked for help" *because* "I am brave."

3. "I am not careless with my body" *because* "I have self-love."

4. "I live peacefully (enough) with my family" *because* "I value community."

Reframe Loss

Changing your brain patterns isn't easy, but no doubt, it is possible. Each challenge is an opportunity to improve. The secret is *practice.*

Neuroscientists continue to unravel the mystery of how changes happen in the brain. We know that we build new connections and that some parts of the brain can grow or shrink, and it seems we can even turn genes on and off. Amazingly, our actions each day, every day of our lives can make those changes happen.

Try this: Don't think of your struggles as failure. Think of them as practice. Just like weight lifting or learning a new dance step, the training and practice of attention and resilience involve fatigue, frustration, and mistakes. Each effort, however, pushes you closer to your goal. Keep practicing, and the pattern will get stronger, building resilience to strengthen you against the effects of external stress.

Tamara Holt is an educator and activist who shares easy and accessible research, tools, and strategies to inspire and motivate others to heal themselves and their worlds. She works with individuals, companies, groups, and online.

Needs, Feelings, and Empathy
Michael Jascz

Bullying is an increasingly serious issue in our society. In a 2017 study conducted at Florida Atlantic University, 73 percent of students reported having been bullied at school, 34 percent experienced cyberbullying, and 67 percent stated that enduring bullying affected their ability to learn. We need to examine the effects of bullying and address the root of the problem.

Some students think that bullying is not their problem because they do not participate in it. However, everyone plays a part when bullying takes place. A person who acts with bullying behavior often needs an audience to entertain. By not speaking up, people who act with bullying behavior might interpret silence as a form of approval.

Bystander intervention can be extremely effective. For example, students can find a person of authority to address the bullying. However, bystanders may fear retaliation or ostracism from the person who is bullying. Bystanders may also intervene in subtle, less intimidating ways, such as attempting to redirect the conversation or serving as support for the person being bullied.

Teachers can address bullying behavior by speaking to all individuals involved and by promoting moral development and empathy in the classroom. When speaking to targets of bullying behavior, teachers can encourage them to open up about their situation and also affirm their self-worth. When speaking to the person who bullies, teachers can reinforce the gravity of the person's actions and also discuss why they are acting with bullying behavior. As an alternative to punishment, the trauma-sensitive school movement recommends asking a child who bullies, "What's going on with you?" instead of "What is wrong with you?"

The National Child Traumatic Stress Network states that close to 40 percent of students in the United States have experienced some form of trauma. It is possible that a child who bullies has been bullied. Such trauma can result in toxic stress that disrupts brain chemistry. Creating an atmosphere of emotional and physical safety for students can reduce bullying and positively impact students personally and academically.

To help address bullying at its root, we can use Marshall Rosenberg's nonviolent communication (NVC) model, which teaches how to articulate needs and feelings without blame and judgment and to listen empathically.

What are needs and feelings? Some needs are purely for survival, like the physical needs for air, food, water, and shelter. There are also needs for connection, such as the need for friendship, community, affection, empathy, love, and respect. The NVC "needs and feelings" vocabulary gives you a better sense of your needs and feelings. If we hear that someone feels grateful, pleased, delighted, curious, or inspired, then we have a clearer understanding of what's going on. When needs are not met, you may feel annoyed, worried, or frustrated. When articulated in these terms, we hear what someone is experiencing.

NVC can enhance your perspective on how people relate with one another. People can break patterns of judging, blaming, and shaming by developing NVC skills. When practiced, the NVC vocabulary of needs and feelings can foster more thriving and fulfilling relationships.

If we want bullying to stop, it is necessary to address it at the root. At the core of bullying is often mistreatment and misunderstanding of the person who is bullying. By using NVC, students can achieve a new and more compassionate understanding of the people who surround them.

From an NVC perspective, bullying is a strategy to meet a need. Instead of judging people as "bullies" and "victims," we can observe and describe the behavior. When we label someone a bully, we make a judgment about their character rather than an observation about their actions. Labeling can prevent us from seeing the nuanced role each person plays in a situation and can make the people we label feel their situation cannot change. Instead, we can say "someone who acted with bullying behavior" and "someone who was the target of bullying behavior."

As students practice expressing their needs and feelings without blame and judgment, youth who bully can make great strides in the way that they treat others. Seeing this self-improvement and growth within themselves can inspire resilience.

Michael Jascz founded the Relationship Foundation and wrote the book and curriculum Healthy Relationships 101 (HR101). *For the last ten years, he and his team have been training teachers, guidance counselors, and administrators on HR101 tenets.*

Going Offline
Anara Katz

I am in my junior year of high school and have never had a cell phone. That is surprising to most people. My friends tell me that I live under a rock, but I am happier this way.

I see my peers talking behind each other's backs on social media. They post snarky and passive-aggressive posts on Snapchat or Instagram. I have seen firsthand how this public humiliation ruins friendships.

In middle school, I had two close friends who were also close with one another. However, when they got into a fight, one of them whom I will call Ann would post about the other on social media. It was obvious who the posts were about. The comments were intentionally embarrassing for my other friend. Eventually, they lost their friendship, and I got stuck in the middle. We broke apart and went separate ways.

Ann shouldn't have posted about my other friend, of course, but having social media creates a platform for that to easily happen, and when people get angry, they sometimes do impulsive things like what Ann did. Instead of a private, resolvable conflict, friends shame one another in front of everyone. This kind of cyberbullying isn't talked about enough.

I'm not saying that everything about social media is bad. Of course, there are benefits, like starting social justice movements, creating awareness, and building networks of people.

However, when everything is online, the risk of making a mistake is greater. Everyone messes up sometimes, but when others post these mishaps on social media, it can become public to millions of viewers. It is scary knowing that nothing on social media ever goes away. If you make one misstep and someone has a phone and takes a video of it, there is a risk that the video will go viral on YouTube. That person can never escape this one moment.

I have friends who have posted things that they regret. One decision, in one moment, can decide whether you can keep a friend or avoid embarrassment and bullying.

The constant use of social media has created a place where people mercilessly compare themselves to others. Many girls in my high school post sexually explicit pictures of themselves on the internet. It seems to me that society is telling us that we need to show off our bodies to be noticed, loved, and accepted. In Snapchat, camera filters will take away blemishes or make someone's eyes bigger. It can be fun to play around with, but I can't help but think that it must make young people think they need a filter to be beautiful. Every part of our body has to look "perfect," and it creates insecurities, jealousies, and body image problems.

There are many ways in which technology creates social barriers too, including a constant fight to get more followers, as if that is the definition of being okay, cool, or liked. I remember sitting with my friends in middle school, and they would brag to one another about their number of followers. It was horrible, because a hierarchy developed, depending on who had the most.

I remember that when I first went on Instagram, I was embarrassed to show it to people because I felt I didn't have enough followers, as silly as that sounds. Now looking back, I see that worrying about where I fit on the social media hierarchy took me away from myself and my real-life friendships. Pressure to be popular online is another way that kids become vulnerable to bullying. Kids want to fit in, and they are looked down on when they don't have enough followers to prove their worth.

Walking down the hall in my high school is striking. At least half of the kids have their neck cranked down, as they stare at their cell phones. It is like something out of a dystopian movie. Everyone is doing the same thing in the same way at the same time. Our cell phones blend into our bodies, creating something of an electromagnetic-field glob.

Cell phones also act as an escape from our thoughts. Growing up without a cell phone has made me feel more secure and less dependent on the illusionary connection to the world that a cell phone brings. Access to the internet creates a disconnect between people and the real world. It acts as a distraction from reality. Without a cell phone, I find that I am more aware of my environment and emotions. When people are always on phones, I think they have little time to think or self-reflect.

One of my teachers commented that few of her students make eye contact. People are losing social functions, because instead of socializing with real people, they are mostly connecting virtually through the web.

On a daily basis, I see people checking their phones out of habit. They carry their phones with them everywhere, play games on them, and visit social media sites out of boredom. My peers do this while sitting at a restaurant, eating dinner, watching television, spending time with their families, and even driving.

Sometimes I do feel out of the loop. I have a laptop where I can check Instagram, but I am not that interested in social media. I am often the last one to hear of any big news, but I am okay with that.

There was a time in seventh grade when I watched too much television. I would get lost in the characters and plot lines. I allowed myself to sink into these other realities and escape my own, and I began to feel empty inside. Cell phones are like TV.

I believe that the abundant use of screens—cell phones, tablets, video games, laptops, and television—has a similar effect on people. Since I have limited myself from that unnatural world (watching television), I am happier and more engaged in my life. I feel more grounded.

I see my peers using drugs daily. The crazy part is that most of them are completely legal and prescribed. Many of my peers are on meds for ADD, attention-deficit/hyperactivity disorder (ADHD), anxiety, and depression. A huge number of youth are chronically prescribed medication, usually for behavioral problems. I started to wonder why they had these difficulties. It is probably partially due to the overprescription of drugs.

There is also another huge difference between the children and adolescents of the twenty-first century compared to those of past generations: the amount of exposure to wireless radiation (microwave radiation) and other electromagnetic fields that surround us.

Many teachers require cell phones and wireless laptops as a part of their curriculum. Even though I made a decision to keep a distance from cell phones, I can't escape the effect of the pervasive radiation at school. Through my childhood, my father warned me about the biological risks of wireless and cell phone radiation. I wanted to find out for myself whether I believed that cell phone radiation could have a negative impact on health.

I was given the opportunity to study this question in my high school research program. In the course of my study, I found that microwave radiation is linked to many neurobehavioral problems including autism (Plourde 2013); depression, ADD, and ADHD (Sage & Burgio 2018, January); short- and long-term memory loss (Sage & Burgio 2018, January); and fatigue, headaches, and sleeping problems (Navarro et al. 2003). Radiation also has a significant impact on stress hormones (Buchner & Eger 2011, January) and can cause DNA damage (Carpenter & Sage 2012, December).

Children are especially susceptible to microwave radiation because of their thinner skulls and developing brains. Studies show that children exposed to wireless radio in utero may have behavioral problems later in their lives (Sage & Burgio 2018, January). One report said, "The most serious health endpoints that have been reported to be associated with extremely low frequency (ELF) and/or RF [microwave radiation] include childhood and adult leukemia, childhood and adult brain tumors, and increased risk of neurodegenerative diseases, Alzheimer's and amyotrophic lateral sclerosis (ALS)" (Sage & Carpenter 2009, August).

I am grateful that I don't use a cell phone. I believe that I have avoided a lot of futile drama as well as possible health issues. My friends' lives are broadcast to the world in their public photos, comments, and stories. They are accessible to everyone. Because I don't use a cell phone, I have no pressure to be reachable. I have more privacy.

I'm perfectly happy under my rock. I am not involved in any cyberbullying or other drama. My mind hasn't been corrupted by filters or online media. I love the time that I get to spend by myself thinking. I also feel very connected with my family. In our downtime, we play games instead of staring at screens.

I don't feel I am missing out because I don't have a cell phone. If anything, I feel it is the opposite.

References

Buchner, K., & Eger, H. (2011, January). Changes of clinically important neurotransmitters under the influence of modulated RF fields—A long-term study under real-life conditions. Research Gate. Retrieved from https://www .researchgate.net/publication/285497186_

Carpenter, D., & Sage, C. (2012, December). Key scientific evidence and public health policy recommendations. *BioIntiative 2012*, section 24. Retrieved from https:// ecfsapi.fcc.gov/file/7520958422.pdf

Navarro, E. A., Segura, J., Portolés, M., & Mateo, C. G. (2003). The microwave syndrome: A preliminary study in Spain. *Electromagnetic Biology and Medicine, 22*(2–3), 161–169. Retrieved from https://www.emrpolicy.org /science/research/docs/navarro_ebm_2003.pdf

Plourde, E. (2013). Autism/behavior. In *EMF Freedom: Solutions for the 21st Century Pollution* (pp. 95–104). Irvine, CA: New Voice Publications.

Sage, C., & Burgio, E. (2018, January). Electromagnetic fields, pulsed radiofrequency radiation, and epigenetics: How wireless technologies may affect childhood development. *Child Development, 89*(1), 129–136. Retrieved from https://www.ncbi.nlm.nih.gov/pubmed /28504324

Sage, C., & Carpenter, D. O. (2009, August). Public health implications of wireless technologies. *Pathophysiology, 16*(2–3), 233–246. Retrieved from http://www .pathophysiologyjournal.com/article/S0928-4680 (09)00017-0/fulltext

Anara Katz is a high school student interested in studying environmental protection in college. Her hobbies include painting, playing guitar, and tennis. She also interns for New Yorkers for Clean Power and is active in school programs such as Environmental Activism, Women's Empowerment through Literature and the National Art Honors Society. She is excited about her ongoing science research project.

Be Kind
Fretta Reitzes

"Be Kind!" is a familiar phrase spoken by parents, teachers, grandparents, coaches, babysitters, and the many caring adults in our children's lives. But what do these words mean when we use them with our children?

How do they learn what it means to be kind and to care for others? Children don't learn as much from our commands as they do from us; we are their role models. They observe and watch everything we do; they listen to and hear what we say. Our behaviors, attitudes, and words—spoken and unspoken—form the foundation for their moral and ethical development. Our moral code sets the standard for theirs.

Kindness conversations can be an antidote to the bullying crisis in today's schools. Authentic moments of kindness are shared through personal stories about compassion, empathy, respect, acceptance, patience, forgiveness, honesty, integrity, and human dignity. They inspire open dialogue about the unique ways that we care for each other. While bullying is fueled by the toxicity, hatred, and narcissism prevalent in today's culture, kindness conversations have the power to nourish the human heart.

I led a series of workshops on kindness sponsored by Jessie Klein's Creating Compassionate Communities program. Participants were K–12 and college students and school staff. Following is a brief overview of the content and outcomes of several workshops, which have since been replicated in schools and community centers across the country.

Workshop Structure

- Participants: Fifteen students from a New York City public high school
- Format: Students sat together in a circle for a two-part series

Workshop Part 1

a. Brief warm-up exercise defining kindness
b. Questions
   1. How old were you when you first began to understand what kindness is?
   2. Who were you with?
   3. What were the circumstances?
c. Participant share and facilitated discussion

Jay's Story

When he was a little boy, Jay attended a day care center a few blocks from his house. Every day his mother picked him up at 5:30 p.m., and they took the same route home. They walked by the same homeless man on the corner who sat on the same blanket with the same hat in front of him for people to give him money.

Every day, Jay's mother dropped a quarter in the man's hat. Jay liked to listen for the clink that her quarter made when it touched the other coins in the hat. He watched his mother carefully. He saw her smile at the homeless man as she leaned down and saw the man acknowledge her quarter with a nod of appreciation.

When Jay was four, he asked his mother why the man always sat on the same blanket and why he never went home. His mother explained what it meant to be homeless. Jay listened and tried to understand what she told him, but he was confused.

A week later, Jay asked his mother if he could put a quarter in the man's hat like she did. His mother said yes. The next day as they approached the corner where the homeless man sat, Jay's mother gave him a quarter to put in the hat. They dropped their quarters in together. The homeless man acknowledged Jay and his mother with that same nod of appreciation. Every day after that, his mother had a quarter ready for Jay. Together they put their quarters in the man's hat.

Jay added that the best part was that every day after they dropped their quarters in the hat, he and his mother talked together about how it made them feel to give the man their quarters.

Meena's Story

Meena's family is originally from India. She grew up in New York, and her family lived close to many aunts, uncles, cousins, and grandparents. From the time that Meena was a small child, she was keenly aware that all the adults and older cousins in the family worked hard to support their extended family and that some of their money was set aside for their summer trip to India. Her family traveled back to India every summer to visit their relatives.

When they were in India, Meena would often accompany her grandfather to the nearest town. He would find a street that was crowded with shops and markets. He would give money to the beggars who extended their hands for money. Meena noticed that many of the beggars were children, often the same age as she was. It seemed to Meena that her grandfather was just squandering their family's money by giving it away to strangers. She felt troubled.

Meena's grandfather was the patriarch of the family. The children were taught to respect him and never to question, challenge, or disagree with him. When she was six years old and went to town with her grandfather, she gathered her courage, looked him squarely in his eyes, and asked him why he was giving their family's money to beggars and to people he didn't know. Her grandfather knelt down, took her gently by her shoulders, and answered her with a warm but serious smile.

"Because Meena," he said, "they need it more than we do."

With these few words, she understood. She felt his resolve and clarity about what he was doing and never questioned it again. Her grandfather had given her the gift of understanding what kindness meant to him and the moral obligation he felt to share what he had with those in need.

Workshop Part 2

a.   Brief reflection on Workshop Part 1

b.   Question posed: Is there anything you do to create a culture of kindness in your school community?

c.   Participant share and facilitated discussion

Nick's Story ("The Door Holder")

Nick sat in his chair, his arms folded, feet extended toward the center of the circle, and eyes closed. From his body language, I was sure he would not participate in the discussion. Then he began to talk.

Nick told us that last fall he had decided to be the "door holder" on the second floor when it was time to change classes in the morning. For several months, he noticed that when the bell rang, the hallway became congested very quickly. All the students had to walk through two big heavy doors that kept closing and didn't stay open by themselves. Nick also noticed that almost no one held the door for the person behind them. And so, every day between 10:50 and 11:05, Nick decided to assume a post as the official self-assigned "door holder." This did, in fact, ease hallway congestion.

I asked Nick what inspired him to do this. His answer was that someone had to do it to make it better for everyone and he knew he could do it well. He then stood up and showed the group (even though they had seen him in action during school) how he positioned himself at the door for fifteen minutes with his arm held out to hold the door open.

One of the students asked Nick if anyone thanked him for holding the door. According to Nick, some students did, and some didn't say anything. He added that he didn't to do this to be thanked. He did it to make the hallways less congested. A heated conversation then followed. Everyone in the group contributed.

Is saying "thank you" necessary? Do we do something kind because we want to be thanked? Do we do something kind because we want to be recognized for our kind act? One of the boys who had not said anything during the entire discussion brought up the golden rule: "Do unto others as you would want them to do unto you."

Students reflected on values from their parents, their religious education, camp counselors, and sports coaches. The conversation ended after forty-five minutes when the fifteen students concluded that saying "thank you" is only necessary when it is authentic and comes from the heart.

Kindness as Connection

When the workshop ended, the feeling of connection in the room was palpable. No one hurried to leave. The students took their time getting their belongings together. They hugged each other, smiled at one another, and spoke to each other calmly and with warmth. The workshop had provided a safe space for them to connect while they explored what kindness meant to them, and this allowed them to engage in honest and vibrant discussion.

The stories that Jay, Meena, and Nick shared about their first experiences with kindness are about connection. In Jay and Meena's stories, an adult played an essential role, creating security and closeness so that the children felt safe asking those difficult "why" questions. For Nick, kindness came from navigating his role in his school community.

Creating time and a safe space helped this group to feel connected to one another and open to speaking honestly and authentically about these profound early experiences. As the facilitator, I was able to honor their stories and hold a space for the students to deepen their relationship to their own kindness values.

Mark Twain wrote, "Kindness is the language that the deaf can hear and the blind can see." Kindness defines our humanity. It comes from the heart. It is what happens when we recognize vulnerability in others, when we pay attention in our everyday lives, and when we build meaningful, authentic connections. These kinds of conversations can help young people feel more connected with their own vulnerabilities and help to create more peaceful and supportive school environments.

Fretta Reitzes is an educational consultant and works with schools, community centers, and universities around the country. She was the director of the Center for Youth and Family at the 92Y in New York City and the director of the 92Y's Parenting Center and Wonderplay Initiative. She coauthored three books and has been an advisor to national educational institutions.

The Constant Needle: How Relentless Bullying Can Contribute to Death by Suicide
Alyssa Relyea

An insult. Calling someone a derogatory name. Berating someone. Teasing. From the outside and even to the perpetrator, I believe that to some people bullying can seem inconsequential. A pinprick. Too often, our natural tendency is to look at bullying incidents as isolated and unrelated. We placate the victim and minimize the impact. What we often fail to acknowledge is that bullying is rarely an isolated event, a single prick. Instead it is a constant needling on the victim's soul in the form of unrelenting and merciless little pricks. Over time, these pricks can drain the victim's sense of self, efficacy, and self-worth. And sometimes the result is suicide.

I was fortunate to not experience much bullying as a youth. My introduction to bullying began at age twenty, via my twin brother's experiences in his new career. A firefighter and emergency medical technician (EMT), my brother was hired by a fire department that was privatizing their emergency response. He was one of the EMTs and paramedics from an outside company who replaced the cross-trained firefighters/paramedics. My brother was called a scab and was berated and ignored. He had unknowingly walked into a workplace full of anger and hostility.

With coworkers' ire directed at him because of what he stood for (the loss of jobs), my brother would beg me to be on my best behavior while visiting him at work because "they already make my life miserable." Coming to believe he was a burden on his family and had no way out of his personal pain, he took his own life. While it would be unfair to say that the workplace bullying was the direct cause of his death, it is reasonable to say it was a factor in his devastating decision. His case is by no means isolated. Workplace bullying is reported by 35 percent of workers, according to Williams (2011, May 3). What many consider to be a childhood problem often continues into adulthood.

I have found that in contemporary American culture, bullying is pervasive and often focused on our youth. It litters our news feeds and peppers parent conversations at one gathering after another. There is always a new bullying incident to discuss, including cyberbullying. Too often, such bullying contributes to a youth's suicide. Society has even devised a new word to describe this—"bullycide"—although some suicide prevention experts decry its use due to its sensationalist nature. Some people automatically link suicide and bullying, but suicide is much more complicated.

Bullying is not new; in all likelihood, its existence was felt among our earliest ancestors. Today, however, it is more common. According to the National Center for Education Statistics, there has been a 25 percent increase in bullying at schools since 2003 (Hartnig n.d.). Further, bullying follows students home, as mother of bullying victim Grace McComas explained in an article about cyberbullying in Maryland: "No longer does a bully say something nasty in a schoolyard and the child goes home to his sanctuary. Instead, [cyberbullying] is pervasive and invasive. . . . It is gossip and hatred at the speed of electronic media, as close as their cell phone or computer screen" (Ebner n.d.).

According to 2011 statistics from the U.S. Department of Education, 28 percent of students reported being bullied during the academic school year. However, when students were asked if they had experienced bullying in their lifetime, 34 percent reported the experience to researchers from www.cyberbullying .org. With so many children aged twelve to seventeen being online, according to Pew Research (2011, November 9) there are many opportunities for bullying to occur. A crisis text line has even been developed (text HOME to 741741) to reach children where they spend so much time.

In order to find a solution, we must first examine bullying more closely. What makes some targets of bullying take their own lives while others are able to survive, albeit often with other kinds of serious consequences? In adults, completed suicides using lethal means is highly correlated with a feeling of being burdensome to others (Joiner et al. 2002). Is the same true for adolescents?

When we think about bullying as a contributor to suicide, one of the most compelling explanations can be found in the Roy Baumeister's (1990) theory of suicide as escape from self. In addition to having a mental health disorder such as depression, suicide that is related to bullying can occur after a flood of overwhelming emotion, writes Jesse Bering (2010, October 20). The victim often feels like a failure and experiences shame, guilt, and humiliation as a result of the bullying. Young people tend to consider suicide as a way to end the personal pain, which only seems achievable through death. To be sure, every individual case is different, and we can't get into every victim's psyche. Yet we can be sure that when a teen with mental illness experiences relentless bullying that they feel cannot be stopped, the desire to escape the situation can contribute to suicidal ideation.

So what is the solution? In order to catch those at immediate risk, the first step is to educate gatekeepers (family, teachers, doctors) to signs of suicidal thoughts, as described by the American Foundation for Suicide Prevention (n.d.). These signs include the following.

Talk
- Being a burden to others
- Feeling trapped
- Experiencing unbearable pain
- Having no reason to live
- Killing themselves

Behaviors
- Increased use of alcohol or drugs
- Looking for a way to kill themselves, such as searching online for materials or means
- Acting recklessly
- Withdrawing from activities
- Isolating from family and friends
- Sleeping too much or too little
- Visiting or calling people to say goodbye
- Giving away prized possessions
- Aggression

Moods

- Depression
- Loss of interest
- Rage
- Irritability
- Humiliation
- Anxiety

Additionally, gatekeepers should be aware that two factors warrant immediate and intensive response. According to Joiner (2009, June), in the interpersonal-psychological theory of suicidal behavior, when individuals communicate a sense of burdensomeness (people are better off without me) and a sense of social alienation (I'm on the outside and don't belong), there is cause for special concern, because these feelings can contribute to suicidal thoughts. Given the isolating nature of bullying, teachers, parents, and anyone else involved with children and teens should be aware of this interplay.

Another kind of education must also occur. As a suicide prevention advocate with the American Foundation for Suicide Prevention, it is my hope that we save those in immediate danger *and* shape society so that suicide is no longer considered a viable option. To that end, we must change the conversation about mental health. We must remove the stigma surrounding mental illness and treat those who are suffering through a bout of *any* ill health, be it mental or physical. All pain is worthy of our compassion, empathy, and attention. We don't need to get rid of the internet or social media, but we do need to teach children to use cyberspace more appropriately so that they become more compassionate and caring individuals.

I believe this is possible and have seen it in action. A student of mine met another boy in online video chat rooms, and on one occasion, the acquaintance expressed suicidal thoughts. This victim of online and real-life bullying, whose parents were uninvolved, spoke about his vague suicidal threat in an online chat room. This thirteen-year-old had a plan, and yet he reached out to strangers in one last effort to save his own life.

My student took him seriously, messaged him privately, and was able to convince him to live and get help. It is this story, among others, that gives me hope for the future. We *can* use social media to save lives, and we *can* raise a generation of compassionate people. We need to exhibit compassionate care toward others in workplaces, schools, and online so that no cry for help goes ignored.

Bullying may or may not be human nature, but it does not have to be a complacent choice. Bullying can become a constant needling to a person's sense of self, one that is destructive and corrosive. According to the Centers for Disease Control and Prevention's (2016, April) latest statistics, youth and adult suicide is on the rise and is a leading cause of death for all Americans.

We know that suicide is preventable. By educating gatekeepers and making compassion and empathy an everyday value instead of something we reserve for when problems arise, we can turn the tide of bullying, self-harm, and related suicide. We all play a part, and we have the solution within us.

References

American Foundation for Suicide Prevention. (n.d.). Risk factors and warning signs. Retrieved from https://afsp.org /about-suicide/risk-factors-and-warning- signs/

Baumeister, R. F. (1990). Suicide as escape from self. *Psychological Review, 97*(1), 90–113.

Bering, J. (2010, October 20). Being suicidal: What it feels like to want to kill yourself. *Scientific American*. Retrieved from https://blogs.scientificamerican.com/bering-in-mind /being-suicidal-what-it-feels-like-to-want-to-kill-yourself/

Centers for Disease Control and Prevention. (2016, April). Increase in suicide in the United States, 1999–2014. Retrieved from https://www.cdc.gov/nchs/products /databriefs/db241.htm

Crisis Text Line. (n.d.). Crisis text line. Retrieved from http://www.crisistextline.org

Ebner, T. (n.d.). Maryland schools focus attention on cyberbullying. Retrieved from http://cnsmaryland.org/interactives/cyberbullying/cyberbullying-in-maryland-schools/index.html

Hartnig, S. (n.d.). Student bullying on increase, federal statistics reveal. Retrieved from http://students.com.miami.edu/netreporting/?page_id=1269

Joiner, T. (2009, June). The interpersonal-psychology theory of suicidal behavior: Current empirical status. American Psychological Association. Retrieved from http://www.apa.org/science/about/psa/2009/06/sci-brief.aspx

Joiner, Jr., T. E., Pettit, J. W., Walker, R. L., Voelz, Z. R., & Cruz, J. (2002). Perceived burdensomeness and suicidality: Two studies on the suicide notes of those attempting and those completing suicide. *Journal of Social and Clinical Psychology, 21*(5), 531–545. Retrieved from https://msrc.fsu.edu/system/files/Joiner%20et%20al%202002%20Perceived%20burdensomeness%20and%20suicidality-%20two%20studies%20on%20the%20suicide%20notes%20of%20those%20attempting%20and%20those%20completing%20suicide.pdf

Pew Research Center. (2011, November 9). Teens, kindness and cruelty on social network sites. Retrieved from http://www.pewinternet.org/2011/11/09/teens-kindness-and-cruelty-on-social-network-sites-2/

Williams, R. (2011, May 3). The silent epidemic: Workplace bullying. *Psychology Today*. Retrieved from https://www.psychologytoday.com/blog/wired-success/201105/the-silent-epidemic-workplace-bullying

Alyssa Relyea, MA, has been a passionate advocate for suicide prevention since 1997 when she lost her twin brother, Andrew, to

suicide. Volunteering with the American Foundation for Suicide Prevention strengthened her dedication. She writes for outlets including the Huffington Post and speaks about suicide prevention and mental health.

Using Restorative Justice to Prevent and Stop Bullying
Nichole Rowe Small

At the University Neighborhood Middle School, where I serve as a school counselor, we believe in restorative practices as a way to prevent school bullying and intervene effectively in conflict. Our three-tiered program of community building, restorative justice circles, and one-on-one support is integrated throughout the school, in all classrooms, and engages every student and community member.

We also do peer mediation when fewer students have a dispute or conflict that they want solved but cannot solve on their own.

Community Building

Community building circles help students and staff build trust and feel comfortable speaking openly, honestly, and constructively with one another. Participants respond to a prompt, such as "tell us how a close friend would describe you" or "roses, thorns, and buds." In the second, roses are highlights, buds are things that are happening that could turn into roses, and thorns are things that made us feel uncomfortable or unhappy.

In their answers and the conversation that follows, participants see and get to know each other's similarities and differences. These conversations also help people recognize and experience one another's vulnerabilities. We also use community circles for classroom discussions, adult and student book clubs, staff meetings, parent meetings, and orientations.

Teachers have community building circle time with one another during our weekly professional development sessions. Each staff member is encouraged to look within to see how their perspectives, worldviews, and experiences affect how they approach their teaching and how this affects the extent to which they are caring for or harming the students.

We discuss biases, stereotypes, racism, and oppression as well as ways in which we can grow equity within our community. We also reflect on the impact these issues have on our interactions with our students.

These circles help students, teachers, and families communicate together. Parents are invited into our circles to discuss community issues, including academic expectations and social-emotional concerns. We encourage willing participants to share their points of view and personal feelings. Anyone is allowed to pass if they do not want to speak. School community members all participate in circles at specific times during the week.

Restorative Justice Circles

We use equity circles, restorative circles, and reentry circles to address and resolve conflicts and other community concerns.

Equity circles are done on a needs basis, when the community is being harmed but we are unclear about the reason (e.g., a student is disrupting the class repeatedly, walking around, or not engaging with tasks). In an equity circle, we learn why the student is behaving this way. For example, it turned out that one student with ADHD wasn't taking her medications. With her paraprofessional present and her family's support, we were able to help this student engage constructively in the school.

Students participating in an equity circle need to commit to being fair and understanding. A school counselor or teacher with extensive restorative training and experience facilitates the equity circle. The leaders listen to the information presented, ask relevant questions, and help the participants come to an agreement that works for everyone involved, including the school community. The panel offers suggestions and techniques to fix the wrongs that need to be righted. Students who run equity circles are trained in conflict resolution. These circles require paperwork and parent consent and can be requested by any community member or group.

Restorative circles take place when someone in the community was harmed. As in all circles, we follow specific circle procedures. For the circle, we need a facilitator, a centerpiece, and a talking piece. The centerpiece in a restorative circle usually has items that are related to the circle members. For example, we use our schools' T-shirts to celebrate community unity, and a talking piece could be a teddy bear, a rock, or an actual Native American talking piece, whatever the group or facilitators decide on.

Participants are asked what they need to feel safe in the circle. These words, such as "compassion" and "honesty," are written on index cards and placed in the center of the circle.

We work to address systemic and structural racism in our circles. We talk about the microaggressions that take place particularly against people from marginalized groups. Students and school staff speak about these painful experiences in the trusting spaces we create. We also hear from individuals who have begun to realize that they were inadvertently or even purposely hurtful to others. Through the bonding experience, members of the circle often become more self-aware and committed to treating themselves and others with new respect and compassion.

This process helps address the underlying factors that may lead children to engage in disturbing behaviors in the first place. We had a student, for instance, who often called other students "gay" and made off-color jokes. We found out in circle with his class that the boy's father was homophobic and made the same kinds of comments in their family. The boy who told these jokes was sharing what he learned at home.

The group became emotional when some students shared about their own gay family members, particularly how painful it was when others made fun of them and how much they loved these family members. The student making homophobic comments and other students with similar biases came to understand how similar they were to the people they were teasing. The discussion helped build the students' capacities to love and respect others. With this self-reflection, the student who was making jokes agreed to stop.

Restorative circles are used when someone has harmed another person or the larger community. The main goal in a restorative justice circle is community safety. The restorative justice circle allows the person who has done harm to become accountable to those they have harmed and enables this person to repair the damage their actions caused. The second goal is accountability. We discuss strategies that help students feel safe, build relationships, and feel empowered in our community.

In restorative circles, we ask four questions:

1. Why are we here?
2. Who was harmed?
3. How will that harm be repaired?
4. What will each person do to repair the harm?

We initiated a restorative circle when one of our students was bullying a girl new to this country. The student was harassing the girl about her sneakers. The students in the circle held the person bullying accountable for her actions. Each student spoke about what it felt like when they experienced, witnessed, or heard about bullying. They also spoke about what the school's expectations and core values were and why bullying is wrong. Both the student who was bullied and the student who did the bullying had a chance to speak.

In this case, an entire class participated in the discussion, and together with the students involved in the incident, they agreed on nonpunitive consequences. The person who was bullying was not suspended. She was helped to stay in our community, learn from her harmful behaviors, and make different and more positive choices about her future behaviors.

New York City's Department of Education is the largest and most segregated school system in America. At the University Neighborhood Middle School, we operate with an awareness and consciousness about the school-to-prison pipeline. We have to interrogate how we treat our students and make sure that we are not participating in this inequitable process even though we are a part of this same system. We use these practices to prevent black and brown students being pushed out of schools for things that warrant community voice and support.

Too often, students' voices, experiences, and challenges go unheard or are misunderstood. Instead of support, care, and help to communicate, resolve issues, build relationships, and move forward in their education, they can be suspended, expelled, shamed, and punished. With these punitive systems, students of color tend to be given harsher consequences for the same negative behaviors that white students exhibit.

We use the Chancellor's Regulations to help us navigate a menu of consequences for bullying, and since this process has been added to the list of possible school responses, we most often choose the restorative route. We have seen the punitive interventions, time and again, undermine student-to-student and teacher-to-student relationships, as well as community morale.

When students acting out against adults or another student are suspended without a conversation among the parties, students tend to remain resentful toward the other(s). Requiring a child to wait many weeks where they may speak with lawyers at a suspension site but not with the person they have wronged most often sets up lasting hostilities between the parties. Instead, providing opportunities for the parties to resolve the matter before it goes to the suspension site can mitigate the anger that students feel about what occurred. When we use restorative justice as an alternative to suspension, we often have parents present.

Reentry circles are used for students who return from being suspended. The circle helps to reintegrate the person(s) who inflicted harm and helps them to rejoin the community as a valuable, contributing member. No one is devalued in this space. Each community member sees how their choices affect the community. They learn that when their choices hurt others, it is necessary and possible to fix it. They are allowed to choose which community members are a part of their reentry circle. All circle members take the role of active support to help this community member take a more positive role in the community and refrain from committing any more harm.

One-on-one support follows the reentry and restorative circles and is crucial for helping students remain accountable and keep their commitments and to help them to make different choices.

I believe that all schools should have a school-wide strategic plan that requires staff, students, and parents to address behavior-related issues through restorative processes. Teen misbehaviors should be used as a means to engage in constructive dialogue that enhances everyone's social skills, including listening, speaking compassionately, showing empathy and forgiveness, and fostering reintegration. Our youth should never be viewed as criminals or be seen through criminal lenses.

Restorative practices work. They help schools become what they are meant to be: a place where people share, learn, and grow together, from the youngest to the eldest person.

These practices also encourage accountability without the stigma or the juvenile justice record that could overshadow a student through adulthood. Instead of building criminal records, we need to capitalize on teachable moments. We should encourage students to treat each other fairly, with love, kindness, and an understanding that we can talk through most things and resolve conflicts using the child-friendly processes that work.

Two organizations that have trained our staff in restorative practices include Talking Peace in California and the Morningside Center for Teaching Social Responsibility in New York City. No one should conduct restorative practices without intensive training from an excellent program. Schools need to make a commitment to doing this right.

Nichole Rowe Small is a school counselor at the University Neighborhood Middle School. Since 1999 she has worked for the New York City Department of Education. She has an M.Ed. from Columbia University in school psychology and an MA in counseling. Her CUNY BA is also in psychology with a minor in black studies. She is the equity liaison at the University Neighborhood Middle School.

The Missing Discourse of Rights: Bullying versus Sexual Harassment in K–12 Schools
Nan Stein

The battles over bullying continue. Some studies report that prevalence surges; other studies report declines, and disagreements over the definition persist. According to a national annual survey of school crime and safety, during the 2013–2014 school year, 16 percent of public schools reported that bullying among students occurred at least weekly. During the 2012–2013 school year, 21.5 percent of students reported being bullied at school. A recent 2017 article in *Pediatrics* reviewing ten years of surveillance data on Maryland youth from 2005 to 2014 found significant improvements and asserted that bullying had declined.

Other studies and meta-analyses look at interventions and find claims of efficacy, while different efforts to help, though popular, have minimal evidence of effectiveness to warrant their usage. Researchers and curriculum developers (and their marketers) line up with their data, fighting it out for relevance and supremacy. It's hard to keep current with all this competition.

Despite these turf wars, some fundamental assumptions continue to be overlooked. This essay will discuss some of those oversights. Specifically, I have three primary concerns about the bullying framework: first, the overly broad use of the term "bullying"; second, the definition(s) of "bullying"; and third, the lack of effective evidence-based interventions for prevention and remediation.

Broad Use of the Term "Bullying"

The term "bullying" is imprecise and vague; it is too often used as a default, as a crutch, and has been stretched to describe everything from meanness to peer aggression to behaviors that might qualify as criminal sexual assault. I consider this word to be a placeholder for what we should call "racism," "sexism," or "homophobia." Unfortunately, all harmful conduct is sometimes collapsed into the simple one-word term "bullying," whether we are talking about social exclusion or sexual assault. All of a sudden, all offensive and aggressive behaviors have been labeled bullying. I believe we need to expand our vocabulary, instead of reducing it to one overused term.

Developmental psychologist Lyn Mikel Brown wrote an article in *Education Week* in 2008 that urged educators to be honest and up-front when identifying behaviors and the terms to describe them. Dr. Brown wrote, "Calling behaviors what they are helps us educate children about their rights, affirms their realities, encourages more complex and meaningful solutions, opens up a dialogue, invites children to participate in social change and ultimately protects them."

In my law review article (Stein 2003), I wrote about my observations regarding school administrators who frequently misled students and their parents in an attempt to disguise their liability for preventing and eliminating sexual harassment in schools. In one way or another, administrators conveyed that the parents of the offending child would be sued for actions that took place in the school. Too many administrators embrace and promote the bullying framework and discourse because they believe they will not end up in federal court if they label behaviors bullying as opposed to naming those behaviors as harassment. By doing this, they conflate harassment behaviors and definitions with bullying, which also displaces the legal rights of students to be free from harassment under federal civil rights education laws, which do not cover bullying.

The Office for Civil Rights of the U.S. Department of Education addressed and clarified this problematic phenomenon in a guidance memorandum that they issued in an October 26, 2010, Dear Colleague letter called "Harassment and Bullying" (Ali 2010; Office for Civil Rights 2010). In the letter, in no uncertain terms, they asserted that bullying cannot override harassment and other civil rights laws.

The media indulges in oversimplification and distortion, as headline after headline flashes the term "bullying." When I read these articles or listen to these news reports, I often learn that youth were charged with criminal violations or school districts were sued in federal court for sexual or racial harassment under federal civil rights laws. So the obvious question arises. Why aren't we calling these alleged bullying behaviors for what they are—alleged criminal actions and/or violations of civil rights?

Using the term "bullying" is talking in shorthand, which does us all a disservice. Instead, I believe that we should encourage students and adults, and especially reporters and journalists, to use more accurate words, not fewer words, when they describe conduct that they think interferes with or disrupts the learning environment.

The Definition(s) of Bullying

The definition of bullying is unclear. When we look at the fifty states that have passed different state laws on bullying, the definition in various dictionaries, and the various ways in which researchers define bullying, we see that there is no single definition.

Even as the Centers for Disease Control and Prevention in 2014 (Gladden, Vivolo-Kantor, Hamburger & Lumpkin, 2014) offered a common definition of bullying "as any unwanted aggressive behavior(s) by another youth or group of youths, who are not siblings or current dating partners, involving an observed or perceived power imbalance and is repeated multiple times or is highly likely to be repeated," state lawmakers as well as researchers seem to utilize their own definitions.

This process of creating a definition is arbitrary and capricious, an inconsistent, almost whimsical process. Some laws and researchers insist that bullying is comprised of "repeated" behaviors; others say it can be a one-time occurrence. Some laws and researchers define it as a differential "imbalance of power," but it is not clear as to how the imbalance is determined or by whom. Most mysterious of all, what comprises "power"? If the behaviors are classified based on severity, what measures are in use to define this condition?

I find it useful to reflect on two cases of Massachusetts students who committed suicide; their trajectories provide painful illustrations of the ways in which school personnel treat and frame student-to-student interactions. Phoebe Prince and Carl Walker-Hoover took their own lives in January 2010 (Phoebe) and April 2009 (Carl), after allegedly being bullied by their peers. I believe both students were sexually harassed by their peers and to call what they endured "bullying" minimizes the perpetrators' behaviors.

Since these two cases, dozens of other young students who have been targets of sexual harassment have committed suicide. This is not just a matter of semantics; denying the discriminatory nature of the conduct directed at these aggrieved students limits the remedies that are owed to them and their families.

I believe that the two school districts in the Massachusetts cases should have been sued in federal court under federal civil rights laws for their disregard of federal law Title IX: the right to receive an education that is free from sex discrimination and harassment. We know from media reports and statements from lawyers who represented the aggrieved and grieving families that the school staff had been contacted by the aggrieved students and their parents about the problems Phoebe and Karl were experiencing.

With the school personnel "on notice," the liability lay with them to create a school environment that would not permit or tolerate behaviors that interfered with those children receiving their civil rights—their equal rights—to go to school in an environment free from racial and sexual discrimination, including sexual harassment.

This legal precedent was settled in the1999 case heard in the U.S. Supreme Court, *Davis v. Monroe County Board of Education (GA) School District*, in which a fifth-grade girl in Macon, Georgia, was sexually harassed by a male classmate over a period of time. She and her parents informed the school district about this harassment, but the district failed to take appropriate actions to address these persistent problems. This case established that school personnel are liable for peer-to-peer sexual harassment when they know about it and fail to take any action. Thus, in both Carl and Phoebe's cases, the school personnel were on notice. And yet they failed to take remedial action. Tragically, both students killed themselves.

Lack of Effective Evidence-Based Interventions for Prevention and Remediation

My final point is about consumer protection. Schools are flooded with flyers and emails with glowing testimonials about bullying curricula and materials. Some of those materials have scientific validity in their development, while other interventions lack this evidence. Many materials and authors promote efficacy claims, yet the research results often do not support such assertions. Many of these interventions and curricula have yet to be evaluated, or if they have undergone evaluation, there are major gaps that raise concerns about the generalizability of their effectiveness (Ttofi & Farrington 2010; Bradshaw 2015).

Some interventions have been evaluated by their author(s), which may present a conflict of interest and inherent bias. Other results, assuming they were effective, have not been replicated with groups beyond the initial group of students. If the effects cannot be replicated in other environments with more diverse populations, then there is doubt about the usefulness of that particular strategy with a wider group of subjects, schools, and youth. The integrity of some of these evaluations must be called into question, as schools volunteered to be included in the studies after having already expressed an interest in these materials.

Any evaluation project that did not utilize a random assignment at the beginning calls the whole enterprise into question and should limit the glowing assertions that flow upon its conclusions. Many of these evaluations have not been published in peer-reviewed journals, which would allow these studies to be scrutinized by other scholars.

Many of the curricula have mixed results despite their popularity, whether they are free like Don't Laugh at Me, developed by Operation Respect, an organization founded by Peter Yarrow of the folk group Peter, Paul, and Mary, or those that cost in four figures like Steps to Respect offered by the Committee for Children or the Olweus Bullying Prevention Program.

The Olweus program in particular has been used widely after its initial effort in rural South Carolina in the mid-1990s. This program remains both expensive and highly touted, but positive results weren't confirmed until their large-scale 2013 study in Pennsylvania (Limber & Olweus 2013). Other programs have been created by parents whose children have committed suicide or were victims in mass shootings, such as Rachel's Challenge, which came from a family whose daughter was killed at Columbine High School.

No matter the understandable motivation of the parents and curriculum creators to pour their grief into something productive, we still need to require evaluations that show intervention efficacy. Some of these programs don't have evaluation sections on their websites—maybe because there aren't any.

The motivation to prevent lost lives should spur action. But this should not result in reckless implementation of unproven programs that respond to isolated issues rather than holistic policy creation, professional development, and comprehensive programming supported by rigorous, unbiased evaluation.

Studying school violence does not mean merely focusing on gangs, guns, and drugs. As my coauthors and I addressed in a 2002 article, there are gendered dimensions to school violence. To make schools gender safe, we need to create a culture that neither permits nor endorses sexual harassment toward students who identify as females, males, questioning, or trans youth. We must appropriately label behaviors and respond effectively to what is really going on in the hallways, bathrooms, and buses. Children's lives and right to learn in a safe environment depend on it.

References

Ali, R. (2010, October 26). Dear colleague letter from assistant secretary for civil rights. U.S. Department of Education. Retrieved from https://www2.ed.gov/about /offices/list/ocr/letters/colleague-201010.html

Bradshaw, C. P. (2015). Translating research to practice in bullying prevention. *American Psychologist, 70*(4), 322–332. doi:10.1037/a0039114.

Brown, L. M. (2008, March 29). 10 ways to move beyond bully prevention (and why we should). *Education Week, 27*(26). Retrieved from http://www.edweek.org/ew/articles /2008/03/05/26brown.h27.html

Carlton, M. (2017, July). Summary of school safety statistics. U.S. Department of Justice, Office of Justice Programs. Retrieved from https://www.ncjrs.gov/pdffiles1/nij/250610 .pdf https://www.ncjrs.gov/pdffiles1/nij/250610.pdf

Davis v. Monroe County Board of Education (GA) School District, 526 U.S. 629. 1999.

Gladden, R. M., Vivolo-Kantor, A. M., Hamburger, M. E., & Lumpkin, C. D. (2014). Bullying surveillance among youths: Uniform definitions for public health and recommended data elements (Version 1.0). Atlanta, GA: Centers for Disease Control and Prevention. Retrieved from https://www.cdc.gov/violenceprevention/pdf/bullying-definitions-final-a.pdf

Limber, S., & Olweus, D. (2013, November 11). Evaluation research on the implementation of the Olweus Bullying Prevention Program in Pennsylvania schools: Summary of findings presented at the annual meeting of the International Bullying Prevention Association.

Office for Civil Rights. (2010, October 26). Dear colleague letter: Harassment and bullying background, summary, and fast facts. U.S. Department of Education. Retrieved from https://www2.ed.gov/about/offices/list/ocr/docs/dcl-factsheet-201010.html

Stein, N. D. (2003). Bullying or sexual harassment? The missing discourse of rights in an era of zero tolerance. *Arizona Law Review, 45*(3), 783–799. Retrieved from http://arizonalawreview.org/pdf/45-3/45arizlrev783.pdf

Ttofi, M. M., & Farrington, D. P. (2010). Effectiveness of school-based programs to reduce bullying: A systematic and meta-analytic review. *Journal of Experimental Criminology, 7*(1), 27–56. doi:10.1007/s11292-010-9109-1.

Nan Stein is a senior research scientist at Wellesley College Center for Research on Women, where she conducts research on sexual harassment in K–12 schools, teen dating violence, and gender violence in educational settings. Her research on peer sexual harassment began in the late 1970s. She has published many articles in peer-reviewed journals, book chapters, and law review articles, and she often serves as an expert witness in Title IX lawsuits. Her research has been funded by the U.S. Department of Justice's National Institute of Justice, the Centers for Disease Control and Prevention, the U.S. Department of Education, the Soros Foundation, the National Educational Association, and other family foundations.

Only Compassion—Not Tough Love—
Can Teach Empathy
Maia Szalavitz

There is a paradox at the heart of the way we think about empathy. Almost instinctively, people expect victims to become sympathetic toward other victims once they have had a personal, painful experience themselves. But in fact, being victimized doesn't automatically create empathy, and some people respond to being abused or hurt by becoming more likely to be bullies or abusers themselves, not less so.

That's because the most callous bullies see victimization through a completely different lens. And we need to understand this way of seeing in order to understand why causing suffering is not a good way to induce empathy and how to really help reduce bullying.

To such bullies, whom some researchers label "callous/unemotional," being bullied is just the price the victim pays for being at the wrong end of a status hierarchy. "It's nothing personal. That's what you get." From this perspective, those on top feel they deserve to lord power over everyone else. Someone with this disposition or perspective tends to believe in their own right to rule the school regardless of prior experiences being bullied or not. If they get bullied themselves, they simply think they need to regain power, not behave better. Power alone motivates them.

This misconception, along with the idea that suffering inspires empathy, is involved in nearly all of the common but misguided approaches to the prevention and treatment of bullying, addiction, and antisocial behavior.

Programs intended to create empathy by imposing pain and humiliation often do the opposite. Research shows that "boot camps" and other "tough love" approaches backfire and aggravate instead of mitigate the behaviors of those with callous and antisocial characteristics. In extreme cases, these punitive approaches cause post-traumatic stress disorder (PTSD) and depression. By looking at why these harsh approaches fail, we can learn about what works.

First, let's consider a child with a typical temperament. This person feels their own pain and that of others and usually responds to victims with sympathy. However, that response doesn't require them to have had the same experience as the other, or even anything like it; once they've passed the appropriate developmental milestones, they are good at empathizing and can easily imagine how bad it would feel to be abused and isolated, even if they haven't themselves had similar pain.

Alternatively consider a child with a sensitive temperament. Here, again, even more than a typical child, a sensitive youth will see why abusing others is wrong without much experience of being bullied. Sensitive children may become so distressed by the pain of others, however, that they don't respond kindly; instead, they may flee the intensity of the situation either physically or by checking out. This is not a lack of empathy. It's a problem of self-regulation.

Now let's look at a child who has "callous/unemotional" traits. These children tend to be fearless and impulsive. They do not worry about what might go wrong if they take a certain action; they just do it. Because they have less fear and tend to be less sensitive to painful experiences (including punishment), such experiences are also less frightening to them. Much of the sting of pain comes from worrying about it, so if an aversive experience doesn't make you anxious, it tends to be less painful.

Another aspect of what makes punishment painful to typical children is social; most children want to avoid punishment not just because it's boring or painful but because they don't want to disappoint people they love and admire or to be isolated from others. However, callous/unemotional children often feel less reward from social contact. They care less about disappointing others.

These children, then, may be less sensitive to negative consequences, whether social or physical. Their social sensitivity is reduced by the lack of reward from positive social interaction, and their physical sensitivity is reduced by their decreased experience of fear and anxiety. This can also affect how they think about other people. If social and physical pain doesn't bother them much, why do others complain so much about it when they inflict it?

What this means is that these children are the worst candidates for tough love. Callous/unemotional kids find both the physical and the social rejection involved in harsh punishment less aversive. Therefore, tough love is unlikely to change the way they relate to others.

Moreover, tough love sends them the implicit message that it is okay for powerful people to make others suffer "for their own good." And that means that when they get such power themselves—which often happens in programs that have "point and level" systems—they are even more inclined to use it. Indeed, the adults running the program have just shown that such behavior is acceptable for those in charge.

For typical and sensitive children, however, tough love can do another sort of harm. In the case of typical children, extreme and adverse experiences like being isolated, undergoing corporal punishment, or being publicly humiliated can lead to less trust in adults, and in severe cases, they can lead to PTSD and depression, just like bullying by peers can. If they have experienced prior trauma, it is more likely that they will develop depression and PTSD.

Sensitive children are even more prone to PTSD and depression without any prior trauma, and prior trauma makes this risk worse. Tough love also does harm by aggravating their difficulties with self-regulation. When they become more distressed, they are even less able to reach out to others who are hurting.

Essentially, while tough love "gives bullies a taste of their own medicine," it is neither necessary nor sufficient to create empathy. And in the children who may be the most dangerous bullies, tough love reinforces the idea that might makes right and creates more of a desire for revenge than for sympathy.

To learn empathy, children need a safe and nurturing environment where they can be taught to understand their own feelings and the ways that their actions affect the feelings of others. Before you can imagine someone else's experiences, you need to be able to describe what it's like to be you. Such self-awareness gives you the language and understanding needed to be empathetic to others.

If we want to help children with different temperaments to empathize and to care, we need to see how they see things and then match that with the way that we approach helping them become more connected. Acting empathetically will come from different places in different temperaments, and differing temperaments present different barriers to kindness. None of these are reduced by tough love, but they can be improved by meeting each child where they are.

Maia Szalavitz is the author of the New York Times *best seller* Unbroken Brain: A Revolutionary New Way of Understanding Addiction. *She also wrote* Help at Any Cost: How the Troubled Teen Industry Cons Parents and Hurts Kids *and, with Bruce D. Perry, MD, PhD, she cowrote* The Boy Who Was Raised as a Dog *and also* Born for Love: Why Empathy Is Essential—and Endangered. *For her thirty years of groundbreaking writing on addiction, drug policy, and neuroscience, she has won awards from the National Institute on Drug Abuse, the Drug Policy Alliance, the American Psychological Association, and the American College of Neuropsychopharmacology.*

Inner Peace Creates Outer Peace
M. Cristina Zaccarini

School bullying on college campuses presents unique challenges. Students tend to be more isolated from family and neighborhood friends due to living in the dormitories or managing a high workload. In addition to hurtful behaviors from peers, students may have anxieties related to exams, professors' expectations, and the pressures of fitting in socially. Students might feel lonely, anxious, or depressed.

Sometimes students channel these frustrations outward. They feel angry because they don't know what to do about feeling so overwhelmed and out of control. Students might then become aggressive toward others, socially exclude, or put down their peers to help themselves feel better about themselves. These students need help to manage their feelings, including anger, their stress, and their ability to focus on the new demands they face in college.

As a college professor, I encounter students who had been excellent students in high school but now seem overwhelmed. What could I do about what is ostensibly a mental health issue when my charge as a history professor is to impart academic knowledge?

Studying leaders in spirituality and mindfulness, I have found, helps my students develop self-awareness and more inner peace. In one of my classes, called History, Herstory, Yourstory, I combine the history of spirituality with contemporary mindfulness practices, shaping my interactive lectures around historical actors and groups who worked toward the antithesis of bullying: compassion for self and others, connection to nature, social justice, and yearning for fair and equitable social relationships in the world.

While spirituality has historically been connected to religion, it is also important to study spirituality separate from religion. Today, a spiritual person can be an atheist or agnostic, and the spirituality of historical figures can be examined in the context of contemporary questions about self-compassion and societal justice.

In this course, I ask students to consider questions related to these historical figures. What is the relationship between an individual's inner peace and that person's ability to foster peace and equitable relations in a household and in society? How can we use meditation to foster self-care so that the flow of anger from inside does not seep into the world, resulting in the bullying of others? These kinds of questions enable students to make connections between historical narratives, contemporary times, and their own lives and relationships with others.

Often students who express difficulties at the start of the semester benefit from the study of spirituality and mindfulness exercises. Students are assigned narratives, including those on shamanism among indigenous peoples of the Americas and Asia. They read about Muslim, Daoist, Buddhist, Jewish, and Christian mystics. The academic readings are combined with in-classroom mindfulness exercises based on the free materials provided by the Palouse Mindfulness website, offering videos, readings, handouts, and a completion certificate, obtainable through https://palousemindfulness.com/.

We begin class with a five-minute meditation. I ask students to observe their experiences and document their thoughts in Palouse's daily journal. They learn to locate where they experience sensations associated with these thoughts in their body. As observers, they often experience a new feeling of peace. Students who had initially reported anxiety feel more relaxed, and they express this in the journal. I show students how these classroom exercises relate to the historical narratives centering on spirituality.

Spirituality, which concerns itself with the individual's relationship to society and our higher being, shares common ground with mindfulness. Jon Kabat Zinn defines mindfulness as awareness that develops by paying attention in the present and without judgment. Both spirituality and mindfulness involve the belief in the interconnectedness of all beings in the universe and an emphasis on a compassion for self and others that is the antithesis of bullying.

Historical narratives provide students with valuable information about what happened in the past and also an understanding about how spiritual and mindful individuals negotiate social, political, and economic challenges to build a compassionate society at odds with bullying. For example, Sojourner Truth, a former slave who gained inspiration from spirituality, worked mindfully against the bullying oppressors of her people, observing their institutions and navigating a complex legal system that perpetuated the bullying of many.

I also discuss mindfulness meditation as a secular practice deriving from Buddhism, as this offers an example of a convergence among spirituality, compassion, and social justice. The word "Buddha" means "awakened or enlightened one." The Hindu prince Siddhartha Gautama, born around 567 BCE in the Nepalese foothills of the Himalayas, challenged the oppressive Hindu caste system that had given him an elite status and comfortable existence. Meditation helped Gautama see the unjustifiable suffering around him.

While some emphasize how the propagation of these ideas, particularly the meditation done in solitude, represents a socially passive turn inward, there is evidence that meditation led the Buddha and his followers not only to see the nature of suffering but to also reduce pain and create compassion. The term "engaged Buddhism" refers to the practices of many Buddhists with a mission of compassion-based social activism that, when fueled, can be a strategy to mitigate bullying.

The work of Thich Nhat Han, a pioneer in engaged Buddhism and mindfulness, offers a valuable synthesis from which students can examine spirituality and social activism while learning history. Through Thich Nhat Han's writings, they also learn about the mindfulness practices he brought to young social workers in Vietnam.

Students often find it interesting that the Buddhist monks played a part in the resistance to the South Vietnamese government that bullied them. Clearly, while Buddhist tenets are grounded in compassion for self and others, the Buddhist majority suffered because these regimes supported an elite group of power holders, oblivious to the needs of the majority of Buddhists.

I ask students to compare and contrast how a similar lack of compassion might coexist alongside bullying in the United States. Whose needs are not represented in the United States?

Where does lack of compassion manifest alongside bullying in neighborhoods, workplaces, households, and classrooms?

Students who reflect deeply upon the historical figures and make connections to their own lives through the practice of mindfulness are given tools that benefit both the grasping of historical material and the historical significance of compassion for self and others. Through these analytical exercises, students can recognize bullying in history and its links to societies lacking in compassion. These activities give students the tools to reduce their stress, anxiety, anger, and misplaced abuse. They become introspective through mindfulness and better understand links among compassion for self, society, and their college community.

By studying the history and practice of mindfulness and compassion, students develop confidence through mastery—made easier and more enjoyable by practicing ancient wisdoms—and they develop inner and outer peace, helping to foster an anti-bullying and caring college classroom that extends into our larger community.

M. Cristina Zaccarini is a history professor and codirector of the Asian Studies Program at Adelphi University, New York. Her courses focus on the history of women, gender, and spirituality. Her most recent publication is "Connecting Histories of Gender, Health, and U.S.-China Relations," in P. S. Nadell & K. Haullman (Eds.), Making Women's Histories: Beyond National Perspectives *(2013).*

This chapter profiles a sample of less well-known empathy-focused programs and some prominent bullying-prevention organizations. It also describes activists, scholars, and victims associated with bullying. The information was collected from articles, websites, and interviews.

Empathy-Focused Programs

Breath-Body-Mind

Breath-Body-Mind (BBM), created by psychiatrists Richard P. Brown and Patricia Gerbarg, is an evidence-based multimodal program of mind-body practices including paced breathing, movement, empathy building, and Dr. Fehmi's Open-Focus Attention Training.

Teachers and school principals in K–12 New York schools where BBM operates, including both highly academic and struggling inner-city schools, report reduced school violence, including decreases in bullying. Instead of hurting others, would-be bullies become more present and less likely to react to triggering stimuli. Witnesses are more likely to get help, rather than take pleasure in seeing others get hurt, and students who are bullied become less anxious, more confident, and less overwhelmed.

Meditation reduces K–12 school bullying. When students learn paced breathing, they tend to experience more self-empathy and empathy for others. (Wave Break Media Ltd/Dreamstime.com)

BBM practices are grounded in neuroscience. Ten clinical trials found BBM safe and effective. Dr. Brown developed the program after integrating his knowledge of neuropsychiatry with ancient breathing, movement, and meditative techniques culled from healing traditions in China, Japan, India, Tibet, Siberia, Korea, and Russian Orthodox monks. Studying these customs, Dr. Brown saw the similarities among the diverse cultures, and together with Dr. Gerberg's psychoanalytic knowledge, they distilled a set of core arts that were easy to teach, rapidly effective for a wide range of psychological and physical conditions, and safe when adapted for individuals with particular vulnerabilities.

A sustained practice helps participants feel calmer, tempers reactive impulses, and reduces symptoms of stress, depression, anxiety, post-traumatic stress disorder (PTSD), and insomnia. By calming the sympathetic part of the autonomic nervous system and activating the parasympathetic part, BBM breathing and movement helps people become less stressed, less over reactive, and more empathetic and open to connecting with others.

In addition to working in schools, Dr. Brown and Dr. Gerberg train therapists and have helped heal stress and trauma in diverse populations, including first responders, Native Americans, South Sudanese, Rwandans, Ugandans, Nigerians, Middle East refugees, Rohingya refugee children, U.S. military veterans, active duty soldiers, and survivors of mass disasters, such as the 9/11 World Trade Center attacks, the Gulf Horizon oil spill, and the earthquake in Haiti.

They also provide programs for the public, workshops for cancer survivors, stress reduction for health care providers and lawyers, and teacher training. Working with nonprofits, including Serving Those Who Serve, Global Grassroots, and No Limit Generation, they use donations to provide scholarships for BBM training and programs for nonprofits, veterans, schools, and disaster relief.

Dr. Brown, associate professor in clinical psychiatry at Columbia University Medical College, has been voted Top New York metro doctor, Super Doctor of New York City physicians, and America's Top Psychiatrist. Dr. Gerbarg, assistant clinical professor in psychiatry at New York Medical College and trained at Harvard Medical School and the Boston Psychoanalytic Society, was also voted a Top doctor in New York state for her work in integrative psychiatry.

Their books include *The Healing Power of the Breath*, translated into many languages; *Complimentary and Integrative Treatments in Psychiatric Practice*, published by the American Psychiatric Association Publishing; and *Non-Drug Treatments for ADHD*.

Challenge Day

Cofounded by Rich and Yvonne Dutra-St. John, Challenge Day and the Be the Change Movement seek to shift a school culture in one day. They focus on building empathy and creating kinder and more emotionally open relationships.

The program helps to demonstrate that participants have more in common than they have differences. Rich Dutra-St. John says, "It is when we compare our outsides to others' insides that we get in trouble. Inside, we all struggle and have deep emotional lives." Challenge Day is designed to transform the competitive social cliques present in most schools to create open heart-to-heart communication.

Facilitators lead activities to help students feel more connected to one other. In one icebreaker, young people stand back-to-back and then turn around and share experiences they have had when they felt hurt or judged. To help reserved and introverted as well as extroverted participants feel comfortable, the exercises take place in large and small groups and also pairs.

An F-word presentation focuses on shifting the too-common belief that "feelings are a bad thing," explained Dutra-St. John. "We use an iceberg metaphor to explain that most people show only about 10 percent of who they are," he continues. "The rest of us remains underneath the waterline. We hide behind labels like 'teacher,' 'counselor,' 'jock,' or 'smart kid.'" In this discussion, students are helped to speak about the cost of being disconnected from one another.

"The problems in schools and in society are not bullying, violence, or even suicide. These are the symptoms of the underlying problems of separation, isolation, and loneliness," Dutra-St. John said. "People are willing to do horrific and mean things to be part of a group. The same mentality that creates 'jocks' or 'popular groups' leads others to join dangerous gangs." On Challenge Day, students get below the waterline, Dutra-John explains. "They express their feelings and get real."

In another activity, called "If you really knew me—you would know...," students share personal aspects of themselves instead of relying on the images they have spent time constructing. "We share heart-to-heart instead of image-to-image." The goal is for people to feel more included. The facilitators do a lot of storytelling and role modeling, and they open up about themselves. In smaller groups, students begin to share with one another.

Students are asked, in another exercise, to step over a line drawn on the floor, if they or someone they know have experienced a particular challenge in their lives. They are asked about being affected by racism or sexism and if they have ever felt left out or hurt because they were different. Most often, by the end of the game, everyone has crossed the line. Then the facilitators lead a follow-up talk: "Why do we hurt each other because of our differences?"

The "miracle" comes when students stand up and speak, says Dutra-John. "They say thank you to people they love and sorry to people they have hurt. Sometimes they apologize to kids they have bullied."

The day ends with appreciation. "Most students say they feel proud of themselves and each other. Then we challenge them to be part of the Be the Change movement in their school. We ask them to do one positive thing for someone each day—something to benefit their school and their family," said Dutra-St. John.

Challenge Day sometimes involves a whole school and other times one class. The school may request that the program start with older students, who are then expected to mentor younger ones. The goal, Dutra-St. John says, is to carry the message to as many schools as possible, to help students feel inspired, and for students to help keep the program going even after they have graduated.

"I'm so proud of what we do," Dutra-St. John says. "There is always something in the room that moves me to tears. I just know the apologies and the gratitude wouldn't have happened without Challenge Day. That's what I love. You see the pain when people cross the line and then you see them using their voice for positive change."

Creating Compassionate Communities (CCC)

To prevent school bullying and to intervene effectively if it occurs, founder Jessie Klein and her team lead K–12 and college workshops that focus on empathy-building games, restorative justice, and breath-focused meditation. The goals include decreasing a range of hurtful behaviors as well as anxiety and depression and to increase empathy and kindness.

Exercises include teaching Marshall Rosenberg's nonviolent communication through activities like Empathy Poker, gratitude journals, and compassionate listening and speaking. Solo, in dyads, triads, and large groups, people "build empathy muscles" via card games and by engaging in walk-around-the-room exercises, role-plays, talking circles, and breath- and compassion-focused mindfulness. Presentations, like Stop Bullying Now: Here's How, integrate video and images that provide instruction and encourage active participation.

Klein's team facilitates the program for school staff, students, and parents, according to schools' interests and needs—long or short-term, monthly, weekly, or in a single "power session."

Schools receive their own CCC curriculum and Needs and Feelings card decks to keep the program going after the workshop(s) ends.

Across demographics and other differences, people laugh, forge connections, experience support, and appreciate one another's similarities as vulnerable human beings. Participants report that the program also positively shifts their relationships with people in other parts of their lives.

The program integrates Klein's research on bullying, including the particular challenges for LGBTQI+ students and for those targeted for issues including abilities, race, class, gender, and weight.

CCC was launched in 2015 in three New York City public schools (elementary, middle, and high school) with a grant from the Adelphi University Center for Health Innovation. A preliminary evaluation using a frequency analysis on responses to questions from over five hundred surveys from the schools where CCC operated for a year showed decreased hurtful behaviors, including gossip and social exclusion, and increased social and physical safety, bonding, and acts of kindness.

Kidsbridge

Executive Director Lynne Azarchi created the Kidsbridge Tolerance Center to support New Jersey students from pre-K through eighth grade. The mission is to "educate and empower children and youths through character education, diversity appreciation and pro-social life skills training." Azarchi says that they try "to create empathetic individuals and caring citizens who live without prejudice or discrimination and who are positive advocates for themselves and others."

Kidsbridge, Azarchi says, envisions an accepting world where people are free to be themselves without being bullied or mistreated. The program invites students to participate in four-hour training sessions focused on civility and kindness, empathy and caring, learning and education, empowerment and leadership, and tolerance and respect.

Azarchi says that she worries about "ineffective programs on empathy, where people put posters on walls and hold an assembly or two and think they are done. Assembly programs don't teach them anything. We need to do something more to save children from the ravages of bullying and hate. Very few social-emotional programs measure and assess. Children are killing themselves all around the world including in New Jersey." Through Kidsbridge, Azarchi facilitates small group discussions and then measures and assesses the impact of the activities. "We find a statistically significant improvement in attitude, or we don't do it," she says.

Dr. James Graham and Dr. Julie Hughes, two psychology professors from the College of New Jersey, regularly analyze the Kidsbridge program. Their undergraduate psychology majors coordinate the pre- and post-visit surveys. Students who go through the Kidsbridge program show improvement in empathy, stereotype knowledge, college aspiration, and sensitivity to religious diversity as well as moral reasoning and empowerment.

From the Kidsbridge learning lab, teachers take tools and collaborate to create more caring classrooms. "A lot of schools are broken," Azarchi explains. "We help teachers create a caring classroom. They leave with activities that reinforce what they have learned. We have social-emotional skill building programs where we go directly into the schools and then we follow up with the kids. We get more involved with students over time and are able to reinforce our upstander/empathy programs."

For elementary school students, the Kidsbridge program facilitates small group discussions, creative icebreakers, and conflict resolution skits with puppets. Middle school students create action plans that they take back to their schools to implement. "We don't use other people's curricula because we have created what we find are highly effective thought-provoking face-to-face discussions that move the needle in diversity and bullying prevention. We measure everything and we are effective according to both student and teacher research," says Azarchi.

Kidsbridge receives lots of letters from children after they complete the program. One letter said, "I didn't realize I was a bully. I didn't realize how hurtful I was being." Another said, "No one should bully me. I'm going to go to a teacher next time. I deserve respect." A third said, "I said something mean and awful so the kids will laugh and now I really feel bad about it."

Kidsbridge programs are customized and engage education professors to advise them on how to stay developmentally appropriate. The program is available to any New Jersey school that is interested. Subsidized by New Jersey foundations and corporations, many low-income schools in Trenton, Camden, Newark, and New Brunswick use the program for free.

The hopeful message Azarchi wants to convey is that "you can teach empathy and empowerment, and the earlier the better. We have accomplished informed, evidence-based, effective and fun education and we keep up with the latest SEL research."

Morningside Center for Teaching Social Responsibility

Founded in 1982, this restorative justice training organization works with educators to create a program tailored for each school. With thirty staff members, they provide interactive workshops and coaching focused on teaching and building restorative practices. Their programs help schools "create a caring school community." The philosophy is that people and their relationships are most important and that when anyone makes a mistake or causes harm, they can be guided through restorative practices to understand how their actions impacted others. Participants are helped to hold themselves accountable for what they have done, constructively heal harm, and repair the affected relationships.

Goals include helping youths and adults to feel heard and valued and to develop and practice social and emotional skills, including managing feelings, relating well to one another, appreciating each other's differences, and resolving conflicts.

Morningside facilitators teach restorative justice practices tailored for specific age groups including for pre-K to fifth grade, "Reading, Writing, Respect, and Resolution"; for grades six to twelve, "Building Belonging"; and for pre-K to twelfth grade, "Social-Emotional Learning/Restorative Practices/Racial Equity." They help schools use restorative practices as an alternative to punishment, and they raise awareness regarding how traditional discipline tends to mostly affect students of color.

Schools are helped to use daily or weekly restorative circles and to help all students participate. Circles are structured and usually include a meaningful centerpiece, a relevant talking object (a person can only speak when they hold this item), and a formal opening and closing to set it apart from the rest of the day. After some practice, students are helped to facilitate circles themselves.

The work focuses on building connections, creating a "kind and productive classroom and school," and teaching problem-solving and conflict-resolution skills.

Circles are the core of both the prevention and intervention work. According to the website, when used consistently, they help everyone "prevent conflicts, mistakes and harm from occurring" and they help community members respond to harm done in a "constructive, restorative way so that resolution, repair, and learning become possible." Any person in the community can request a circle.

School staff are supported and guided throughout the program. Principals are helped to rethink their approach to school discipline and to integrate social-emotional learning and restorative work. Parents are also encouraged to participate in some of the circles that affect their children in order to support the youths' positive growth.

With the New York City Department of Education, the program is charged with bringing restorative practices to NYC schools. According to hundreds of participating schools, the introductory training and coaching as well as the advanced training promoting racial equity have improved school climate and significantly reduced suspensions.

New York City Children's Theater (NYCCT)

The New York City Children's Theater is "a leader in educational programming that engages students through theater and role-play," according to its creator, Brooke Boertzel. "Kids have a great time while learning valuable lessons on how to deal with difficult situations whether they are being bullied or just witnessing bullying in their school or community."

NYCCT presents live theater in four productions a year in Times Square and in low-income neighborhoods (Title 1 schools). In the five boroughs, for pre-K through fifth grade, the NYCCT education department offers a variety of interactive theater performances and workshops. They show their productions annually in seventy to one hundred schools and community centers.

Boertzel says she felt discouraged when she saw the anti-bullying programs her nephews received in middle school, because they were "didactic, lecture-based assemblies serving hundreds of students at a time." Drawing upon her experience studying applied theater, Boertzel helped to create their two best known anti-bullying programs, Alice's Story (for first through third grade) and Fair and Square (for third through fifth grade), as a way to engage small student groups to openly explore the sensitive topic of bullying through the lens of their own experiences.

The residency program, Literature at Play, helps students adapt a teacher-selected book into an original play or musical. The work is connected to the New York state English Language Arts curriculum and supports the New York City Department of Education Theater Blueprint benchmarks.

Boertzel says their work uses theater as an educational tool to explore academic, social, and emotional content. By getting the audience actively involved, no one is expected to be a passive observer. They hope children will share what goes on in their classrooms and incorporate their responsive ideas into a narrative.

NYCCT has thirty-five teaching artists on their roster, twelve of whom are trained to facilitate the anti-bullying program. Both Alice's Story and Fair and Square use a format that incorporates a script and explores an issue of bullying in a fictional school setting. The actors put on a short performance and then come out of the role to ask advice from the student audience. Helping the students empathize with the characters, the actors ask, "What would you say to the character in this dilemma?" Then they replay the performance with the children's suggestions.

Boertzel said that they found this format effective because "it creates an aesthetic distance which allows the children to explore the topic of bullying in a safe environment. The students don't have to get too personal or reveal too much from their own experience, but they can be honest about their concerns as they connect with the characters and reflect on the narrative and the characters' experiences."

In the first play, Alice is bullied at school. The actress playing Alice asks the students for advice: "Who can I reach out to when I'm being bullied?" The students then talk about what they have done or would do in that moment. "We are trying to cultivate their natural sense of empathy by requiring them to put themselves in someone else's shoes," Boertzel says. "We ask them, how would you feel if someone did this to you?

"The wonderful thing about theater is that it gives students a chance to explore different roles and practice these situations in a safe environment. The Alice character replays the scene multiple times—each time trying different approaches that the students suggest in order to change the outcome," she explains. "This provides a platform to make mistakes, rewind, and try something again. It also prepares children to have multiple and accessible tools to manage tough situations when they experience difficulties in their own lives."

She says, "In the third-through-fifth-grade play, Fair and Square, the bullying looks different, the issues are blurrier at that age." Boertzel explains, "Kids go in and out of many roles including victim, bystander and bully. The workshop provides them with tools for how they can manage their emotions safely and responsibly. We help them become accountable for how they handle situations, including how they might respond to emotionally charged situations that involve decision-making without escalating the conflict."

When the main character finds himself in an argument with another classmate, he reacts emotionally and physically, making the situation even worse. "We ask kids to deconstruct the situation and talk about ways they or the characters could handle the situation better. We ask them to reflect on what they do when they get so worked up that they want to react angrily." Boertzel says. "Learning how to responsibly manage these emotionally charged situations is more relevant for the third through fifth graders than the classic case of teasing used for the first through third graders."

During Alice's Story, students take a class oath, promising to cultivate communities of respect and inclusion. In Fair and Square, students learn the PICK trick, an acronym the children can draw upon when managing their emotions in a charged situation: "Pause, Inhale, Consider the consequences, and Keep yourself and others safe." They are also encouraged to tell others when they feel upset or angry. Teachers have reported that their students utilize the PICK trick throughout the school year.

During each workshop, the artists spend forty-five minutes with a class. Boertzel explains, "We are realistic about how much we can achieve in this short amount of time, so the teachers need to continue the conversation with their students. We provide a resource guide to help teachers prompt, frame, and support those discussions."

She says, "The content is sensitive, and sometimes it brings up personal stories. The teaching artists are trained to manage those situations and identify students who need to speak more with teachers or guidance counselors after the workshops. Our work is meant to function as a platform for discussion and a conversation starter."

Peace in Schools

Peace in Schools is the first U.S. elective full-credit course on mindful meditation and conscious communication. In ninety-minute sessions two to three times a week, classes use mindful meditation to decrease bullying behaviors.

Caverly Morgan, the founder and lead teacher of the program, says that she created Peace in Schools because of her own high school experiences: "When I was in high school, I had panic attacks. I didn't know what they were. I would have loved to have tools to come back to my center and work with my anxieties."

Morgan trained for eight years in a Zen monastic setting and "wanted to bring mindful practice to young people so they could access these tools at an earlier age than I had." She continues, "Any student who is bullying another student is confused about who they are. They are maintaining a world-view of separation in their relationship with other students, a 'me versus you' dynamic. We seek to dissolve this separation. By the time teens finish the course, they feel grounded. They can work with stress, communicate with others from a place of compassion, and recognize their interconnections with others."

In Pillar One, the facilitators introduce "mindful tools," including sitting and walking meditation. Students learn how to experience a body scan as well as mindful eating.

In Pillar Two, the program teaches self-compassion, kind self-talk, and they learn how to "dis-identify from the conditioned mind." Teens learn how to recognize how the mind creates and maintains limitations and how not to identify with these negative thoughts. The facilitators help students to come back to their center, "to a recognition of who they authentically are rather than who they have been conditioned to believe themselves to be," Morgan explains.

In Pillar Three, the facilitators talk about how to bring mindfulness practices into their everyday lives. At this stage, Peace in Schools teaches Marshall Rosenberg's nonviolent communication, a model of compassionate speaking based on identifying feelings and needs in one self and others. "Teens meet each other from essence to essence," Morgan says. "They learn to see each other from a place of authenticity and release the temptation to maintain identity masks."

The course is based on what Morgan calls CARE: confidentiality, acceptance, reverence and empathy. It operates in six schools in Portland, Oregon, and is expanding through a training program called the Peace in Schools Teacher Training Institute.

Peace in Schools facilitators stay at the schools where the program operates, working with students for seventy-five hours over the semester while building bridges with the counselors. According to Morgan, "It is difficult for the school counselors to track the mental health of the two hundred to three hundred teens for whom they are responsible. It is virtually impossible. We keep constant communication open with the counselors so we can send kids in need to them and they can let us know about those who need our support."

Morgan started the program by creating an after-school program at Wilson High School in Portland, Oregon. She explains, "The principal came to me and said he recognized the power of the tools that I was bringing to the students, and he wanted more teens to have access to the program. They decided to make it a semester-long class so that students who have plans after school or play sports or have to take care of siblings could also take the program."

Morgan says that they advertised the class as a physical education course and expected twenty teens to sign up; instead, they had three hundred teens who wanted to register. "We were confident that we had struck a real need," she says. "I see the transformative capacity that a mindful study can have in a classroom. I hope that mindfulness will be in every high school and we'll see the benefits in a large way. It shouldn't be forced, but it would be incredible for it to be offered in every school as an elective."

Rachel's Challenge

Rachel's Challenge is a K–12 bullying prevention program named after seventeen-year-old Rachel Scott, who was killed in the Columbine High School massacre. It is a secular nonprofit, created in 2001 by Rachel's father, Darell Scott. He was inspired to start the program after reading the essays and journals his daughter wrote.

"She was known as a devout Christian at Columbine, and teased and ostracized because of her religious convictions," explains Rachel's youngest brother, Mike Scott. Students shared Rachel's last words with reporters. Eric Harris, one of the shooters, asked her, "Do you believe in God?" She replied, "You know I do." Harris said, "Well, go be with him," and shot her in the head.

Rachel left behind notebooks on the simple principles by which she lived, Scott says, including a two-page essay that she wrote a month before her murder that she titled "My Ethics: My Codes of Life." Rachel advocated compassion, Scott continued, as "the greatest form of love humans have to offer. One of her essays was written for a fifth period class where she talked about her commitment to living with kindness and compassion, helping and forgiving others, showing mercy, and changing the world."

Scott says that "Rachel acted on her beliefs. An example is when she defended Adam Kyler, a student with special needs at Columbine. He had a rough time in middle and high school, where he was picked on and bullied. One day Rachel saw two boys bullying Adam. She marched over, got between them, and said, 'If you touch him again, you are going to have to fight me.' Adam told us he was planning on committing suicide, and instead he and Rachel became friends."

Rachel's Challenge is about the power of small acts of kindness. Saying "hi" or giving an encouraging word can make a big difference in someone's life. The program persuades people that how you act affects those around you. Students are asked to stop being prejudiced, seek only the best in others, keep a journal, and, through kindness, commit to bringing positive changes to their home, school, and community. They are expected to show care and compassion to those who are vulnerable, ridiculed or otherwise in need. Then students are asked to commit to these pledges and to ask their family, friends, and peers to help spread Rachel's wisdom.

Facilitators share stories about how Rachel helped other children when she was alive. She focused on three groups of people: those who didn't have friends, those who were bullied and teased, and those with special needs. Through Rachel's stories, Scott says, "Kids awaken to a new part of themselves. They connect with each other more easily because they see what they have in common and understand better what others are going through."

The program also does an adult evening event, where speakers tell stories and show photos and video clips. "The result is that those who are labeled as a bully are able to change that part of themselves. We believe that what you put your focus on is what you give power to, so we focus on the positive," says Scott.

Additionally, Rachel's Challenge operates in colleges and businesses. Over forty presenters travel around the world to share Rachel's story and to help participants set up a Friends of Rachel club. "Another goal," says Scott, "is to create a permanent climate and culture change in the education system." He says that the program, still based in Littleton, Colorado, builds deeper relationships and teaches students the importance of connecting with others.

Organizations

Centers for Disease Control and Prevention (CDC)

This government agency creates resources to support the health of people and communities including preventing disease, injury, and disability and preparing for new threats to our health. The CDC page "Preventing Bullying" states the official U.S. definition, which is also paraphrased on the federal website StopBullying.gov:

> Bullying is a form of youth violence. CDC defines bullying as any unwanted aggressive behavior(s) by another youth or group of youths, who are not siblings or current dating partners that involves an observed or perceived power imbalance and is repeated multiple times or is highly likely to be repeated. Bullying may inflict harm or distress on the targeted youth including physical, psychological, social, or educational.
>
> Bullying can include aggression that is physical (hitting, tripping), verbal (name calling, teasing), or relational/social (spreading rumors, leaving out of group). Bullying can also occur through technology and is called electronic bullying or cyberbullying. A young person can be a perpetrator, a victim, or both (also known as "bully/victim").

The CDC states that bullying negatively impacts students who bully, those who are bullied, and witnesses to bullying. In public schools, bullying is the most frequently reported discipline problem. To prevent bullying and other school violence, the CDC makes evidence-based recommendations to strengthen youths' social learning, help youths develop relationships with other caring adults via after-school and mentoring programs, prioritize "street outreach" and "community norm change," and commit to school violence prevention strategies.

Gay, Lesbian, and Straight Education Network (GLSEN)

GLSEN is a national K–12-focused education organization committed to creating safe schools. They educate people about how LGBTQI+ students are particularly at risk for being bullied and harassed. The organization tries to help all people in school communities feel valued and respected. They also document incidents directed against students because of their sexual orientation, gender identity, and gender expression.

Every two years, GLSEN releases a National School Climate Survey, which presents data about the extent to which these students hear biased language from other students and educators, experience harassment and assault, and endure anti-LGBTQI+ discrimination. This report details the effects of this hostile school climate on students' educational outcomes and psychological well-being, as well as the extent to which supportive school resources are available and useful.

GLSEN's work includes sex education, activism, parent advocacy, and sharing student experiences. It informs people about how they can help make schools safer, including learning about LGBTQI+ experiences, standing up to bias, joining activists, teaching others, and supporting and connecting with LGBTQI+ students and their supporters. GLSEN provides resources for students, such as helping them lead Ally Week, where LGBTQI+ K–12 students are helped to lead conversations on how allies in their schools can support them.

GLSEN also calls for schools to provide professional development that guides educators on how to help targeted LGBTQI+ students, use inclusive curricula, enforce policies that protect students from being bullied with specific mention of students most often targeted, and support gay-straight alliances and other programs that work to make schools safer and improve school climate.

National Council on Disability

The National Council on Disability recommends new policies to the president and Congress, generates research and reports on bullying of students with disabilities.

In the briefing paper "Bullying and Students with Disabilities," by Jonathan Young, Ari Ne'eman, and Sara Gelser for a White House Conference on Bullying Prevention, the council reported that students with both visible and nonvisible disabilities are bullied because of their disabilities; they are bullied more than students who are not disabled. In 2003, a study found that 34 percent of students taking ADHD medication are bullied two to three times a month—significantly more than other students.

The National Council is concerned that policy makers, educators, and researchers have not addressed this problem. A Massachusetts Advocates for Children (2009) survey of families with children on the autism spectrum found that close to 40 percent of these children endured bullying for over a year. Ninety-two percent of the parents told school officials, and 68 percent said the schools did not sufficiently help.

The briefing paper notes that the Department of Education now includes disability as a protected class (along with race and gender), as per civil rights laws, including Section 504 of the Rehabilitation Act and Title II of the American with Disabilities Act. In its "Dear Colleague" letter, the Department of Education states that schools are required to respond when they become aware that students with disabilities are bullied or harassed.

National Suicide Prevention Lifeline

The National Suicide Prevention Lifeline provides a website, phone number, and free and confidential support for anyone feeling distressed. It provides suicide prevention and intervention resources and best practices for professionals.

The lifeline is a U.S.-based crisis network, available twenty-four hours a day, seven days a week, that provides confidential help for those who need emotional support or who are experiencing a suicide crisis. For counseling, the U.S. hotline connects callers with the closest available accredited crisis centers within forty-nine states.

A web page dedicated to youth cautions that "Suicide is the second leading cause of death for young people between 10 to 24." At the top of the website is a statement about the relationship between bullying and suicide. Youths can click directly to get more information from StopBullying.gov.

The "Youth" page offers information on "How to Take Care of Yourself," including links on asking for help, making a safety plan, and learning how painful feelings can be overcome.

The "How to Help" link tells loved ones to take threats seriously. It cautions that adults should not assume that youths who are speaking about suicide are just trying to get attention. They ask family members to learn the warning signs—for instance, if someone's behavior changes, they talk about a suicide plan, or they confide in someone that they are contemplating it. The website recommends giving empathy and support even if the adult doesn't understand why the young person is taking a particular concern so seriously.

The National Action Alliance for Suicide Prevention created a partnership with Facebook so that a person from the United States or from Canada using the social media site can report suicidal comments posted by their friends. Once reported, the user who posted the comment will receive an email from Facebook encouraging them to call the lifeline or to click on a direct link to engage in live chat services.

For individuals, friends, and families, the lifeline provides safety recommendations and help to develop action plans that address emotional crises when they occur. They include special sections for veterans, young adults, and those concerned about bullying. The "With Hope Comes Help" part of the website provides stories and emotional support directly from suicide survivors.

In 2005, the U.S. Substance Abuse and Mental Health Services Administration and the Mental Health Association of New York City created the National Suicide Prevention Lifeline funded by grants and private donations. It also trains individuals and groups and teaches suicide intervention skills.

There is also a Spanish-language hotline and a tele-interpreter service that allows network crisis centers to translate calls into more than 150 languages. Special tabs exist for the hearing impaired, LGBTQI+ youth, and Native Americans.

Federally funded Columbia University evaluators regularly assess the lifeline.

Peace Alliance

The Peace Alliance supports peace-building school and community-building practices and policies. They use educational efforts and grassroots political power to support programs and policies that decrease violence, transform conflict, and enhance cooperation.

According to Dan Kahn, the organization's national field director, one example of a successful peace-building practice is in West Philadelphia High School. Kahn says that for six straight years, this school had been on Pennsylvania's list of the most dangerous schools. They now have a restorative discipline program, and in two years, the number of violent incidents decreased by 65 percent. The Peace Alliance shines a light on this and other anti-bullying, peace-building programs. They work with Congress and in the media to organize citizens who want to serve as school advocates. Peace Alliance volunteers also promote peace-building practices in local communities, and they advocate for statewide and federal policies.

The alliance supports programs focused on utilizing restorative talking circles and other restorative justice practices, Kahn said, that help students accused of bullying become positive and contributing community members, instead of being excluded through suspension, expulsion, or similar interventions, which can create anger, hostility and violent recidivism.

To create more restorative justice in schools, the Peace Alliance collaborated with Colorado coalitions and provided tools, resources, and a grassroots nationwide database of sixty thousand people. They sent 1,500 email blasts to potential supporters, including sample letters that people could edit to write to their own legislators. Parents of children who benefited, victim advocacy organizations, and law enforcement supporters joined the Peace Alliance project and advocated for restorative justice practices.

According to Kahn, due to Peace Alliance work supporting restorative justice practices both in and outside schools, thousands of people have been diverted from jail and are engaged in productive and community-building work: "It takes $100,000 per year to pay for each incarcerated adult and $150,000 per year for each juvenile. It makes more sense financially and practically to get these people back in their communities, and leading productive and service-focused lives."

Kahn says that "back in society, they are taking care of their families and paying taxes. These are the kinds of results legislatures understand. They see how our work is efficient, cost-effective and powerful in its ability to reduce violence in schools and communities."

Peace Alliance volunteers and staff also lobbied the federal legislature to support bills that include the Youth Promise Act, created to decrease prison time for young people by increasing mentoring, support, and education programs. According to Kahn, because of the West Philadelphia High School success, the Peace Alliance was able to get restorative justice practices included in the act, which makes it possible for schools to choose restorative justice as a component of their discipline plan.

StopBullying.gov

StopBullying.gov is a federal government website managed by the U.S. Department of Health and Human Services. It defines bullying and cyberbullying, lists students most at risk, and recommends ways to prevent and respond to bullying. Its website content is provided by the Department of Education, the Department of Health and Human Services, the Centers for Disease Control and Prevention, Health Resources and Services Administration, Substance Abuse and Mental Health Services Administration, and the Department of Justice.

StopBullying.gov provides videos and games that teach youths about bullying. It offers step-by-step bullying solutions and provides an online bullying-prevention course. The site encourages people to report all forms of bullying to school administrators or criminal justice authorities when appropriate. A "Stop Bullying on the Spot" tab provides tips and advice for adults regarding what they can do and when to call for outside help.

The website also lists United States state and federal laws as each state addresses bullying differently, in either single or multiple policies.

Acknowledging that LGBTQI+ youths are among the most common bullying targets, StopBullying.gov provides links to create safer environments for these youths and information to educate people on the sexual orientation federal civil rights laws.

The website also has a separate link for students with special needs, who are also at greater risk than general population students, and provides information on how to create safe environments for youth with disabilities and for youth with special health needs. Resources include federal civil rights laws that apply to protecting youths with disabilities.

StopBullying.gov also provides a list of evidence-based bullying prevention and intervention programs.

Activists

Eloise Jamison Berdahl-Baldwin

Eloise Jamison Berdahl-Baldwin is the "secret teen advisor" behind Pacer Center's Teens Against Bullying's popular website Ask Jamie. She provides information and support when teens write to her with questions and concerns about their experiences with bullying.

When Berdahl-Baldwin was sixteen years old, she was cyberbullied. This inspired her to help other youths. Berdahl-Baldwin explains what happened when she was eighteen years old in her senior year of high school:

> I had a relationship with this person. It was on the verge of something serious. Then I found out hurtful information about him, and I chose to break off the relationship.

After that, tensions brewed, and at the end of sophomore year someone showed me the really offensive, sexist, and violent messages he had sent about me to one of my classmates. It wasn't directed towards me, but I saw it because someone showed it to me.

It was clear from the messages that he wanted me to read them and that it would give him pleasure to see me in pain. I will never forget reading those words for the first time. I was shocked by how it affected me. The words he used replayed in my mind and become ingrained in my brain.

Berdahl-Baldwin says that the experience shattered her self-concept:

People told me I was weak for being so hurt by the bullying and they blamed it all on me. The community chose to condone the bullying and ignore my experience. It was incredibly isolating because the school is so small and this person who bullied me was very popular. Bullying is not just the momentary action between the bully and the target. It extends into the social network of a community and impacts physical and mental health. I had headaches and stomach aches, and severe anxiety. It was a life-changing experience. Before I was bullied, I never had a panic attack, and now I still get panic attacks. I'm doing much better, but I feel devastated by how normal bullying is.

She began her bullying prevention work in a summer internship at Pacer's National Bullying Prevention Center in Bloomington, Minnesota. Berdahl-Baldwin says, "I didn't have any expectations going into it. I contacted the director and asked to volunteer. I wanted to do something online that could have a far-reaching effect. With the director of the program, I created Ask Jamie in the fall of 2015, and ever since, I have been receiving online questions about bullying and responding to them."

Berdahl-Baldwin is able to write informed and compassionate emails to the teens who write to her because of her own traumatic experiences. She says, "I couldn't sleep. It affected my eating. I lost my appetite. I couldn't focus in school. I would read a chapter of a book, and I couldn't tell you what I read. It affected my friendships or what I thought were my friendships."

To keep informed, Berdahl-Baldwin reads books and goes to bullying prevention conferences. She went to hear the FBI speak about sexting, for instance, so that she could respond to someone's email who felt pressured to send a nude photo of herself via text messaging:

> When I heard the FBI speak, it was the first time I had heard about these dangers. I think most kids don't know what they are doing or how they are making themselves vulnerable by engaging in this behavior. For me, it took independent research to find out how destructive this behavior can be. It wasn't taught in my health class, and it wasn't discussed in my internet safety lessons at school.
>
> In my opinion, this trend is damaging and disturbing, but it is incredibly normalized and widespread. Parents and other adults don't really know about it. I think it exploits girls and their sexuality, and it can be seriously dangerous when the images get into the wrong hands.

After Berdahl-Baldwin went to the FBI presentation, she wrote back to the student who told her that she was being pressured to send someone a nude picture of herself. Listening to the FBI, Berdahl-Baldwin learned that over 70 percent of nudes sent online will end up on a child pornography site. These images are also used to bully and blackmail. The FBI calls this "sextortion." A 2016 FBI report explained that sextortion is a type of online and sexual exploitation in which individuals coerce victims into providing sexually explicit images or videos of themselves and then post the images publicly or send the images to victims' friends and family.

Berdahl-Baldwin encouraged the student who wrote to her about the sexting concern to speak to a trusted adult about her predicament and to report it to law enforcement. Her most frequent feedback is to talk to a professional:

> I'm a stepping stone to the next step. I'm not a professional. I can't contact parents. I'm not trained to deal with mental health. I can help them tell an adult, receive support from a counselor or report something to the police. I can guide the writer on whom to contact. Mostly, I give support and kindness. I'm anonymous and I do not judge them. I also give them resources and advice on how to take care of their physical and mental health.

Anxiety is a big issue for many teens grappling with bullying experiences, Berdahl-Baldwin says. She posts many of her responses so that teens who visit her page are able to find some answers even if they don't write her a letter. She receives about three to five questions each week. Her answers got longer, as she learned more about the "nuances of bullying." One time, she says, she wrote nine pages, single spaced, to answer three questions.

"I get more letters before school starts," she says, "because there is often a lot of anxiety about facing certain people. During school breaks, I don't get as many letters."

By spending forced time alone and feeling abandoned by her former friends, Berdahl-Baldwin learned a lot of what she tells her writers:

> Through my own bullying experience, I learned that it is so important to take care of yourself. Bullying is isolating. I found I had a lot of time to learn how to be comfortable being alone and to foster a good relationship with myself. I won't invest in relationships that are hurtful anymore.

I would rather be alone than be with someone who is mean.

Treat yourself as you would treat a best friend. Nix the negative self-thought. Bullying can create low self-esteem and we make it worse by calling ourselves names. I tell them to never say anything negative about themselves, like "I am stupid or ugly." It is really important to talk positively to yourself in order to build confidence and to feel better.

Berdahl-Baldwin also says that she advocates physical health. "I tell people to exercise. Exercise is very helpful. The endorphin release helps curb anxiety and depression." And she suggests that her writers practice regular self-care. "People should carve out at least thirty minutes a day for a routine that they find relaxing and enjoyable. I tell them to do something that makes them smile and work on being okay being by themselves."

Another concern for Berdahl-Baldwin is social media. When people write to her about it, "I tell them to refrain from believing that everyone is doing something fun with another person. It is easy to feel pressure that you should be doing something constantly with others. I'm not buying into that. Everyone feels lonely sometimes. Everyone has down days, and I highlight that. What it looks like on social media is not always what it seems."

She also encourages her writers to ask an adult to intervene. "My dad helped a lot," she says. "He contacted the school and eventually the parents of the boy, and then he talked with the boy's parents about the situation. That led to a meeting with the person who bullied me. He finally apologized and that was how it ended."

"I still have anxiety," she says. "It is still something I'm dealing with. I'm in therapy now, and I wasn't expecting that going to a counselor would be so useful, but it has helped me in the aftermath of the bullying." Berdahl-Baldwin is now a bullying prevention public speaker. As a teen, she spoke to 250 people at a Minnesota Department of Education conference for educators, and she hopes that what she does will inspire others to help too.

Ellen DeGeneres

Ellen DeGeneres, a comedian, actress, and television talk-show host, is also an activist who focuses on animal rights and bullying, especially against LGBTQI+ teens.

DeGeneres starred in her own sitcom series, *Ellen*, which was broadcast from 1994 to 1998. The series broke new cultural ground when DeGeneres's character—and DeGeneres herself—came out as a lesbian. That episode, which won an Emmy Award, marked the first time a sitcom lead character was openly gay. The controversial move motivated some of the show's sponsors to withdraw their advertisements. An ABC Alabama affiliate refused to air the episode. Subsequent shows continued to feature gay-friendly themes, leading to praise from the LGBTQI+ community and criticism from some conservative groups.

In 2003 DeGeneres launched the syndicated daytime *Ellen DeGeneres Show*. Though politically liberal, she is known for welcoming guests of all beliefs and engaging them in friendly, funny, and respectful dialogue. Her talk show received a Genesis Award (for highlighting animal protections issues) and GLAAD media promotion and support.

One of the earliest American celebrities to come out as lesbian, she married actress Portia de Rossi in August 2008, the year after same-sex marriage was legalized.

In 2016, President Obama presented DeGeneres with the Presidential Medal of Freedom. Referring to the *Ellen* episode that revealed DeGeneres's sexual orientation, Obama noted, "It's easy to forget now just how much courage was required for Ellen to come out on the most public of stages twenty years ago." Today, that episode is considered a cultural milestone in advancing LGBTQI+ awareness. A nationwide 2015 *Variety* public survey concluded that DeGeneres is credited with doing more to advance gay rights than any other American celebrity.

DeGeneres often interviews guests on her show who are working against bullying and related prejudice and trying to stop it.

Tim Field

As a victim of bullying and harassment, Tim Field became a self-taught, widely recognized anti-bullying authority.

After recovering from workplace bullying that sent him into a deep depression, he began to exhaustively research bullying. From 1996 to 2004, he established and ran the UK National Workplace Bullying Advice Line. The popularity of the help line exploded after the British newspaper *Sunday Independent* published an article about workplace bullying. During those eight years of operation, Fields recorded 8,125 cases of bullying. In 1997, he published his best-selling book *Bully in Sight*. In 2001, he and Neil Marr released their book *Bullycide: Death at Playtime*, an exposé of child suicide associated with bullying.

He also set up the website Bully Online, a comprehensive website based on all aspects of bullying, including news, case histories, links, resources, and policy development. Described as the world's largest resource on workplace bullying and related issues, the site also includes ways to recognize, tackle, and escape bullying. Field also established Success Unlimited, a publishing company aimed at addressing bullying-related matters.

The Tim Field Foundation website states that it strives to help people "develop conscious awareness and evolve beyond their need to exhibit the behaviors of bullying." The website provides information about the myths and misperceptions of bullying and supplies research tools and online activities to equip bullying victims.

In 2006, Field died from cancer. His work remains influential.

Lee Hirsch

Lee Hirsch is a documentary filmmaker and author. He wrote, directed, and produced the award-winning 2012 film *Bully*, a documentary investigating bullying in schools across the United States. The movie follows five families of varying ethnicities, cultures, and geographic regions as they deal with the fallout from bullying. It was shot over the course of the 2009–2010 school year and confronts issues including suicide and homophobia. Hirsch has said that the film was close to his heart, as he had been a victim of childhood bullying and he did not receive the support he had wished for at the time.

In addition to garnering critical and audience acclaim, Hirsch also launched a grassroots social action campaign against bullying, the Bully Project. The goal of this project is to bring the film to more than ten million youths nationwide and to build empathy and take action against all forms of bullying.

Lady Gaga

Lady Gaga is a singer, songwriter, and anti-bullying activist. In a 2012 *New York Times* interview, she described being bullied herself as a child: "I was called really horrible, profane names very loudly in front of huge crowds of people, and my schoolwork suffered at one point," she stated. "I didn't want to go to class. And I was a straight-A student, so there was a certain point in my high school years where I just couldn't even focus on class because I was so embarrassed all the time. I was so ashamed of who I was." Lady Gaga recounted how she had many experiences that are similar to what young people experience today, including being shoved in a trash can and excluded from social gatherings.

With her mother, Lady Gaga created the Born This Way Foundation to empower people and to create a more supportive environment in and out of schools. Lady Gaga's music fans are encouraged to join a "bottom-up movement" to try to make it cooler for young people to be nice and to raise awareness about bullying and youth cruelty as a human rights abuse.

The foundation supports rigorous academic research and works to create partnerships that provide young people both online and offline with kinder communities, improved mental health resources, and more positive environments.

As one of the most-followed celebrities on Twitter, Lady Gaga encourages young people to open up and share both their experiences and the impact those experiences had on their emotional health. She wrote a public letter announcing that she still suffers from post-traumatic stress disorder related to the bullying she experienced, and she encourages others who suffer symptoms of extreme anxiety and panic to seek help.

Researchers

Donna Gaines

Donna Gaines is the author of *Teenage Wasteland: Suburbia's Dead End Kids*, about a quadruple teen suicide involving four youths in Bergenfield, New Jersey. Alienated at home, in school, and in their community, the students had dropped out of high school and were part of a subculture known as "the Burnouts." Gaines says that even after they were dead, many members of the community and school continued to label them with taunts including "losers," "dirt bags," "druggies," and "dropouts."

Gaines analyzed the social culture around this tragic event, where many adults in this "upper-poor" white suburban town had experienced job loss and struggled financially. Hopeless, helpless, and powerless, and seeing a dim economic future, many young people became increasingly depressed, angry and rebellious.

Yet, instead of looking at the larger social context in which this suicide pact occurred, many people in Bergenfield blamed the parents, the youths' peer group, favorite musical bands, and drugs, Gaines recounts,

> They were different from the mainstream kids. They weren't into sports. They loved music—heavy metal, hardcore and hard rock. They were good kids, yet they

were diminished in the status hierarchy of the high school which valorized the jocks and more conforming students.

The bullying was structural. They weren't beat up—but they were systematically beaten down and considered worthless. Like racism, sexism, and homophobia, it is a form of social intolerance and prejudice. It is similar to people who are harassed on the street, beaten, even shot just for being who they are. These kids committed the 'crime' of embracing defiant music subcultures and styles instead of more mainstream all-American activities. They were dismissed, and devalued because they were different. This is still happening in schools across the country.

Bullying doesn't just happen because people are mean. It happens because people can get away with it. The schools sanction the behavior and sometimes rely on bullying to control deviant behavior. By design or default, the Bergenfield school condoned and encouraged this systematic disrespect.

Gaines says that she is still working to bring attention to the plight of youths who experience similar isolation and alienation. Gaines retired recently from her work as an assistant professor of social science and interdisciplinary studies at the State University of New York, Empire State College on Long Island. Having established herself as an expert on youth culture, she encouraged students to join her in youth advocacy and community activism.

She taught Youth Studies courses, such as Child Welfare; Youth, Community and Culture; Youth and Society; and Youth at Risk, where she addressed bullying, LGBTQI+ discrimination, suicide, teen pregnancy, gangs, and immigration. She discussed the structural position of youths as the "minority of minorities" and focused on youth subcultures that empower and enrich young people in everyday life.

Gaines says that her students are concerned about school bullying for many reasons. Some are parents of children being bullied or of LGBTQI+ kids. They work in schools and in their communities. "They see bullying everywhere," says Gaines. "I never imagined when I wrote *Teenage Wasteland* that it would get even worse for kids. That kids would be systematically bullied into suicide, or blowing up their schools."

Gaines says she also understands bullying from her own experiences as a child. She discussed those experiences in her book, *A Misfit's Manifesto: The Sociological Memoir of a Rock & Roll Heart*:

> I was an only child, I wore orthopedic shoes. I was clumsy and overweight. Kids called me a fat slob. They wouldn't sit next to me, I withered every day with shame and self-hatred. The experiences still haunt me. I have a happy, healthy life. Nobody would look at me and call me fat, and yet those names still make me cringe. I was filled with rage until I realized, as long as you are angry, the bullies are still calling the shots. Why give them any power? So now I channel that rage into a passion for social justice and loud music.

A former social worker with Child Protective Services, Gaines also worked against bullying by teaching her students to be sensitive to young peoples' needs and to be open to diversity, subcultures, and alternative values.

"Being bullied can turn you into a depressed, angry adult. "I didn't want that to be my life story. I wasted a lot of time being angry when I could have been learning interesting new things about the world. So much of my emotional energy was caught up in surviving and fighting for my dignity," she says. "I was lucky my parents stood up for me and that I found meaning and love in the world. Instead of thinking about how I was ridiculed, I think about the support I've had. That's a strength-based social work intervention strategy. You get to throw off the labels and rewrite your story."

Most important, "we have to transform the schools that isolate and label people who are different and struggling," Gaines says. "We need to train people to be kind. Without proactive efforts, we are not going to have kind people."

Dan Olweus

Dan Olweus, a professor of psychology at the University of Bergen in Norway, is known as the pioneer of research on bullying and peer harassment. His first book, translated into English in 1978 as *Aggression in the Schools: Bullies and Whipping Boys*, is widely regarded as the first large-scale study of bullying.

For a long time, school administrators and parents tended to overlook bullying and dismiss it as age-appropriate or even normal behavior. Olweus reported on the negative consequences of bullying, and in 1983, he developed and implemented the Olweus Bullying Prevention Program (OBPP).

Evaluations of the OBPP found that the program decreased bullying by 50 percent in Norway, where it was first launched. It was quickly translated into multiple languages and implemented across Europe, and the program is still known internationally for reducing bullying.

The OBPP focuses on systemic change to create a safe and positive school climate with an intentional focus on bullying prevention. The K–12 program addresses the problem of bullying at four levels: school-wide, classroom, individual, and community. It is designed to involve students, staff, and parents as well as members of nearby organizations and businesses.

In the United States, the program has been shown to be effective but with a lower bullying reduction rate than in Norway. Jan Urbanski, director of Safe and Humane Schools at Clemson University, oversees training and implementation of the OBPP in North, Central, and South America. According to Urbanski, the lower reduction is due in part because Norway has less of a bullying problem. In Norway, the bullying rate was 6 percent and was decreased to 3 percent (a decrease of three percentage points). In the United States, the bullying rate is about 24 percent—almost one out of every four children is bullied. It would be a bigger challenge to decrease this number by half (or twelve percentage points).

Norway also has a different school structure, especially in middle and high schools, and the fidelity of the OBPP implementation is much higher there. U.S. schools have found it more difficult to find time in the school day for training, class meetings, and staff discussion. Additionally, Norway has a more homogenous culture and less income inequality. "These do not necessarily make it more difficult to implement the OBPP in the U.S.," says Urbanski, "just different."

Before the Olweus trainer-consultants work with a given school, they provide a readiness survey to ascertain whether the school is adequately prepared for the OBPP implementation. If a school has no process in place to address inappropriate behaviors, they are not ready for the OBPP, Urbanski said. "We give them some direction on what to consider before implementing the OBPP. We give them resources. But realistically at a minimum the school should have a code of conduct to address problem behavior. Without one, it would be a red flag that they may not be ready. Program fidelity is higher if the school is motivated to make a full system change as an ongoing effort."

Once a school is ready, a certified OBPP trainer-consultant conducts a two-day training for the school's newly formed Bullying Prevention Coordinating Committee. This is followed by twelve to eighteen months of consultation to implement the program. A trainer works a minimum of twelve hours with the school—at least once a month, and sometimes every other week.

Schools receive an annual questionnaire to measure the program's effectiveness and to assess the school's ongoing needs. With the school's Prevention Coordinating Committee, the OBPP conducts teacher training, creates a "kickoff" for the students, and examines the school's anti-bullying policy. The OBPP trainer-consultant also helps the committee to actively involve the whole school community.

One of the first parts of the OBPP work is to understand how Dan Olweus defines bullying. The OBPP website states the following:

1. Bullying is aggressive behavior that involves unwanted, negative actions.

2. Bullying often involves a pattern of behavior repeated over time.

3. Bullying involves an imbalance of power or strength.

Urbanski explains that the definition of bullying is discussed in class meetings so that the difference between bullying and other forms of conflict is clear. Kids being kids and fooling around and joking needs to be handled differently, she says. "Saying or doing hurtful things to another student who has a hard time defending him or herself is more clearly bullying." In bullying, "no one is having fun. They are not generally friends, but they could be. There is a difference in power between the person who is bullying and the person who is being bullied. The person who is bullying might be stronger, older, have higher status, be an athlete, have more money or have better grades. In a conflict, on the other hand, there is equal power. The aggression takes place on a level playing field."

In the classroom, students learn the school rules about bullying, the reporting procedure, and actions they should take if it happens to them or they see it happening. "The majority of students are bystanders," Urbanski says. The program helps students become more empathetic and "to empower the bystanders to be part of the prevention effort to help create a safe and respectful climate."

If the situation is more of a conflict than a bullying incident, the students are encouraged to work it out between the two of them—perhaps through peer mediation. That's a whole different program that isn't taught through the OBPP. Urbanski says, "We do say that you shouldn't handle bullying situations in peer mediation because of the difference in power between the people involved. In a conflict, equal parties talk about their side of the story. In bullying the person who is being bullied doesn't have the same power or strength, so it is less likely to end in a win-win solution."

The OBPP encourages schools to use their existing processes to address general forms of conflict. "We don't tell schools what that has to be. We also don't require specific positive or negative consequences for things that happen. We share what other schools are doing. We provide resources, but we don't have those kinds of requirements," Urbanski explains.

In class meetings with teachers, students are engaged in discussions about social-emotional issues depending on where the school chooses to focus, including friendships, getting along with others, or anger management. Teachers are given lessons they can use, or they can develop their own plans. The goal is to provide enough prevention so that the norm in the school is that students do not bully one another.

If a bullying problem does develop, the school staff is given a six-step On the Spot intervention model to use if they see the behavior firsthand. The plan is different if staff members hear about a bullying incident from others. There are separate follow-up meetings with the student who bullied and the student who was bullied. There are also follow-up meetings with the parents of the students involved. A safety plan may be developed, and there may also be a review to help determine whether the incident needs to be examined at another level of investigation, as per school policy.

The OBPP works with the outside community to support the school in their bullying prevention work. They provide information to the community and posters to put up in local businesses, and they invite guest speakers for community participation. "We want students to see the bullying prevention message in the community as well as in the school," Urbanski said. They also provide training to implement the OBPP in community youth organizations like "Mom and Pop dance studios" and "YMCA after-school programs."

The Olweus program certifies trainer-consultants through-out the country. To date, since 1995, they have trained over 1,500 people throughout the United States as well as in Mexico, Barbados, Brazil, Canada, the Dominican Republic, Guam, Panama, Slovenia, United Arab Emirates, and the U.S. Virgin Islands.

The OBPP has thirty-five years of research based on questionnaires they have given their schools. Their national database includes the demographics of the school and the school's bullying prevalence rate. Urbanski said, "We see effectiveness, a reduction in bullying and a reduction in other antisocial behaviors. It all depends on the fidelity of the implementation, the more the schools follow the model, the better the results." The OBPP did a large-scale study in Pennsylvania and other research in South Carolina. In South Carolina, they implemented a parallel program called Positive Behavior Intervention Support. Funded by the National Institute of Justice, this research looks at how effective it is to combine the programs versus doing the OBPP program alone or not doing it at all.

Students are also helped to develop a voice in their schools. "We often hear that people are just nicer," Urbanski says. "Teachers say that the classroom is more manageable, though others say that the program takes too much time." High school teachers are expected to facilitate a weekly or biweekly class meeting. "If the program is fully implemented, the teachers are not dealing with other behavior issues in the classroom so they should be getting the time back," Urbanski says. "We do get various responses from, 'We love it,' to 'It's not part of my job and I don't want to do it.'" Mostly, though, "we hear back that there is a safer and more empathetic climate in the school where everyone can learn."

The Center for the Study and Prevention of Violence at the University of Colorado at Boulder, which uses rigorous scientific evaluations to recognize programs that have solid empirical success, designated the OBPP as a Blueprint Model Program.

Deborah Temkin

Deborah Temkin is an American child development and bullying research authority who was the first person in the federal government to head an effort to stop childhood bullying. She suffered from bullying when she was in middle school, according to news reports, and the experience made her determined to help prevent others from suffering the same fate.

In her Tucson, Arizona, middle school, Temkin was asked to be editor of the school paper. When she accepted the position, a feud developed that managed to turn most of Temkin's classmates against her. Temkin was socially isolated, and verbally and physically bullied. Despite Temkin and her parents' complaints, the school did little to stop the bullying. Her parents enrolled her in a private school at the beginning of ninth grade to help her to have a new start. Temkin became determined to understand bullying and ways to prevent it.

In November 2009, Temkin attended the International Bullying Prevention Association conference in Pittsburgh, where Kevin Jennings was the keynote speaker. President Obama had made Jennings, a civil and gay rights activist, the assistant deputy secretary for the Office of Safe and Drug-Free Schools in the Department of Education. Jennings focused on school shootings and drug abuse. After his speech, Temkin approached Jennings and said she would like to work for him.

Jennings gave Temkin an unpaid internship, which led to Temkin planning the first annual Federal Partners in Bullying Prevention Summit. Temkin was then hired as research and policy coordinator for bullying prevention initiatives. She managed anti-bullying activities in nine federal departments. She also coordinated the 2011 White House Conference on Bullying Prevention and the 2011 and 2012 Federal Partners in Bullying Prevention Summits. Temkin's other responsibilities included overseeing the collection and development of materials on bullying for StopBullying.gov.

She was nominated for the Samuel J. Heyman Service to America Medal and recognized for her outstanding federal service.

Temkin left her federal position in 2012 (the same year she finished her PhD) and launched a new anti-bullying initiative at the Robert F. Kennedy Center for Justice and Human Rights, called Project SEATBELT (Safe Environment Achieved through Bullying Prevention, Engagement, Leadership, and Teaching). In 2014, she became a senior research scientist at Child Trends.

Victims

Tyler Clementi

At age eighteen, Tyler Clementi committed suicide after being cyberharassed because he was gay. He had asked his roommate, Dharun Ravi, for privacy because he had a date. Ravi left, but before leaving, he pointed his computer's webcam at Clementi's bed. Ravi urged friends and Twitter followers to watch the videos he secretly made and posted of Clementi's sexual interactions.

In the summer before his high school graduation, Clementi started to come out about being gay to his close family members and friends. People who knew Clementi reported that he was still vulnerable as a freshman in college and that he was pained by the trick Ravi played on him. He had only recently become comfortable about living openly as a young gay man.

Clementi discovered what Ravi did when he viewed his roommate's Twitter feed. News reports stated that Clementi was devastated when he realized he had become a topic of ridicule at his new school and that he was also upset at the lack of support he experienced. The people who saw the videos had not reported the harassment to authorities.

Clementi's story brought national attention to issues of cyberbullying and the specific struggles facing lesbian, gay, bisexual, transgender, intersex, and queer youth. Clementi's parents, Jane and Joseph Clementi, established the Tyler Clementi Foundation in 2011 in order to promote acceptance of LGBTQI+ teens and others who face discrimination and prejudice. They provide education around bullying and cyber-bullying and promote research into the causes and prevention of teen suicide. In 2015, the foundation launched #Day1, an anti-bullying campaign that aims to stop bullying before it begins.

In 2016, Ravi pleaded guilty to one count of attempted privacy invasion.

Ryan Halligan

Ryan Patrick Halligan was a thirteen-year-old student from Poughkeepsie, New York, who committed suicide after several years of schoolyard and internet bullying.

His father described him as a gentle and sensitive child. During his early years, educators noticed that Halligan struggled more than other students and placed him on an alternative learning track. Halligan had advanced past special education by the time he reached fifth grade, but that same year, he encountered a bully who mocked his coordination skills.

By the beginning of seventh grade, Halligan began to encounter new bullying problems. According to news reports, he convinced his parents to buy him kickboxing training tapes, along with boxing gloves and a punching bag, so that he could better defend himself. He fought with the main person who bullied him, and his parents reported that they were surprised that their son became friends with the person soon thereafter.

That summer, Halligan started to like one of the more popular girls at school, and he shared private information about his life with her. When school resumed, Halligan approached the girl he had spoken to all summer. Instead of returning his interest, she mocked him. He discovered that she had divulged his secrets to her friends and that they were laughing at his expense.

Halligan was crushed. He visited several websites that described ways to commit suicide. In his yearbook, he drew a hangman on the flagpole of his school. He even said to the girl on the

Internet, "It's girls like you that make me want to kill myself." She told him that it was about time, according to news reports.

Without a note, Halligan committed suicide. After his death, his father pushed for the passage of a state anti-bullying bill that would require schools to develop policies to protect students from harassment. Vermont Act 117, An Act Relating to Bullying Prevention Policies was signed into law in 2004 by Vermont's governor. Halligan's father also tried to gain passage of a second law, the Vermont Act 114, mandating suicide prevention education in the state's schools; in 2006, this Act was also signed into law. His father speaks at schools around the country to stop cyberbullying.

David Knight

David Knight, born in Ontario, Canada, had been physically bullied since elementary school. In high school, he became a victim of online bullying when a classmate created a website called Welcome to the Page that Makes Fun of Dave Knight.

According to media reports, the creator of the site posted that Knight was a gay pedophile who used a date rape drug on younger boys. The site encouraged others to join in and leave messages about how much they disliked Knight.

A classmate brought the website to Knight's attention, and Knight learned that many other students had viewed the site and had joined in the mocking. Knight said that it would have been easier to deal with the face-to-face bullying in front of thirty people in a cafeteria. The cyberbullying was devastating. Knight became withdrawn and depressed. He left in the middle of his senior year to become homeschooled.

Knight's parents learned that Yahoo.com hosted the website that bullied their son. Since Yahoo did not have any policies regarding what people posted, the torment on the website continued. Knight and his family tried to shut down the website, but Yahoo ignored their request. When the family threatened Yahoo with a lawsuit, Yahoo removed the page.

In 2002, the Knights filed suit against the school board alleging that school officials were aware of the bullying but did nothing to address it. They also filed criminal charges against the person who bullied their son during senior year, punched Knight in the face, and shoved him into a locker. The bully was ordered to perform community service and later committed suicide.

David Knight went on to train as a fighter pilot for the Canadian Armed Forces.

Megan Meier

Megan Meier, who lived in Dardenne Prairie, a small suburb of St. Louis, Missouri, received hateful messages on her Myspace account from a fictional sixteen-year-old boyfriend, "Josh Evans."

In court, witnesses testified that Lori Drew, the mother of one of Meier's former friends, created the fictional account with her daughter, Sarah, and with an eighteen-year old employee in order to get back at Meier for allegedly spreading gossip about Sarah.

The witnesses said that Drew created the fictional boy to humiliate Meier. The last message that Meier received from "Josh" ended, "The world would be a better place without you." Meier's mother said that her daughter was hysterical when she received the message. Twenty minutes later, she hanged herself in her bedroom closet, three weeks before she would have turned fourteen years old.

Drew was indicted in 2008 and acquitted in 2009. Newspaper reports suggested that Drew became "America's most reviled mother." Bloggers posted photographs of Drew, telephone numbers, email details, and addresses of the Drews on various websites. The Drews left Missouri.

The incident inspired legislation against harassment on the internet, including Missouri's Megan's Law, which made it a felony if someone twenty-one years or older communicates with someone seventeen years or younger by electronic means or by phone in order to frighten, intimidate, or cause emotional distress to that person.

Christina Meier, Megan's mother, started the Megan Meier Foundation in Chesterfield, Missouri, to "support and inspire actions to end bullying, cyberbullying, and suicide."

Phoebe Prince

Two groups of students bullied Phoebe Prince in her South Hadley High School, according to media reports, soon after she immigrated to Massachusetts from Ireland. The torment started after Prince went out with football star Sean Mulveyhill, who was still in an "on-again, off-again" relationship with another girl, Kayla Narey.

When Mulveyhill and Narey started to date exclusively, Prince apologized to Narey, revealing that Prince and Mulveyhill had been together. Narey broke off her relationship with Mulveyhill. Mulveyhill took Narey's side and they soon became part of a group of students that bullied Prince.

One day a student threw an empty can at Prince's head and yelled insults at her. Narey and Mulveyhill were there and laughed. Soon after, at age fifteen, Prince hanged herself in the stairway leading to her apartment with a scarf her younger sister had given her for Christmas. Students posted more hostile and crude comments on Prince's Facebook memorial page even after her death.

Six of the teenagers faced criminal prosecution for civil rights violations. Five of the teenagers involved were sentenced to probation and community service.

A year after Prince's death, the state passed stricter antibullying legislation. The law bans bullying on school grounds, buses, and other school activities, and it requires reporting and investigation of every bullying incident.

The bullying Prince experienced attracted international attention, controversy, and more awareness about suicide associated with school bullying.

Ghyslain Raza

In 2003, after classmates leaked a video Ghyslain Raza made of himself reenacting scenes from a *Star Wars* movie, the fifteen-year-old Canadian student was dubbed the "Star Wars Kid" at his school, Séminaire Saint-Joseph.

Raza had used school equipment to film the infamous video, according to media reports. It showed Raza using a golf ball retriever as an imaginary light saber, which he brandished in mock battle like the *Star Wars* character Darth Maul. The tape, which Raza never intended to become public, was discovered by classmates, who digitized the footage and uploaded it to the file-sharing network Kazaa. Raza's peers mocked and bullied him until Raza dropped out of school and began working with a private tutor.

The video continued to receive millions of hits shortly after being uploaded and it became one of the first viral internet videos. The phenomenon made Raza an international pop culture icon. It is also one of the first widely publicized cyberbullying cases. As the video grew in fame, a Quebec television station revealed his identity, and Raza began to receive media attention.

Although some people showed affection for Raza by setting up Star Wars Kid fan sites and petitioning George Lucas to give the teen a cameo role in a future *Star Wars* film, others poked fun at him by ridiculing his weight or adding special effects to the original footage. Some online commenters told him to commit suicide and one called him a "pox on humanity."

Raza was diagnosed with depression, and his parents, who felt that their son had suffered undue humiliation and loss of privacy, filed a lawsuit against the families of the classmates who uploaded the video. In 2006, the families settled out of court for an undisclosed amount.

According to some estimates, Raza's video had been viewed almost a billion times, making it one of the most popular videos in online history. Besides inspiring several spoofs on the internet, the "Star Wars Kid" was referenced in many forms of mainstream entertainment, including episodes of the television series *Arrested Development, American Dad,* and *The Colbert Report.*

In 2013, as a law school graduate of McGill University and president of a local historic preservation group, Raza broke his long press silence and spoke with two of Canada's leading news magazines about cyberbullying. Raza said he was motivated to speak to the press due to the many cyberbullying-prompted suicides. Raza encouraged victims to persevere and survive.

This section includes information related to bullying in the form of graphs, charts, legislative actions, court cases, and presidential speeches.

Data

Females were more often the object of name-calling and rumors. Males and females were both excluded from activities. More males had their property destroyed. In many categories, black students were bullied most often. Sixth grade students experienced the most bullying compared with those in other grades, and bullying decreased substantially in eleventh and twelfth grade.

Seventy-five percent of school shootings are linked to bullying, according to the FBI. Across demographics, people are joining the student-led movement, March for Our Lives, to end bullying-related gun violence. (Arienne Davey/Dreamstime.com)

Table 5.1 Demographics of Students Being Bullied at School—Types of Bullying (2015)

Types of Bullying: Percentage of Students (ages 12–18) Who Reported Being . . .

	Made Fun of, Called Names, or Insulted	Subject of Rumors	Threatened with Harm	Pushed, Shoved, Tripped, or Spat Upon	Tried to Make Do Things They Did Not Want to Do	Excluded from Activities on Purpose	Property Destroyed on Purpose
Sex							
Male	12.7	9.1	4.8	2.7	4.4	1.9	6.0
Female	13.9	15.5	2.9	2.3	5.7	1.8	4.2
Race/ethnicity							
White	14.2	12.8	3.9	2.1	5.6	1.6	5.3
Black	17.2	14.3	5.2	3.4	4.9	1.6	5.6
Hispanic	9.5	10.4	2.9	2.1	3.4	2.0	3.7
Asian	10.1	4.9	N/A	N/A	N/A	N/A	3.9
Other	16.4	18.6	8.9	9.1	9.8	N/A	11.2
Grade							
6th	21.4	17.7	7.3	5.2	10.1	4.0	13.1
7th	18.6	12.9	3.8	2.9	6.4	2.7	7.8
8th	15.6	13.1	5.1	2.9	5.1	3.1	7.5
9th	12.5	10.6	2.8	2.7	4.4	1.3	4.4
10th	12.6	12.9	2.9	1.7	5.7	1.2	2.2
11th	8.8	10.2	4.2	N/A	3.0	N/A	2.1
12th	6.2	10.8	2.5	2.4	2.4	N/A	1.6
Location							
Urban	14.5	11.4	3.9	2.9	5.1	2.4	5.6
Suburban	13.3	13.2	3.9	2.6	5.4	1.6	4.8
Rural	10.9	10.6	3.8	N/A	3.7	N/A	5.2
Type of school							
Public	13.4	12.5	4.0	2.6	5.0	1.8	5.2
Private	11.5	8.6	N/A	N/A	5.0	N/A	3.6

Source: Musu-Gillette, L., Zhang, A., Wang, K., Zhang, J., Kemp, J., Diliberti, M., & Oudekerk, B. A. (2018). *Indicators of school crime and safety: 2017.* NCES 2018-036/NCJ 251413. Washington, DC: National Center for Education Statistics, U.S. Department of Education, and Bureau of Justice Statistics, Office of Justice Programs, U.S. Department of Justice.

Females experienced most of the different types of cyberbullying. Males endured more cyberbullying while gaming online.

Table 5.2 Sex of Students Who Reported Being Cyberbullied—Types of Cyberbullying (2013)

Types of Cyberbullying: Percentage of Students (ages 12–18) Who Reported . . .

	Male	Female
Hurtful information on internet	1.2	4.5
Private information purposely shared on internet	0.4	1.5
Subject of harassing instant messages	1.0	3.4
Subject of harassing text messages	1.6	4.9
Subject of harassing emails	0.2	1.7
Subject of harassment while gaming online	2.5	0.4
Excluded online	1.9	0.9

Source: Musu-Gillette, L., Zhang, A., Wang, K., Zhang, J., Kemp, J., Diliberti, M., & Oudekerk, B. A. (2018). *Indicators of school crime and safety: 2017*. NCES 2018-036/NCJ 251413. Washington, DC: National Center for Education Statistics, U.S. Department of Education, and Bureau of Justice Statistics, Office of Justice Programs, U.S. Department of Justice.

Females were bullied and cyberbullied more than males. Students whose families made below $15,000 were bullied and cyberbullied more than higher-income students.

Table 5.3 Demographics of Students Bullied and Cyberbullied (School Year 2012–2013)

Student Characteristic	Number of Students	Percent Bullied	Percent Cyberbullied
Total	25,013,000	21.5	6.9
Sex			
Male	12,862,000	19.5	5.2
Female	12,151,000	23.7	8.6
Race/ethnicity			
White, not Hispanic or Latino	13,317,000	23.7	7.6
Black, not Hispanic or Latino	3,842,000	20.3	4.5
Hispanic or Latino	5,770,000	19.2	5.8
Asian, not Hispanic or Latino	1,180,000	9.2	5.8
All other races, not Hispanic or Latino	903,000	25.2	13.4

(continued)

Table 5.3   (continued)

Student Characteristic	Number of Students	Percent Bullied	Percent Cyberbullied
Grade			
6th	2,078,000	27.8	5.9
7th	4,018,000	26.4	7.0
8th	3,812,000	21.7	6.4
9th	3,897,000	23.0	6.7
10th	4,047,000	19.5	8.6
11th	3,795,000	20.0	6.8
12th	3,366,000	14.1	5.9
Household income			
Less than $7,500	927,000	25.5	9.5
$7,500 to 14,999	1,103,000	26.3	8.1
$15,000 to 24,999	1,918,000	21.5	4.9
$25,000 to 34,999	2,512,000	21.5	6.7
$35,000 to 49,999	3,274,000	21.8	6.3
$50,000 or more	10,706,000	21.7	7.4

Source: U.S. Department of Justice, Bureau of Justice Statistics. (2013). *School crime supplement to the National Crime Victimization Survey*.

Bullying remained high from middle school through high school.

Table 5.4   Grade of Students Who Reported Being Bullied—Location of Bullying (2015)

Percentage of Students (ages 12–18) Who Reported Being Bullied . . .							
	In a Classroom	In a Hallway or Stairwell	In a Bathroom/ Locker Room	Cafeteria	Outside on School Grounds	On School Bus	Online or by Text
Total	33.6	41.7	9.4	22.2	19.3	10.0	11.5
Grade							
6th	37.4	26.3	8.2	21.1	34.0	16.1	N/A
7th	39.1	45.5	12.2	22.2	22.4	14.1	8.1
8th	30.3	51.1	13.3	26.0	15.7	8.7	15.5
9th	38.4	37.0	13.8	23.3	N/A	14.2	N/A
10th	33.5	40.6	N/A	17.7	14.4	N/A	18.1
11th	29.4	39.9	10.1	17.5	30.9	N/A	11.2
12th	21.1	49.0	N/A	28.6	14.2	N/A	18.7

Source: Musu-Gillette, L., Zhang, A., Wang, K., Zhang, J., Kemp, J., Diliberti, M., & Oudekerk, B. A. (2018). *Indicators of school crime and safety: 2017*. NCES 2018-036/NCJ 251413. Washington, DC: National Center for Education Statistics, U.S. Department of Education, and Bureau of Justice Statistics, Office of Justice Programs, U.S. Department of Justice.

Adults were notified more often about face-to-face bullying compared with cyberbullying, especially in grades six and seven. Injuries were most common in sixth and seventh grades. Adults were notified about cyberbullying least often in ninth grade.

Table 5.5 Results by Grade of Bullying and Cyberbullying (School Year 2012–2013)

	Bullying		Cyberbullying
	Percent of Cases Where . . .		
	Adult Was Notified	Student Was Injured	Adult Was Notified
Total	38.9	5.8	23.3
Grade			
6th	58.3	10.6	17.5
7th	52.3	10.5	28.0
8th	38.1	6.2	30.4
9th	35.2	3.9	12.4
10th	34.6	4.0	23.9
11th	25.8	N/A	26.7
12th	22.4	N/A	21.0

Source: U.S. Department of Justice, Bureau of Justice Statistics. (2013). School crime supplement to the National Crime Victimization Survey.

This table shows victims' various responses to bullying; some avoided specific places at school, and others fought back.

Table 5.6 Percentage of Students Who Reported Being Bullied and Cyberbullied, by Student Reports of Fear, Avoidance, and Responses (School Year 2012–2013)

	Feared Attack or Harm	Skipped School	Skipped Class	Avoided School Activities	Avoided a Specific Place at School	Engaged in a Physical Fight	Carried a Weapon to School
Total	3.5	0.9	0.5	1.0	3.7	3.6	2.1
Bullied	10.5	3.6	2.0	3.4	11.3	11.4	4.3
Not bullied	1.6	0.2	0.1	0.4	1.6	1.5	1.5
Cyberbullied	11.7	6.3	3.3	6.1	15.4	10.1	6.0
Not cyberbullied	2.9	0.5	0.3	0.7	2.8	3.1	1.8

Source: U.S. Department of Justice, Bureau of Justice Statistics. (2013). School crime supplement to the National Crime Victimization Survey.

This table shows the type of hate speech used in bullying. Most of the hate speech focused on race and was most frequent in sixth grade.

Table 5.7 Percentage of Students Who Reported Hate-Related Words, by Type (2015)

| | Total, Any Hate-Related Words | Type of Hate-Related Words | | | | | |
		Race	Ethnicity	Religion	Disability	Gender	Sexual Orientation
Total	7.2	3.2	1.8	1.0	0.7	1.3	1.0
Grade							
6th	10.1	5.2	2.5	N/A	N/A	1.6	1.9
7th	7.0	3.2	2.0	0.5	0.8	0.7	0.7
8th	9.2	3.8	1.5	1.4	0.7	1.9	0.9
9th	7.4	3.1	2.0	0.9	N/A	1.5	0.8
10th	6.5	2.7	1.8	0.7	N/A	0.9	1.2
11th	6.0	2.2	0.9	N/A	N/A	1.4	1.1
12th	5.4	2.8	1.9	1.6	0.8	1.0	N/A

Source: U.S. Department of Justice, Bureau of Justice Statistics. (2016, August). *School crime supplement (SCS) to the National Crime Victimization Survey, selected years, 2005 through 2015.* Retrieved from https://nces.ed.gov/programs/digest/d16/tables/dt16_230.35.asp

Those who identified as lesbian, gay, or bisexual were face-to-face and electronically bullied significantly more than those who identified as heterosexual.

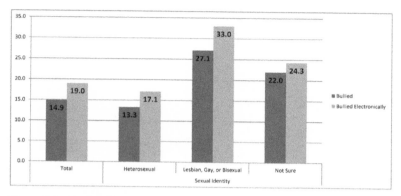

Figure 5.1   Percentage of High School Students Who Were Bullied at School or Electronically Bullied, by Sexual Identity (2017)

Source: Centers for Disease Control and Prevention. (2018). *Youth Risk Behavior Survey, data summary & trends report, 2007–2017*. Retrieved from https://www.cdc.gov/nchhstp/newsroom/2018/2017-YRBS.html#Summaries

School shootings include any incident when a person fired a gun in K–12th grade or college.

Shootings more than doubled from 1979 to 1988 (27) to 1989 to 1998 (55) and continued to increase from 1999 to 2008 (66). There were 148 shootings in the three decades from 1979 to 2008.

The first three years of the decade starting in 2009 had more shootings (43) than the decade between 1979 and 1988 and almost as many as the decade between 1989 and 1998 (Klein 2012).

Recent reports show that there were 175 shootings from 2009 to 2018, more than the previous three decades combined.

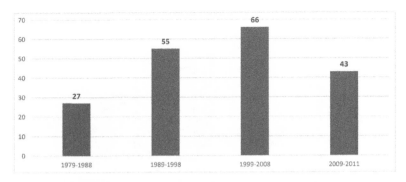

Figure 5.2   Numbers of School Shootings by Decade (1979–2011)

Source: Klein, J. (2012). *For educators: The bully society: School shootings and the crisis of bullying in America's schools*. New York: NYU Press. Retrieved from https://nyupress.org/resources/for-educators/ or jessieklein.com

This table categorizes school shooting motives. Most school shooting perpetrators reacted to having their masculinity challenged.

Table 5.8   Motives in 148 School Shootings (1979–2008)

Catalyst	Further Detail
Gay-bashing	In 12 of the cases, heterosexually identified perpetrators committed shootings after being called gay or some other reference to homosexuality (almost 10%).
Violence against girls/women	In 31 of the shootings, perpetrators specifically targeted girls/women (over 20%).
Dating/domestic violence	In 19 of the shootings, perpetrators attacked girls and/or women with whom they were in a relationship (almost 15%).
Antischool	From 1979 to 1988, there were 8 shootings related to bad grades or being disciplined (e.g., suspended or expelled), doubling from 1989 to 1988 to 16, and increasing between 1999 and 2008, to 19, making a total of 43 shootings (almost 30%).
Racism	Racism played a role in 11 of the shootings (almost 10%).

Source: Klein, J. (2012). *For educators: The bully society: School shootings and the crisis of bullying in America's schools*. New York: NYU Press. Retrieved from https://nyupress.org/resources/for-educators/or jessieklein.com

This table describes some of the legal recourses for students who are bullied. At the time of publication, there is no federal anti-bullying policy.

Table 5.9   Civil Rights Statutes Relevant to Bullying

Civil Rights Act of 1964	Protects targets if the harassment is deemed to be discrimination based on sex, race, color, national origin, and religion.
Title VI of the Civil Rights Act of 1964	Prohibits discrimination on the basis of race, color, and national origin for programs and activities receiving federal financial assistance.
Title IX of the Education Amendments of 1972	No person in the United States shall, on the basis of sex, be excluded from participation in, be denied the benefits of, or be subjected to discrimination under any education program or activity receiving federal financial assistance.
Section 504 of the Rehabilitation Act of 1973	No otherwise qualified individual with a disability in the United States, as defined in section 705(20) of this title, shall, solely by reason of her or his disability, be excluded from the participation in, be denied the benefits of, or be subjected to discrimination under any program or activity receiving federal financial assistance.
Titles II and III of the Americans with Disabilities Act	Title II: Prohibits disability discrimination by all public entities at the local level—for example, school district, municipal, city, county, and state level. Title III: No individual may be discriminated against on the basis of disability with regards to the full and equal enjoyment of the goods, services, facilities, or accommodations of any place of public accommodation by any person who owns, leases, or operates a place of public accommodation. Public accommodations include most places of lodging (such as inns and hotels), recreation, transportation, education, and dining, along with stores, care providers, and places of public displays.
Individuals with Disabilities Education Act (IDEA)	A four-part (A—D) piece of American legislation that ensures that students with a disability are provided with free appropriate public education (FAPE) that is tailored to their individual needs.

Documents

Davis v. Monroe County Board of Education (1999)

In this case, a family sued a school for not preventing sexual harassment. The Supreme Court decided on their behalf, stating that due to Title IX, the school system can be held accountable for failing to prevent bullying that includes sexual harassment.

JUSTICE O'CONNOR delivered the opinion of the Court.

Petitioner brought suit against the Monroe County Board of Education and other defendants, alleging that her fifth-grade daughter had been the victim of sexual harassment by another student in her class. Among petitioner's claims was a claim for monetary and injunctive relief under Title IX of the Education Amendments of 1972 (Title IX). The District Court dismissed petitioner's Title IX claim on the ground that "student-on-student," or peer, harassment provides no ground for a private cause of action under the statute. The Court of Appeals for the Eleventh Circuit, sitting en banc, affirmed. We consider here whether a private damages action may lie against the school board in cases of student-on-student harassment. We conclude that it may, but only where the funding recipient acts with deliberate indifference to known acts of harassment in its programs or activities. Moreover, we conclude that such an action will lie only for harassment that is so severe, pervasive, and objectively offensive that it effectively bars the victim's access to an educational opportunity or benefit.

. . .

We consider here whether the misconduct identified in Gebser—deliberate indifference to known acts of harassment—amounts to an intentional violation of Title IX, capable of supporting a private damages action, when the harasser is a student rather than a teacher. We conclude that, in certain limited circumstances, it does. As an initial matter, in *Gebser* we expressly rejected the use of agency principles in the Title IX context, noting the textual differences between Title IX and Title VII. Additionally, the regulatory scheme surrounding Title IX has long provided funding recipients with notice that they may be liable for their failure to respond to the discriminatory acts of certain nonagents. The Department of Education requires recipients to monitor third parties for discrimination in specified circumstances and to refrain from particular forms of interaction with outside entities that are known to discriminate.

The common law, too, has put schools on notice that they may be held responsible under state law for their failure to protect students from the tortious acts of third parties. In fact, state courts routinely uphold claims alleging that schools have been negligent in failing to protect their students from the torts of their peers.

This is not to say that the identity of the harasser is irrelevant. On the contrary, both the "deliberate indifference" standard and the language of Title IX narrowly circumscribe the set of parties whose known acts of sexual harassment can trigger some duty to respond on the part of funding recipients. Deliberate indifference makes sense as a theory of direct liability under Title IX only where the funding recipient has some control over the alleged harassment. A recipient cannot be directly liable for its indifference where it lacks the authority to take remedial action.

. . .

Applying this standard to the facts at issue here, we conclude that the Eleventh Circuit erred in dismissing petitioner's complaint. Petitioner alleges that her daughter was the victim of repeated acts of sexual harassment by G. F. over a 5-month period, and there are allegations in support of the conclusion that G. F.'s misconduct was severe, pervasive, and objectively offensive. The harassment was not only verbal; it included numerous acts of objectively offensive touching, and, indeed, G. F. ultimately pleaded guilty to criminal sexual misconduct. Moreover, the complaint alleges that there were multiple victims who were sufficiently disturbed by G. F.'s misconduct to seek an audience with the school principal. Further, petitioner contends that the harassment had a concrete, negative effect on her daughter's ability to receive an education. The complaint also suggests that petitioner may be able to show both actual knowledge and deliberate indifference on the part of the Board, which made no effort whatsoever either to investigate or to put an end to the harassment.

. . . Accordingly, the judgment of the United States Court of Appeals for the Eleventh Circuit is reversed, and the case is remanded for further proceedings consistent with this opinion.

It is so ordered.

Source: *Davis v. Monroe County Board of Education*, 526 U.S. 629 (1999).

President Barack Obama's Statement on Bullying Prevention (2011)

In March 2011, President Obama hosted a White House Conference on Bullying Prevention.

I want to reiterate what Michelle said: Preventing bullying isn't just important to us as President and First Lady, it's important for us as parents. It's something we care deeply about.

We're joined here by several Members of Congress who've shown real leadership in taking up this cause. We've got a number of members of my administration with us today who are going to help us head up the efforts that come out of the White House on this issue. . . .

Now, bullying isn't a problem that makes headlines every day. But every day it touches the lives of young people all across this country. I want to thank all of you for participating in this conference. But more importantly, I want to thank you for being part of what's a growing movement—led by young people themselves—to put a stop to bullying, whether it takes place in school or it's taking place online.

And that's why we're here today. If there's one goal of this conference, it's to dispel the myth that bullying is just a harmless rite of passage or an inevitable part of growing up. It's not. Bullying can have destructive consequences for our young people, and it's not something we have to accept. As parents and students, as teachers and members of the community, we can take steps—all of us—to help prevent bullying and create a climate in our schools in which all of our children can feel safe, a climate in which they all can feel like they belong.

As adults, we all remember what it was like to see kids picked on in the hallways or in the schoolyard. And I have to say, with big ears and the name that I have, I wasn't immune. I didn't emerge unscathed. But because it's something that happens a lot and it's something that's always been around, sometimes we've turned our blind eye to the problem. We've said, "Kids will be kids." And so sometimes, we overlook the real damage that bullying can do, especially when young people face harassment day after day, week after week.

So, consider these statistics: A third of middle school and high school students have reported being bullied during the school year; almost 3 million students have said they were pushed, shoved, tripped, even spit on. It's also more likely to affect kids that are seen as different, whether it's because of the color of their skin, the clothes they wear, the disability they may have, or sexual orientation.

And bullying has been shown to lead to absences and poor performance in the classroom. And that alone should give us pause, since no child should be afraid to go to school in this country.

Today, bullying doesn't even end at the school bell. It can follow our children from the hallways to their cell phones to their computer screens. And in recent months, a series of tragedies has drawn attention to just how devastating bullying can be. We have just been heartbroken by the stories of young people who endured harassment and ridicule day after day at school and who ultimately took their own lives. These were kids brimming with promise—kids like Ty Field, kids like Carl Walker-Hoover—who should have felt nothing but excitement for the future. Instead, they felt like they had nowhere to turn, as if they had no escape from taunting and bullying that made school something they feared. I want to recognize Ty's mom and dad, who are here today, Carl's mother and sister, who are here today. They've shown incredible courage as advocates against bullying in memory of the sons and the brother that they've lost. And so we're so proud of them, and we're grateful to them for being here today.

No family should have to go through what these families have gone through. No child should feel that alone. We've got to make sure our young people know that if they're in trouble, there are caring adults who can help and young adults that can help, that even if they're having a tough time, they're going to get through it, and there's a whole world full of possibility waiting for them. We also have to make sure we're doing everything we can so that no child is in that position in the first place. And this is a responsibility we all share, a responsibility we have to teach all children the Golden Rule: We should treat others the way we want to be treated.

The good news is, people are stepping up and accepting responsibility. They're refusing to turn a blind eye to this problem. The PTA is launching a new campaign to get resources and information into the hands of parents. MTV is leading a new coalition to fight bullying online, and they're launching a series of ads to talk about the damage that's done when kids are bullied for the color of their skin or their religion or being gay or just being who they are. Others are leading their own efforts here today. And across the country, parents and students and teachers at the local level are talking—taking action as well. They're fighting not only to change rules and policies, but also to create a stronger sense of community and respect in their schools.

Joining this conference today is a young man I just had a chance to meet, Brandon Greene from Rhode Island. Brandon's 14 years old. Back in sixth grade, when he was just a kid, he did a class project on bullying. Now, 2 years later, it's a school-wide organization with 80 members. They do monthly surveys in their school to track bullying rates. And what they realized is that stopping bullying isn't just about preventing bad behavior, it's also about working together and creating a positive atmosphere. So Brandon and his fellow committee members are now also doing activities like coat drives and community service at their school. And it's making a real difference. So we're very proud of Brandon and the great work he's doing.

There are stories like this all across the country, where young people and their schools have refused to accept the status quo. And I want you all to know that you have a partner in the White House. As the former head of Chicago's public schools, nobody understands this issue better than my Education Secretary, Arne Duncan. He's going to be working on it, along with our Health Secretary, Kathleen Sebelius. Arne's going to head up our administration's efforts, which began last year with a first-of-its-kind summit on bullying.

And we're also launching a new resource called stopbullying .gov, which has more information for parents and for teachers. And as part of our education reform efforts, we're encouraging schools to ask students themselves about school safety and how we can address bullying and other related problems, because as every parent knows, sometimes the best way to find out what's happening with our kids is to ask, even if you have to—if it's in the case of Sasha, you have to keep on asking.

Now, as adults, we can lose sight of how hard it can be sometimes to be a kid. And it's easy for us to forget what it was like to be teased or bullied. But it's also easy to forget the natural compassion and the sense of decency that our children display each and every day, when they're given a chance.

A couple other young people that I just had a chance to meet, Sarah and Emily Buder, who are here from California, they're right here next to the First Lady. And Sarah and Emily, they read a story about a girl named Olivia in a nearby town—this is a girl they didn't know—who had faced a lot of cruel taunting in school and online because she had had an epileptic seizure in class. So they decided to write Olivia a letter and asked their friends to do the same.

They figured they'd send Olivia about 50 letters. But in the months that followed, thousands and thousands of letters poured in from every corner of the country. It really tapped into something. A lot of the letters were from young people, and they wanted to wish Olivia well and let her know that somebody out there was talking—was thinking about her and let her know that she wasn't alone. And because those children treated Olivia with that small measure of kindness, it helped Olivia see that there was a light at the end of the tunnel.

The fact is, sometimes, kids are going to make mistakes; sometimes, they're going to make bad decisions. That's part of growing up. But it's our job to be there for them, to guide them, and to ensure that they can grow up in an environment that not only encourages their talents and intelligence, but also their sense of empathy and their regard for one another.

And that's what ultimately this conference is all about. And that's why all the issues that we're talking about really matter. And that's how we're going to prevent bullying and create an environment where every single one of our children can thrive.

So thank you for the good work that you're already doing, and I'm sure you're going to come up with some terrific ideas during the course of this conference. Thank you very much.

Source: Obama, B. (2011). Remarks at the White House Conference on Bullying Prevention, March 10, 2011. *Public Papers of the Presidents of the United States, Barack Obama, 2011, Book 1.* Washington, DC: Government Printing Office, 213–216.

New Jersey's Anti-Bullying Policy (2011)

Known as the New Jersey Anti-Bullying Bill of Rights Act, this policy defines bullying, requires reporting and investigation of bullying incidents, and mandates training for identifying and addressing bullying. In 2011 when this policy passed, it was considered the toughest U.S. anti-bullying policy.

BE IT ENACTED by the Senate and General Assembly of the State of New Jersey:

1. Sections 1, 2, and 16 through 30 of this act and P.L.2002, c.83 (C.18A:37-13 et seq.) shall be known and may be cited as the "Anti-Bullying Bill of Rights Act."

2. The Legislature finds and declares that:

    a. A 2009 study by the United States Departments of Justice and Education, "Indicators of School Crime and Safety," reported that 32% of students aged 12 through 18 were bullied in the previous school year. The study reported that 25% of the responding public schools indicated that bullying was a daily or weekly problem;

    b. A 2009 study by the United States Centers for Disease Control and Prevention, "Youth Risk Behavior Surveillance," reported that the percentage of students bullied in New Jersey is 1 percentage point higher than the national median;

    c. In 2010, the chronic persistence of school bullying has led to student suicides across the country, including in New Jersey;

    d. Significant research has emerged since New Jersey enacted its public school antibullying statute in 2002, and since the State amended that law in 2007 to include cyberbullying and in 2008 to require each school district to post its anti-bullying policy on its website and distribute it annually to parents or guardians of students enrolled in the district;

    e. School districts and their students, parents, teachers, principals, other school staff, and board of education members would benefit by the establishment of clearer standards on what constitutes harassment, intimidation, and bullying, and clearer standards on how to prevent, report, investigate, and respond to incidents of harassment, intimidation, and bullying;

f. It is the intent of the Legislature in enacting this legislation to strengthen the standards and procedures for preventing, reporting, investigating, and responding to incidents of harassment, intimidation, and bullying of students that occur in school and off school premises;

g. Fiscal responsibility requires New Jersey to take a smarter, clearer approach to fight school bullying by ensuring that existing resources are better managed and used to make our schools safer for students;

h. In keeping with the aforementioned goal of fiscal responsibility and in an effort to minimize any burden placed on schools and school districts, existing personnel and resources shall be utilized in every possible instance to accomplish the goals of increased prevention, reporting, and responsiveness to incidents of harassment, intimidation, or bullying, including in the appointment of school anti-bullying specialists and district anti-bullying coordinators;

i. By strengthening standards for preventing, reporting, investigating, and responding to incidents of bullying this act will help to reduce the risk of suicide among students and avert not only the needless loss of a young life, but also the tragedy that such loss represents to the student's family and the community at large; and

j. Harassment, intimidation, and bullying is also a problem which occurs on the campuses of institutions of higher education in this State, and by requiring the public institutions to include in their student codes of conduct a specific prohibition against bullying, this act will be a significant step in reducing incidents of such activity.

. . .

C.18A:6-112 Instruction in suicide prevention for public school teaching staff.

2. The State Board of Education, in consultation with the New Jersey Youth Suicide Prevention Advisory Council established in the Department of Children and Families pursuant to P.L.2003, c.214 (C.30:9A-22 et seq.), shall, as part of the professional development requirement established by the State board for public school teaching staff members, require each public school teaching staff member to complete at least two hours of instruction in suicide prevention, to be provided by a licensed health care professional with training and experience in mental health issues, in each professional development period. The instruction in suicide prevention shall include information on the relationship between the risk of suicide and incidents of harassment, intimidation, and bullying and information on reducing the risk of suicide in students who are members of communities identified as having members at high risk of suicide.

. . .

C.18A:17-46 Reporting of certain acts by school employee; report; public hearing.

1. Any school employee observing or having direct knowledge from a participant or victim of an act of violence shall, in accordance with standards established by the commissioner, file a report describing the incident to the school principal in a manner prescribed by the commissioner, and copy of same shall be forwarded to the district superintendent. The principal shall notify the district superintendent of schools of the action taken regarding the incident. Two times each school year, between September 1 and January 1 and between January 1 and June 30, at a public hearing, the superintendent of schools shall report to the board of education all acts of violence, vandalism, and harassment, intimidation, or bullying which occurred during the previous reporting period. The report shall include the number of reports of harassment, intimidation, or bullying, the status of all investigations, the nature of the bullying based on one

of the protected categories identified in section 2 of P.L.2002, c.83 (C.18A:37-14), the names of the investigators, the type and nature of any discipline imposed on any student engaged in harassment, intimidation, or bullying, and any other measures imposed, training conducted, or programs implemented, to reduce harassment, intimidation, or bullying. The information shall also be reported once during each reporting period to the Department of Education. The report must include data broken down by the enumerated categories as listed in section 2 of P.L.2002, c.83 (C.18A:37-14), and data broken down by each school in the district, in addition to district-wide data. It shall be a violation to improperly release any confidential information not authorized by federal or State law for public release. The report shall be used to grade each school for the purpose of assessing its effort to implement policies and programs consistent with the provisions of P.L.2002, c.83.

(C.18A:37-13 et seq.). The district shall receive a grade determined by averaging the grades of all the schools in the district. The commissioner shall promulgate guidelines for a program to grade schools for the purposes of this section. The grade received by a school and the district shall be posted on the homepage of the school's website. The grade for the district and each school of the district shall be posted on the homepage of the district's website. A link to the report shall be available on the district's website. The information shall be posted on the websites within 10 days of the receipt of a grade by the school and district. Verification of the reports on violence, vandalism, and harassment, intimidation, or bullying shall be part of the State's monitoring of the school district, and the State Board of Education shall adopt regulations that impose a penalty on a school employee who knowingly falsifies the report. A board of education shall provide ongoing staff training, in cooperation with the Department of Education, in fulfilling the reporting requirements pursuant to this section. The majority representative of the school employees shall have access monthly to the number and disposition of all reported acts of school violence, vandalism, and harassment, intimidation, or bullying.

C.18A:17-48 Annual report to Legislature.

3. The Commissioner of Education shall each year submit a report to the Education Committees of the Senate and General Assembly detailing the extent of violence, vandalism, and harassment, intimidation, or bullying in the public schools and making recommendations to alleviate the problem. The report shall be made available annually to the public no later than October 1, and shall be posted on the department's website.

. . .

b. A school leader shall complete training on issues of school ethics, school law, and school governance as part of the professional development for school leaders required pursuant to State Board of Education regulations. Information on the prevention of harassment, intimidation, and bullying shall also be included in the training. The training shall be offered through a collaborative training model as identified by the Commissioner of Education, in consultation with the State Advisory Committee on Professional Development for School Leaders.

Conduct which shall constitute good cause for suspension or expulsion of a pupil guilty of such conduct shall include, but not be limited to, any of the following:

    a.   Continued and willful disobedience;

    b.   Open defiance of the authority of any teacher or person, having authority over him;

    c.   Conduct of such character as to constitute a continuing danger to the physical wellbeing of other pupils;

 d. Physical assault upon another pupil;

 e. Taking, or attempting to take, personal property or money from another pupil, or from his presence, by means of force or fear;

 f. Willfully causing, or attempting to cause, substantial damage to school property;

 g. Participation in an unauthorized occupancy by any group of pupils or others of any part of any school or other building owned by any school district, and failure to leave such school or other facility promptly after having been directed to do so by the principal or other person then in charge of such building or facility;

 h. Incitement which is intended to and does result in unauthorized occupation by any group of pupils or others of any part of a school or other facility owned by any school district;

 i. Incitement which is intended to and does result in truancy by other pupils;

 j. Knowing possession or knowing consumption without legal authority of alcoholic beverages or controlled dangerous substances on school premises, or being under the influence of intoxicating liquor or controlled dangerous substances while on school premises; and

 k. Harassment, intimidation, or bullying.

2. As used in this act:
"Electronic communication" means a communication transmitted by means of an electronic device, including, but not limited to, a telephone, cellular phone, computer, or pager;

"Harassment, intimidation or bullying" means any gesture, any written, verbal or physical act, or any electronic communication, whether it be a single incident or a series of incidents, that is reasonably perceived as being motivated either by any actual or perceived characteristic, such as race, color, religion, ancestry, national origin, gender, sexual orientation, gender identity and expression, or a mental, physical or sensory disability, or by any other distinguishing characteristic, that takes place on school property, at any school-sponsored function, on a school bus, or off school grounds as provided for in section 16 of P.L.2010, c.122 (C.18A:37-15.3), that substantially disrupts or interferes with the orderly operation of the school or the rights of other students and that:

a. a reasonable person should know, under the circumstances, will have the effect of physically or emotionally harming a student or damaging the student's property, or placing a student in reasonable fear of physical or emotional harm to his person or damage to his property;

b. has the effect of insulting or demeaning any student or group of students; or

c. creates a hostile educational environment for the student by interfering with a student's education or by severely or pervasively causing physical or emotional harm to the student.

. . .

3. a. Each school district shall adopt a policy prohibiting harassment, intimidation or bullying on school property, at a school-sponsored function or on a school bus. The school district shall adopt the policy through a process that includes representation of parents or guardians, school employees, volunteers, students, administrators, and community representatives.

b. A school district shall have local control over the content of the policy, except that the policy shall contain, at a minimum, the following components:

(1) a statement prohibiting harassment, intimidation or bullying of a student;

(2) a definition of harassment, intimidation or bullying no less inclusive than that set forth in section 2 of P.L.2002, c.83 (C.18A:37-14);

(3) a description of the type of behavior expected from each student;

(4) consequences and appropriate remedial action for a person who commits an act of harassment, intimidation or bullying;

(5) a procedure for reporting an act of harassment, intimidation or bullying, including a provision that permits a person to report an act of harassment, intimidation or bullying anonymously; however, this shall not be construed to permit formal disciplinary action solely on the basis of an anonymous report.

All acts of harassment, intimidation, or bullying shall be reported verbally to the school principal on the same day when the school employee or contracted service provider witnessed or received reliable information regarding any such incident. The principal shall inform the parents or guardians of all students involved in the alleged incident, and may discuss, as appropriate, the availability of counseling and other intervention services. All acts of harassment, intimidation, or bullying shall be reported in writing to the school principal within two school days of when the school employee or contracted service provider witnessed or received reliable information that a student had been subject to harassment, intimidation, or bullying;

(6) a procedure for prompt investigation of reports of violations and complaints, which procedure shall at a minimum provide that:

(a) the investigation shall be initiated by the principal or the principal's designee within one school day of the report of the incident and shall be conducted by a school anti-bullying specialist. The principal may appoint additional personnel who are not school anti-bullying specialists to assist in the investigation. The investigation shall be completed as soon as possible, but not later than 10 school days from the date of the written report of the incident of harassment, intimidation, or bullying. In the event that there is information relative to the investigation that is anticipated but not yet received by the end of the 10-day period, the school anti-bullying specialist may amend the original report of the results of the investigation to reflect the information;

(b) the results of the investigation shall be reported to the superintendent of schools within two school days of the completion of the investigation, and in accordance with regulations promulgated by the State Board of Education pursuant to the "Administrative Procedure Act," P.L.1968, c.410 (C.52:14B-1 et seq.), the superintendent may decide to provide intervention services, establish training programs to reduce harassment, intimidation, or bullying and enhance school climate, impose discipline, order counseling as a result of the findings of the investigation, or take or recommend other appropriate action;

(c) the results of each investigation shall be reported to the board of education no later than the date of the board of education meeting next following the completion of the investigation, along with information on any services provided, training established, discipline imposed, or other action taken or recommended by the superintendent;

(d) parents or guardians of the students who are parties to the investigation shall be entitled to receive information about the investigation, in accordance with federal and State law and regulation, including the nature of the investigation, whether the district found evidence of harassment, intimidation, or bullying, or whether discipline was imposed or services provided to address the incident of harassment, intimidation, or bullying. This information shall be provided in writing within 5 school days after the results of the investigation are reported to the board. A parent or guardian may request a hearing before the board after receiving the information, and the hearing shall be held within 10 days of the request. The board shall meet in executive session for the hearing to protect the confidentiality of the students. At the hearing the board may hear from the school antibullying specialist about the incident, recommendations for discipline or services, and any programs instituted to reduce such incidents;

(e) at the next board of education meeting following its receipt of the report, the board shall issue a decision, in writing, to affirm, reject, or modify the superintendent's decision. The board's decision may be appealed to the Commissioner of Education, in accordance with the procedures set forth in law and regulation, no later than 90 days after the issuance of the board's decision; and

(f) a parent, student, guardian, or organization may file a complaint with the Division on Civil Rights within 180 days of the occurrence of any incident of harassment, intimidation, or bullying based on membership in a protected group as enumerated in the "Law Against Discrimination," P.L.1945, c.169 (C.10:5-1 et seq.);

(7) the range of ways in which a school will respond once an incident of harassment, intimidation or bullying is identified, which shall be defined by the principal in conjunction with the school anti-bullying specialist, but shall include an appropriate combination of counseling, support services, intervention services, and other programs, as defined by the commissioner;

(8) a statement that prohibits reprisal or retaliation against any person who reports an act of harassment, intimidation or

bullying and the consequence and appropriate remedial action for a person who engages in reprisal or retaliation;

(9) consequences and appropriate remedial action for a person found to have falsely accused another as a means of retaliation or as a means of harassment, intimidation or bullying;

(10) a statement of how the policy is to be publicized, including notice that the policy applies to participation in school-sponsored functions;

(11) a requirement that a link to the policy be prominently posted on the home page of the school district's website and distributed annually to parents and guardians who have children enrolled in a school in the school district; and

(12) a requirement that the name, school phone number, school address and school email address of the district anti-bullying coordinator be listed on the home page of the school district's website and that on the home page of each school's website the name, school phone number, school address and school email address of the school anti-bullying specialist and the district anti-bullying coordinator be listed. The information concerning the district antibullying coordinator and the school anti-bullying specialists shall also be maintained on the department's website.

Source: New Jersey Anti-Bullying Bill of Rights Act, P.L. 2010, Chapter 122 (2011).

Bullying-Free Schools: How Local, State, and Federal Efforts Can Help (2012)

This hearing, held by the Senate's Committee on Health, Education, Labor, and Pensions, chaired by Senator Tom Harking (D-Iowa), discusses strategies and issues related to bullying in schools.

Senator Harkin:

All children deserve equitable access to quality public schools where they can learn and thrive. Yet, every day countless students are denied this opportunity because they don't feel safe.

While the rate of serious violent crime among youth has actually gone down a little bit, there's another statistic that's going up, and that's the percentage of young people who have been bullied at school.

Approximately 20 percent of kids from all walks of life experience bullying. It is alarming that 85 percent of students with disabilities have been bullied. Even higher than that, 94 percent of students with Asperger's syndrome have been bullied. Lesbian, bisexual, gay and transgender youth are also at heightened risk. According to data released just yesterday by the Human Rights Campaign, LGBT youth are more than two times more likely to be verbally harassed and called names at school, physically assaulted, kicked or shoved, or excluded by their peers because they are "different."

The top concerns of non-LGBT students in school, when they're polled, are grades, college, and career. LGBT students, when they're polled, say they're most concerned about their non-accepting families and bullying at school.

Being the victim of bullying has adverse effects on mental health, concentration, and, of course, academic outcomes. And as Iowans, we have been reminded recently that bullying can lead to suicide in some cases. Our hearts go out to the family of Ken Weishuhn of Primghar who took his own life earlier this spring after coming out as gay and being bullied for it.

It's also tragic that many students are unable to access their education because bullying makes it unbearable for them to go to school. I've heard from all too many young people who were compelled to drop out of school because of the hostile climate and lack of protections at schools. We will hear from one such student today who is very brave to come forward and talk about her experiences.

Some were able to complete their education only through GED classes because they were denied the high school experiences that their peers were able to enjoy.

We all need to be a part of the solution. We need to teach children to respect differences. As adults, we have to set the examples by modeling civility and empathy for others. Research shows that efforts to foster positive conditions for learning result in higher academic outcomes for students.

The wrong approach and, quite frankly, the irresponsible approach is to just brush it off by saying it's a rite of passage or it's just kids being kids.

Russlynn Ali, Assistant Secretary for Civil Rights, Department of Education:

I, too, have been heartbroken to learn about what far too many students experience in our schools: suicides, torture, mental confinement that leads to depression and sadness and, particularly for our purposes, the inability to learn. If students do not feel safe, they simply cannot learn.

I had the honor of meeting very early on in the administration with the mother of a young suicide victim, Carl Walker-Hoover. I met Ms. Walker-Hoover on what would have been the week of her son's 11th birthday. He was bullied and harassed to the point where he believed he needed to take his own life to escape from it. And I will never forget that day in the very early spring in March 2009, as we were leaving, and Ms. Walker said to me, "He didn't even know he was gay. He was bullied because he was gay, so they thought, but he didn't even know he was gay." He was 10 years old. He might not know whether he was gay.

And it dawned on me then, and until now, those young students, in far too many instances, actually aren't bullied because of their sexual orientation. They're bullied because of the perception that they are not acting like a boy enough, or they are not acting feminine enough if they are females.

When we as a society tolerate a culture in which children bully and harass each other, we fail to live up to the principles of fairness and equality upon which our schools and our country were founded. It is particularly true when bullying is based on personal characteristics such as race, sex, sexual orientation, gender identity, religion or disability.

We are working on this issue in a number of ways, and have been for the last 3 years in particular. I know you are familiar, as are many in the audience I'm sure, with the White House Conference on Bullying Prevention. We are actually having our third annual summit coming soon where we are bringing together, from across the country, educators and students and community groups to learn more about this issue and to help prevent it going forward.

The President has explained that bullying is not something we have to accept. As parents, as teachers, as students, as members of the community, he said we can, all of us, take steps. Everyone needs to feel like they exist in a climate in which they belong.

The way we are doing this in the Department is—I'd like to talk about three things in particular. One, ensuring resources and support in training and technical assistance for educators in order to help them both understand the issue and how to eradicate a culture in their schools that might give rise to bullying and harassment, to help the courageous leaders like Paul Gausman, who I know we will hear from later today.

Now, of course, there is no universal one-size-fits-all approach to fixing this. We recognize the pervasiveness of the problem. The data you cited is illustrative. We have also seen recent data that shows that over 3 million students have also been physically assaulted behind bullying and harassment. It is not, in other words, just teasing.

We are stressing this first through ensuring that those with the greatest responsibility and that are in the position to best help change at the local level, local educators and local community members, have some support. We have distributed funds through the Safe and Supportive School grants to 11 States. That fund in Iowa has been put to some extraordinarily good use, and I know we will hear from Penny later on today, who will give us details.

We are also moving forward on technical assistance, ensuring that everyone everywhere can come to us, ask us how to help, that there's a place to go for best practices on how to stop what's happening in our Nation's schools. We have launched a Web site. You can visit that at stopbullying.gov. We have also produced a resource document analyzing all of the bullying laws across the country and gleaning best practices from States that are doing amazing things.

We still have a long way to go. There are, fortunately, 49 States today that have some kind of bullying law on the books, but no one, no two share the same definition. We do not have a common definition yet for what bullying is, certainly not at the Federal level.

It is also, though, about vigorously enforcing the Nation's civil rights laws where they apply, protections based on race, ethnicity, color, sex discrimination and disability discrimination. We have seen, though, that we don't have jurisdiction over sexual orientation, that the civil rights laws can help for precisely what I talked with you about a few minutes ago and what I learned from Ms. Hoover-Walker.

Those young children, if they are not bullied because of their sexual orientation but because of gender stereotyping, then the civil rights laws can help. It was the first time the Department of Education ever addressed this issue under title 9 in this way.

We have launched a number of proactive investigations. We have received nearly 2,000 complaints just in the last 2 years alleging harassment across all the statutes in our jurisdiction. That is more than ever before and, in fact, was a 34 percent increase just from last year alone. As we track the data this year, it looks like by the end of this fiscal year we will receive even more.

We have launched proactive investigations to ensure that we find out the systemic discrimination where it is happening, not waiting for citizens to file complaints with our office. And we are also, due in no small part to your support and leadership, finally able to collect data across our Nation's schools about incidents of bullying and harassment across the statutes in our jurisdiction and those students that were disciplined for it. This was the first year we collected the data. Next year we will have data across all schools in the country.

Despite the fact that schools are still struggling with how to even report these data or collecting it internally, we've seen about 85 percent of the Nation's school children represented in our survey and over 100,000 incidences of students subjected to harassment, over 160,000 instances of students disciplined for some kind of harassment.

These are but some ways to help. We have a lot more to do. In working with you and with communities across the country, we hope to see some real progress.

Emily Domayer, Student, Morningside College, Sioux City, IA:
The boy pointed at people and said, "Dumb, dumber, and dumbest." When he said "dumbest," he pointed at me.

I was 7 years old the first time I was bullied. I was so shocked and stunned that I didn't know how to react or what to do. All I really knew was that what he had said was wrong and that his words stung like vinegar on a cut.

It was in second grade that I first realized I was different. I felt like I was in and from a different world from my classmates. Sometimes they would talk about me as if I wasn't there, condescendingly explaining my behavior to each other, saying "she always does that."

It was the kids who were in the popular crowd who picked on me the most. They were a small group of girls and boys, kids who seemed to be well-liked by the teachers. Later, I looked back at these early experiences and knew that I was so confused about everything, who I was, why I behaved the way I did, why I didn't understand how to make friends. I was perceived by others to be the shy kid. I was not diagnosed with Asperger's syndrome, an autism spectrum disorder, until I was 12, which is a very late diagnosis.

I wanted to tell my parents that I was getting bullied but I did not know how to explain what was happening. Thankfully, when I was in third grade, the bullies were in the other class. We had two classrooms for each grade. Unfortunately, the bullying got worse when I was in fourth grade. A new girl moved into my neighborhood—I'll call her Girl A—and she behaved well in front of my parents and other adults. But when their backs were turned, she had the personality of a vicious junkyard dog. It took me many years to realize that she chose me because I was vulnerable. I didn't have any friends, and it was difficult for me to make friends. The rules of friendship were completely foreign to me.

One time, she and another student picked on me when the teacher was out of the room. They called me Queen of the Dorks and put an imaginary crown on my head. I was very hurt by their actions.

Our teacher once said, after discovering that some of the students were arguing, that we should all get along because we were all friends. I knew even then that wasn't going to fix anything.

In second, fourth and fifth grade, my peers verbally abused me almost every day about the clothes I wore. I didn't dress like they did. I didn't wear the latest cool clothes. I was not a cool kid. I didn't pay attention to celebrities in the news or watch the same TV shows the other kids watched.

In my childhood, I just wanted to be a happy kid who felt free to be myself. I wanted to be a kid, but my classmates were not OK with that. They knew I wasn't cool, and they used every opportunity they could find to make me feel like I would never be good enough to be their friend.

They were relentless. They made fun of the speech I wrote at the end of the year for the anti-drug program DARE. My Halloween costume wasn't cool. When I gave a presentation in Social Studies, they laughed at me and asked me questions in a mocking tone of voice. I always hated PE because I wasn't very coordinated and my peers were impatient and unkind toward me. I always felt like I was never good enough.

The only reason I ever felt comfortable going to school when I was being bullied was that I got along very well with my teachers. In fifth grade, my teacher gave me a hug every day after school was over. I needed it.

Fifth grade was the worst of all. There was another girl, Girl B, who chose me as her target. The whole school year, she seemed to enjoy treating me like garbage. She pulled my hair, kicked me in line, and made fun of my clothes whenever she could. One time my mom came to school, and after she left, Girl B made fun of my mom wearing a scarf on her head. It was winter time. I was furious, but because I didn't know how to handle the situation, I kept my rage inside.

Recess is hell for most students on the autism spectrum because it is about socialization, an area people on the spectrum struggle with most often. I usually spent most of my time during recess talking with either the recess monitor, who was also one of the lunch ladies, or one of my few friends. I felt comfortable talking with the monitor because she was nice to me, unlike my peers.

One day on the playground I was standing around just talking with someone when Girl B suddenly came up to me and told me to come with her. I told her I didn't want to. She started to ask me why, and she wouldn't stop it. After not being satisfied with my answers, she grabbed me by the arm and gave it a snake bite, twisting my arm very hard with both her hands and causing severe pain. I found a teacher, and she sent Girl B to the principal's office. After my mom learned about the incident, she came to school to speak to the principal, who said that Girl B was having issues at home. Not much else was done.

I am particularly concerned about students who are unable to communicate that they are being bullied. Before I was able to advocate for my disability, I had no idea how to let the adults around me know that I was being bullied. How can students with autism who have little or no verbal abilities inform responsible adults if they are being bullied?

I wished that my elementary school teachers and administrators had done more to address bullying. I felt so alone. It doesn't matter who you are, what you look like, how you dress, what faith you believe, how you learn, whatever, no one should have to feel afraid to go to school. Bullying is not a rite of passage.

It is so heartbreaking to me to think of young children and teens who have committed suicide because they were bullied so much they felt the only solution was to end their lives. Every student has the right to have a safe learning environment. School should be a place where students feel comfortable to be themselves. A school's No. 1 priority above all else should be safety. When students don't feel safe, how can they learn?

Bullying will become less prevalent when teachers, school administrators and parents are honest and open about what behavior is tolerated and what is not. Bullying will go away when schools, parents and students work together so that kids understand that bullying will not be tolerated.

Source: Field Hearing of the Committee on Health, Education, Labor, and Pensions. (2104). Examining solutions to create bullying-free schools, focusing on how local, state, and federal efforts can help. U.S. Senate, 112th Congress, 2nd Session, June 8, 2012. Senate Hearing 112-913. Washington, DC: Government Printing Office.

Bullying of Students with Disabilities (2014)

In this part of a "Dear Colleague" letter, the U.S. Department of Education issued guidance on disability discrimination, including bullying.

II. Schools' Obligations to Address Disability-Based Harassment

Bullying of a student on the basis of his or her disability may result in a disability-based harassment violation under Section 504 and Title II. As explained in OCR's 2010 Dear

Colleague Letter on Harassment and Bullying, when a school knows or should know of bullying conduct based on a student's disability, it must take immediate and appropriate action to investigate or otherwise determine what occurred. If a school's investigation reveals that bullying based on disability created a hostile environment—i.e., the conduct was sufficiently serious to interfere with or limit a student's ability to participate in or benefit from the services, activities, or opportunities offered by a school—the school must take prompt and effective steps reasonably calculated to end the bullying, eliminate the hostile environment, prevent it from recurring, and, as appropriate, remedy its effects. Therefore, OCR would find a disability-based harassment violation under Section 504 and Title II when: (1) a student is bullied based on a disability; (2) the bullying is sufficiently serious to create a hostile environment; (3) school officials know or should know about the bullying; and (4) the school does not respond appropriately.

As explained in Section III, below, for the student with a disability who is receiving IDEA FAPE services or Section 504 FAPE services, a school's investigation should include determining whether that student's receipt of appropriate services may have been affected by the bullying. If the school's investigation reveals that the bullying created a hostile environment and there is reason to believe that the student's IDEA FAPE services or Section 504 FAPE services may have been affected by the bullying, the school has an obligation to remedy those effects on the student's receipt of FAPE. Even if the school finds that the bullying did not create a hostile environment, the school would still have an obligation to address any FAPE-related concerns, if, for example, the school's initial investigation revealed that the bullying may have had some impact on the student's receipt of FAPE services.

III. Bullying and the Denial of a Free Appropriate Public Education

The bullying on any basis of a student with a disability who is receiving IDEA FAPE services or Section 504 FAPE services can result in the denial of FAPE that must be remedied under Section 504. The OSERS 2013 Dear Colleague Letter clarified that, under IDEA, as part of a school's appropriate response to bullying on any basis, the school should convene the IEP team to determine whether, as a result of the effects of the bullying, the student's needs have changed such that the IEP is no longer designed to provide a meaningful educational benefit. If the IEP is no longer designed to provide a meaningful educational benefit to the student, the IEP team must determine the extent to which additional or different IDEA FAPE services are needed to address the student's individualized needs and then revise the IEP accordingly. Any decisions made by the IEP team must be consistent with the IDEA provisions addressing parental participation and should keep the student with a disability in the original placement or setting (e.g., the same school and classroom) unless the student can no longer receive FAPE in that placement or setting. Under IDEA, schools have an ongoing obligation to ensure that a student with a disability who is the target of bullying continues to receive FAPE in accordance with his or her IEP—an obligation that exists whether the student is being bullied based on his or her disability or is being bullied based on other reasons.

Similarly, under Section 504, schools have an ongoing obligation to ensure that a qualified student with a disability who receives IDEA FAPE services or Section 504 FAPE services and who is the target of bullying continues to receive FAPE—an obligation that exists regardless of why the student is being bullied. Accordingly, under Section 504, as part of a school's appropriate response to bullying on *any* basis, the school should convene the IEP team or the Section 504 team to determine whether, as a result of the effects of the bullying, the student's needs have changed such that the student is no longer receiving FAPE. The effects of bullying could include, for example, adverse changes in the student's academic performance or behavior. If the school suspects the student's needs have changed, the IEP team or the Section 504 team must determine the extent to which additional or different services are needed, ensure that any needed changes are made promptly, and safeguard against putting the onus on the student with the disability to avoid or handle the bullying. In addition, when considering a change of placement, schools must continue to ensure that Section 504 FAPE services are provided in an educational setting with persons who do not have disabilities to the maximum extent appropriate to the needs of the student with a disability.

Although there are no hard and fast rules regarding how much of a change in academic performance or behavior is necessary to trigger the school's obligation to convene the IEP team or Section 504 team, a sudden decline in grades, the onset of emotional outbursts, an increase in the frequency or intensity of behavioral interruptions, or a rise in missed classes or sessions of Section 504 services would generally be sufficient. By contrast, one low grade for an otherwise straight-A student who shows no other changes in academic progress or behavior will generally not, standing alone, trigger the school's obligation to determine whether the student's needs are still being met. Nonetheless, in addition to addressing the bullying under the school's anti-bullying policies, schools should promptly convene the IEP team or Section 504 team to determine whether FAPE is being provided to a student with a disability who has been bullied and who is experiencing any adverse changes in academic performance or behavior.

When bullying results in a disability-based harassment violation, it will not always result in a denial of FAPE. Although all students with disabilities are protected from disability-based harassment, the requirement to provide FAPE applies only to those students with disabilities who need or may need FAPE services because of their disability. This means that if a student is the target of bullying resulting in a disability-based harassment violation, but that student is not eligible to receive IDEA or Section 504 FAPE services, there could be no FAPE violation.

When a student who receives IDEA FAPE services or Section 504 FAPE services has experienced bullying resulting in a disability-based harassment violation, however, there is a strong likelihood that the student was denied FAPE. This is because when bullying is sufficiently serious to create a hostile environment and the school fails to respond appropriately, there is a strong likelihood both that the effects of the bullying included an impact on the student's receipt of FAPE and that the school's failure to remedy the effects of the bullying included its failure to address these FAPE-related concerns.

Ultimately, unless it is clear from the school's investigation into the bullying conduct that there was no effect on the student with a disability's receipt of FAPE, the school should, as a best practice, promptly convene the IEP team or the Section 504 team to determine whether, and to what extent: (1) the student's educational needs have changed; (2) the bullying impacted the student's receipt of IDEA FAPE services or Section 504 FAPE services; and (3) additional or different services, if any, are needed, and to ensure any needed changes are made promptly. By doing so, the school will be in the best position to ensure the student's ongoing receipt of FAPE.

Source: U.S. Department of Education. (2014, October 21). *Guidance on bullying of students with disabilities.* Retrieved from https://www2.ed.gov/about/offices/list/ocr/frontpage/pro -students/issues/dis-issue08.html

Safe Schools Improvement Act (2017)

In 2017, this bill was introduced into the U.S. House by Representative Linda Sanchez (D-California), with the purpose of taking action to prevent bullying and harassment of students. It did not come up for a vote.

SEC. 2. FINDINGS.

Congress finds the following:

(1) Bullying and harassment foster a climate of fear and disrespect that can seriously impair the physical and

psychological health of its victims and create conditions that negatively affect learning, thereby undermining the ability of students to achieve their full potential.

(2) Bullying and harassment contribute to high dropout rates, increased absenteeism, and academic underachievement.

(3) Bullying and harassment include a range of behaviors that negatively impact a student's ability to learn and participate in educational opportunities and activities that schools offer. Such behaviors can include hitting or punching, name-calling, intimidation through gestures or social exclusion, and sending insulting or offensive messages through electronic communications, such as Internet sites, e-mail, instant messaging, mobile phones and messaging, telephone, or any other means.

(4) Schools with enumerated anti-bullying and harassment policies have an increased level of reporting and teacher intervention in incidents of bullying and harassment, thereby reducing the overall frequency and number of such incidents.

(5) Students have been particularly singled out for bullying and harassment on the basis of their actual or perceived race, color, national origin, sex, disability status, sexual orientation, gender identity, or religion, among other categories.

(6) Some young people experience a form of bullying called relational aggression or psychological bullying, which harms individuals by damaging, threatening, or manipulating their relationships with their peers, or by injuring their feelings of social acceptance.

(7) Interventions to address bullying and harassment conduct to create a positive and safe school climate, combined with evidence-based discipline policies and practices, such as Positive Behavior Interventions and Supports (PBIS) and restorative practices, can minimize suspensions, expulsions, and other exclusionary discipline policies to ensure

that students are not "pushed-out" or diverted to the juvenile justice system.

(8) According to one poll, 85 percent of Americans strongly support or somewhat support a Federal law to require schools to enforce specific rules to prevent bullying.

(9) Students, parents, educators, and policymakers have come together to call for leadership and action to address the national crisis of bullying and harassment.

SEC. 4701. PURPOSE.

The purpose of this part is to address the problem of bullying and harassment conduct of students in public elementary schools and secondary schools.

SEC. 4702. ANTI-BULLYING POLICIES.

(a) Bullying.—In this part, the term 'bullying' includes cyberbullying through electronic communications.

(b) Policies.—A State that receives a grant under this title shall require all local educational agencies in the State to carry out the following:

(1) Establish policies that prevent and prohibit conduct, including bullying and harassment, that is sufficiently severe, persistent, or pervasive—

(A) to limit a student's ability to participate in, or benefit from, a program or activity of a public school or local educational agency; or

(B) to create a hostile or abusive educational environment, adversely affecting a student's education, at a program or activity of a public school or local educational agency, including acts of verbal, nonverbal, or physical aggression or intimidation.

(2) The policies required under paragraph (1) shall include a prohibition of bullying or harassment conduct based on—

(A) a student's actual or perceived race, color, national origin, sex, disability, sexual orientation, gender identity, or religion;

(B) the actual or perceived race, color, national origin, sex, disability, sexual orientation, gender identity, or religion of a person with whom a student associates or has associated; or

(C) any other distinguishing characteristics that may be defined by the State or local educational agency, including being homeless or the child or ward of a member of the Armed Forces.

(3) Provide—

(A) annual notice to students, parents, and educational professionals describing the full range of prohibited conduct contained in such local educational agency's discipline policies; and

(B) grievance procedures for students or parents to register complaints regarding the prohibited conduct contained in such local educational agency's discipline policies, including—

(i) the name of the local educational agency officials who are designated as responsible for receiving such complaints; and

(ii) timelines that the local educational agency will establish in the resolution of such complaints.

(4) Collect annual incidence and frequency of incidents data about the conduct prohibited by the policies described in paragraph (1) at the school building level that are accurate and complete and publicly report such data at the school level and local educational agency

level. The local educational agency shall ensure that victims or persons responsible for such conduct are not identifiable.

(5) Encourage positive and preventative approaches to school discipline that minimize students' removal from instruction and ensure that students, including students described in paragraph (2), are not subject to disproportionate punishment.

SEC. 4703. STATE REPORTS.

The chief executive officer of a State that receives a grant under this title, in cooperation with the State educational agency, shall submit a biennial report to the Secretary—

(1) on the information reported by local educational agencies in the State pursuant to section 4702(b)(4); and

(2) describing the State's plans for supporting local educational agency efforts to address the conduct prohibited by the policies described in section 4702(b)(1).

SEC. 4704. EVALUATION.

(a) Biennial Evaluation.—The Secretary shall conduct an independent biennial evaluation of programs and policies to combat bullying and harassment in elementary schools and secondary schools, including implementation of the requirements described in section 4702, including whether such requirements have appreciably reduced the level of the prohibited conduct and have conducted effective parent involvement and training programs.

(b) Data Collection.—The Commissioner for Education Statistics shall collect data from States, that are subject to independent review, to determine the incidence and frequency of conduct prohibited by the policies described in section 4702.

(c) Biennial Report.—Not later than January 1, 2019, and every 2 years thereafter, the Secretary shall submit to the President and Congress a report on the findings of the evaluation conducted under subsection (a) together with the data collected under subsection (b) and data submitted by the States under section 4703.

Source: H.R. 1957 (IH). (2107, April 5). 115th Congress, 1st Session.

Introduction

Information on these peer-reviewed journal articles, popular writings, books, films, and organizations is provided to help launch school-bullying research.

Peer-Reviewed Journal Articles

Bai, S., & Repetti, R. L. (2015, February). Short-term resilience processes in the family. *Family Relations, 64*(1), 108–119.
   Family interactions that are warm and supportive help children bounce back more easily from high-stress experiences.

Baldry, A. C., & Farrington, D. P. (2005, September). Protective factors as moderators of risk factors in adolescence bullying. *Social Psychology of Education, 8*(3), 263–284.
   When parents are extremely punitive, children tend to be more involved in bullying incidents as aggressors or victims. Supportive parents can protect children from being involved in bullying.

A young person promotes an anti-bullying book, organization, and national movement. When students organize they can make powerful and important changes to prevent and stop bullying. (AP Photo/Diane Bondareff/ Invision for Monster High)

Bastiaensens, S., Pabian, S., Vandebosch, H., Poels, K., Van Cleemput, K., & DeSmet, A. (2015, June). From normative influence to social pressure: How relevant others affect whether bystanders join in cyberbullying. *Social Development, 25*(1), 1–19.

　　Analyzes the factors that might cause witnesses to experience social pressure to join in cyberbullying.

Beale, A. V., & Scott, P. C. (2001, April). "Bullybusters": Using drama to empower students to take a stand against bullying behavior. *Professional School Counseling, 4*(4), 300–305.

　　Discusses the use of psychoeducational drama to empower students to take a stand against bullying.

Borowsky, I. W., Taliaferro, L. A., & McMorris, B. J. (2013, July). Suicidal thinking and behavior among youth involved in verbal and social bullying: Risk and protective factors. *Supplement, 53*(1), S4–12.

　　Identifies risks associated with verbal and social bullying, including suicide.

Bradshaw, C. P., Sawyer, A. L., & O'Brennan, L. M. (2007, September). Bullying and peer victimization at school: Perceptual differences between students and school staff. *School Psychology Review, 36*(3), 361–382.

　　Examines the differences between student and staff perceptions of frequency of bullying, social norms related to bullying, and responses to witnessing bullying. Results indicate that school staff often underestimate how often students are involved in bullying.

Brubacher, M. R., Fondacaro, M. R., Brank, E. M., Brown, V. E., & Miller, S. A. (2009, August). Procedural justice in resolving family disputes: Implications for childhood bullying. *Psychology, Public Policy, and Law, 15*(3), 149–167.

When youth perceive that familial disputes are handled fairly, they are less likely to bully others.

Carnagey, N. L., Anderson, C. A., & Bushman, B. J. (2007, May). The effect of video game violence on physiological desensitization to real-life violence. *Journal of Experimental Social Psychology, 43*(3), 489–496.
>Playing violent video games can cause less sensitivity to real-life violence.

Citron, D. K. (2009, December). Law's expressive value in combating cyber gender harassment. *Michigan Law Review, 108*(3), 373–415.
>Online harassment of females tends to be overlooked or trivialized. This harassment may impede women from being online and sometimes drives them offline. Law enforcement often marginalizes female experiences by considering the harassment harmless teasing. The authors make legal recommendations and suggestions for changing online behavior norms.

Coburn, P. I., Connolly, D. A., & Roesch, R. (2015, October). Cyberbullying: Is federal criminal legislation the solution? *Canadian Journal of Criminology & Criminal Justice, 57*(4), 566–579.
>Suggests that a proposed Canadian federal law would send too many youths through the criminal justice system. The authors recommend that schools teach conflict resolution models and encourage youths to report cyberabuses.

Darden, E. C. (2015). ED Law: Courts join crackdown on school bullies. *Phi Delta Kappan, 96*(7), 76–77.
>Schools and districts are getting tough on bullying, including cyberbullying. The fight against bullying is being waged in the courts.

Demaray, M. K., & Malecki, C. K. (2006). A review of the use of social support in anti-bullying programs. *Journal of School Violence, 5*(3), 51–70.

    Analyzes the role of social support in six anti-bullying programs.

Duong, M. T., Schwartz, D., Chang, L., Kelly, B. M., & Tom, S. R. (2009, October). Association between maternal physical discipline and peer victimization among Hong Kong Chinese children: The moderating role of child aggression. *Journal of Abnormal Child Psychology, 37*(7), 957–966.

    Discusses the role of maternal physical discipline and its impact on peer victimization in Hong Kong Chinese children.

Einarsen, S. (1999). The nature and causes of bullying at work. *International Journal of Manpower, 20*(1/2), 16–27.

    Analyzes the role of bullying at work and explores differences between dispute-related and predatory bullying.

Espelage, D. L., Bosworth, K., & Simon T. R. (2000). Examining the social context of bullying behaviors in early adolesence. *Journal of Counseling and Development, 78*(3), 326–333.

    Parental physical discipline, time without adult supervision, negative peer influences, and safety concerns in the neighborhood predict bullying. Positive role models help to decrease these behaviors. The authors suggest that school counselors focus on these issues to prevent bullying.

Evans, C., & Smokowski, P. (2016, August). Theoretical explanations for bullying in school: How ecological processes propagate perpetration and victimization. *Child & Adolescent Social Work Journal, 33*(4), 365–375.

Uses theoretical paradigms to understand bullying, especially the desire to acquire social capital and dominate others. Lack of social capital tends to keep bullied students in the victim role and prevents them from gaining social status. The humiliation can cause anger and depression lasting into adulthood.

Fraser, A. M., Padilla-Walker, L. M., Coyne, S. M., Nelson, L. J., & Stockdale, L. A. (2012, May). Associations between violent video gaming, empathic concern, and prosocial behavior toward strangers, friends, and family members. *Journal of Youth and Adolescence, 41*(5), 636–649.
    Exposure to media violence, including violent video games, predicts lower empathetic concern for victims and lower socially positive behavior. Such exposure and lack of empathy also has implications for emerging adulthood.

Garby, L. (2013, Summer). Direct bullying: Criminal act or mimicking what has been learned? *Education, 4*(3), 448–450.
    Examining the push for legislation to put bullies behind bars, the authors explore the extent to which bullies belong in jail or are mimicking behaviors they learn in school that they can also unlearn.

Gini, G., Albiero, P., Benelli, B., & Altoe, G. (2007, April 5). Does empathy predict adolescents' bullying and defending behavior? *Aggressive Behavior, 33*(5), 467–476.
    Low levels of empathy are associated with students' involvement in bullying others. In contrast, empathy is positively associated with helping victimized schoolmates.

Goldweber, A., Waasdorp, T. E., & Bradshaw, C. P. (2013, February). Examining associations between race, urbanicity, and patterns of bullying involvement. *Journal of Youth and Adolescence, 42*(2), 206–219.

Being African American increases the chances of being bullied. Urbanicity is an important consideration for creating culturally sensitive bullying-prevention programs.

Gómez-Ortiz, O., Romera, M., & Ortega-Ruiz, R. (2016, January). Parenting styles and bullying: The mediating role of parental psychological aggression and physical punishment. *Child Abuse & Neglect, 51*, 132–143.
Children disciplined via punishment are at greater risk for bullying and being bullied.

Greene, M. B. (2006). Bullying in schools: A plea for measure of human rights. *Journal of Social Issues, 62*(1), 63–79.
Infusing a human rights framework into bullying prevention efforts can overcome common obstacles to effectively implementing anti-bullying programs.

Harel-Fisch, Y., Walsh, S. D., Fogel-Grinvald, H., Dostaler, S., Hetland, J., Simons-Morton, B., & Pickett, W. (2009, September). A cross-national profile of bullying and victimization among adolescents in 40 countries. *International Journal of Public Health, 54*(2), 216–224.
A cross-national analysis of bullying across forty European and North American countries. The countries are ranked according to the severity of their bullying problem.

Husak, D. (2004, July). The criminal law as last resort. *Oxford Journal of Legal Studies, 24*(2), 207–235.
Alternative measures should be implemented before relying on criminal law.

Jan, A., & Husain, S. (2015, November). Bullying in elementary schools: Its causes and effects on students. *Journal of Education and Practice, 6*(19), 43–56.
Discusses bullying causes and strategies to decrease this behavior in order to optimize learning.

Jeong, S., & Lee, B. H. (2013). A multilevel examination of peer victimization and bullying preventions in schools. *Journal of Criminology*, 10 pages.

Schools with bullying prevention programs are more likely to have students who have been bullied.

Jolliffe, D., & Farrington, D. P. (2006, October). Examining the relationship between low empathy and bullying. *Aggressive Behavior, 32*(6), 540–550.

Examines the relationship between empathy and bullying. Low empathy was related to males' violent bullying and to females' indirect bullying.

Jones, L. M., Mitchell, K. J., & Turner, H. A. (2015, December). Victim reports of bystander reactions to in-person and online peer harassment: A national survey of adolescents. *Journal of Youth and Adolescence, 44*(12), 2308–2330.

Bullying prevention programs would be more effective if they helped bystanders and victims' confidants.

Juvonen, J., & Graham, S. (2014). Bullying in schools: The power of bullies and the plight of victims. *Annual Review of Psychology, 65*, 159–185.

Highlights the social dominance involved in bullying, the inflated self-views of students who bully, and the effects of their behavior on bullied students. The authors critique common intervention approaches designed to reduce bullying, and they make recommendations for a nuanced approach to school-based interventions.

Kimmel, M., & Mahler, M. (2003, June). Adolescent masculinity, homophobia, and violence: Random school shootings, 1982–2001. *American Behavioral Scientist, 46*(10), 1439–1458.

It is mostly white males who commit school shootings, often in response to homophobic bullying. These cases are most common in Republican-dominated "red" states, where more traditional definitions of masculinity are prominent.

Klein, J. (2005). America is from Mars, Europe is from Venus: How the United States can learn from Europe's social work response to school shootings. *School Social Work Journal, 30*(1), 1–24.

In response to school shootings, the United States tends to implement punishment and security measures (masculine-associated responses), while European countries are more likely to work on building student-teacher relationships and prevention (feminine-associated strategies).

Klein, J. (2006). Sexuality and school shootings: What role does teasing play in school massacres? *Journal of Homosexuality, 51*(4), 39–62.

Lax gun-control laws and media violence are insufficient school shooting explanations. In a significant portion of school shootings, young boys sought revenge against other boys who called them gay and other names referring to homosexuality.

Klein, J. (2006, May). An invisible problem: Daily violence against girls in school. *Theoretical Criminology, 10*(2), 147–177.

Violence against girls in the form of dating violence and sexual harassment is so common that it is barely visible to students and school staff, and yet these assaults are implicated repeatedly in school shootings where perpetrators specifically targeted females.

Klein, J. (2006, July). Cultural capital and high school bullies: How social inequality impacts school violence. *Men and Masculinities, 9*(1), 53–75.

Battles for cultural capital among young males are a significant causal factor in U.S. school shootings. Male youths are pressured to demonstrate hyper-masculinity by participating in athletics, fighting, and dominating girls. These pressures include bullying others to prove manhood and social worth.

Konrath, S. H., O'Brien, E. H., & Hsing, C. (2011). Changes in dispositional empathy in American college students over time: A meta-analysis. *Personality and Social Psychology Review, 15*(2), 180–198.
People are not as empathetic as they were in previous generations, which is of concern because empathy promotes cooperation and unity and its lack is associated with conflict and isolation. People tend to be healthier when they are connected with others. Increasing empathy is an important social goal.

Kowalski, R. M., & Limber, S. P. (2013, July). Psychological, physical, and academic correlates of cyberbullying and traditional bullying. *Supplement, 53*(1), S13–S20.
In both cyberbullying and face-to-face bullying, "bully-victims" have the most negative scores for psychological and physical health and academic performance.

Land, D. (2003, May 1). Teasing apart secondary students' conceptualizations of peer teasing, bullying and sexual harassment. *School Psychology International, 24*(2), 147–165.
Examining how high school students think about school bullying and sexual harassment, the authors found little difference between the kinds of bullying that occur among males when compared with females.

Langos, C. (2012, June). Cyberbullying: The challenge to define. *Cyberpsychology, Behavior, and Social Networking, 15*(6), 285–289.

The authors define cyberbullying by using the face-to face bullying definition as a starting point.

Lee, C. H., & Song, J. (2012, August). Functions of parental involvement and effects of school climate on bullying behaviors among South Korean middle school students. *Journal of Interpersonal Violence, 27*(12), 2437–2464.

Analyzes the impact of parental involvement and school climate on bullying among South Korean middle school students. The authors found that positive school climate was negatively correlated with school bullying.

Lereya, S. T., Samara, M., & Wolke, D. (2013, December). Parenting behavior and the risk of becoming a victim and a bully/victim: A meta-analysis study. *Child Abuse & Neglect, 37*(12), 1091–1108.

Negative parenting, including abuse and neglect, is associated with risks for becoming a bully and/or a victim. The authors suggest that intervention models should include families and start even before children enter school.

Lewis, S. V., Robinson III, E. H., & Hays, B. G. (2012, July). Implementing an authentic character education curriculum. *Journal of Childhood Education, 87*(4), 227–231.

Given the widespread mandate for character education across the United States, we should have a clearer definition of what character education entails and develop the most effective curriculum for delivering excellent character education.

Marini, Z. (1999). Peer victimization in middle childhood: Characteristics, causes and consequences of school bullying. *Brock Education Journal, 9*(1), 32–47.

Examines recent research and suggests that the number of students affected by bullying is much higher than previously believed, the range of behaviors involved is more severe, and the consequences are longer lasting. The authors provide an overview of four aspects of bullying, including the myths, characteristics, causes, and consequences.

Marx, R., & Kettrey, H. (2016, July). Gay-straight alliances are associated with lower levels of school-based victimization of LGBTQ+ youth: A systematic review and meta-analysis. *Journal of Youth & Adolescence, 45*(7), 1269–1282.

Lesbian, gay, bisexual, transgender, and queer youth are less likely to be victimized in schools with gay-straight alliance programs.

McPherson, M., Smith-Lovin, L., & Vrashears, M. E. (2006, June). Social isolation in America: Changes in core discussion networks over two decades. *American Sociological Review, 71*(3), 353–375.

Using the General Social Surveys of 1985 and 2004, the authors examine how the core discussion networks of Americans have changed in the past two decades. Discussion networks are smaller in 2004 than in 1985. The number of people saying there is no one with whom they discuss important matters nearly tripled. Both kin and nonkin confidants were lost in the past two decades, but the greater decrease of nonkin ties leads to more confidant networks centered on spouses and parents, with fewer contacts through voluntary associations and neighborhoods.

Mrug, S., Madan, A., Cook, E. W., & Wright, R. A. (2015, May). Emotional and physiological desensitization to real-life and movie violence. *Journal of Youth & Adolescence, 44*(5), 1092–1108.

Youths who see high levels of real life and/or media violence are likely to become less empathetic and emotionally reactive to violence.

Mullet, J. H. (2014, July). Restorative discipline: From getting even to getting well. *Children & Schools, 26*(3), 157–162.

> Youths often respond to traditional punitive discipline with violent retaliation. Restorative justice heals conflicts by focusing on mending relationships and creating restitution.

Nansel, T. R., Overpeck, M., Pilla, R. S., Ruan, W. J., Simons-Morton, B., & Scheidt, P. (2001, April). Bullying behaviors among US youth: Prevalence and association with psychosocial adjustment. *JAMA, 285*(16), 2094–2100.

> Given how many behavioral and emotional difficulties are associated with bullying, including long-term negative outcomes, bullying merits serious attention for both research and prevention intervention.

Olthof, T., Goossens, F. A., Vermande, M. M., Aleva, E. A., & van der Meulen, M. (2011, June). Bullying as strategic behavior: Relations with desired and acquired dominance in the peer group. *Journal of School Psychology, 49*(3), 339–359.

> The authors find that those who bully tend to use it as a strategy to obtain social dominance. To effectively address bullying, this functional aspect of youth violence should be addressed.

Olweus, D. (1997). Bully/victim problems in school: Facts and intervention. *European Journal of Psychology of Education, 12*(4), 495–510. doi:10.1007/BF03172807.

> This landmark study evaluated bullying in Scandinavia. Estimates indicated that 9 percent of students through grade nine were regularly bullied, and 6 to 7 percent of students bully often. The author argues that children have a democratic right to be spared oppression and humiliation in school. His OBPP intervention program is

evaluated in forty-two schools and decreased bullying by 50 to 70 percent.

Olweus, D. (2003). A profile of bullying at school. *Educational Leadership, 60*(6), 12–17.
  The often-described "founder of bullying research" relates bullying facts and myths and discusses Norway's approach to bullying.

Olweus, D. (2005). A useful evaluation design, and effects of the Olweus Bullying Prevention Program. *Psychology, Crime & Law, 11*(4), 389–402.
  The study found that the Olweus Bully/Victim Questionnaire is an effective assessment for evaluating the Olweus Bullying Prevention Program (OBPP).

Olweus, D. (2011). Bullying at school and later criminality: Findings from three Swedish community samples of males. *Criminal Behaviour and Mental Health, 21*(2), 151–156.
  Adolescent bullying predicts adult criminality.

Olweus, D. (2013). School bullying: Development and some important challenges. *Annual Review of Clinical Psychology, 9*(1), 751–780.
  Olweus addresses controversial issues about bullying, including how to distinguish between bullying and other aggression, why bullying is a serious public issue, and why bullying research took a long time to reach the United States.

Olweus, D., & Limber, S. P. (2010). Bullying in school: Evaluation and dissemination of the Olweus Bullying Prevention Program. *American Journal of Orthopsychiatry, 80*(1), 124–134.
  Evaluations of the efficacy of OBPP in the United States are inconsistent but show that it has a positive impact on

self-reported involvement in bullying and other antisocial behaviors.

O'Moore, M., & Kirkham, C. (2001, July). Self-esteem and its relationship to bullying behaviour. *Aggressive Behavior, 27*(4), 269–283.
Low self-esteem is related to being involved in bullying. High self-esteem protects children and adolescents from being involved in bullying.

Orue, I., & Calvete, E. (2012, February). Justification of violence as a mediator between exposure to violence and aggressive behavior in children. *Psicothema, 24*(1), 42–47.
Exposure to violence at home and media violence tend to increase aggressive behavior. In both cases, justifying violence was a mediating factor.

Poteat, P., Kimmel, M., & Wilchins, R. (2010, September). The moderating effects of support for violence beliefs on masculine norms, aggression, and homophobic behavior during adolescence. *Journal of Research on Adolescence, 21*(2), 434–447.
The extent to which youths believe violence is appropriate and effective predicts bullying, fighting, and relational aggression. The authors conclude that adherence to masculine norms and homophobic belief systems also predict aggressive behavior.

Rigby, K., & Cox, I. (1996, October). The contribution of bullying at school and low self-esteem to acts of delinquency among Australian teenagers. *Personality and Individual Differences, 21*(4), 609–612.
Low self-esteem is associated with bullying.

Salmivalli, C. (1999, August). Participant role approach to school bullying: Implications for interventions. *Journal of Adolescence, 22*(4), 453–459.

Roles involved in bullying include assistants, reinforcers, and outsiders. The author suggests that bolstering constructive "peer group power" should be part of bullying interventions. Peers can become informal supports or take formal helper roles such as peer counselors.

Salmivalli, C. (2010, March–April). Bullying and the peer group: A review. *Aggression and Violent Behavior, 15*(2), 112–150. doi:10.1016/j.avb.2009.08.007
Insights into school bullying motives and how the ways victims adjust depend on peer cultures. Discusses interventions that target the peer group and suggest directions for research on peer processes in bullying.

Sanchez, E., Robertson T. R., Lewis, C. M., Rosenbluth, B., Bohman, T., & Casey, D. M. (2001). Preventing bullying and sexual harassment in elementary schools. *Journal of Emotional Abuse, 2*(2–3), 157–180.
Examines an educational project funded by the U.S. Centers for Disease Control and Prevention that tries to prevent dating violence by targeting bullying and sexual harassment on public school campuses. The authors find that when bullying and sexual harassment fester in elementary schools, students learn to accept mistreatment in both peer and future dating relationships.

Schacter, H. L., White, S. J., Chang V. Y., & Juvonen, J. (2015). "Why me?": Characterological self-blame and continued victimization in the first year of middle school. *Journal of Clinical Child & Adolescent Psychology, 44*(3), 446–455.
Students who self-blame and those suffering from depression are at risk for being bullied in the first year of middle school.

Seals, D., & Young, J. (2003, winter). Bullying and victimization: Prevalence and relationship to gender, grade level, ethnicity, self-esteem, and depression. *Adolescence, 38*(152), 735–747.

> Boys are involved in bullying more often than girls. Seventh graders are more involved than eighth graders. Both bullies and victims tend to have higher levels of depression than those not involved in bullying.

Skiba, R. J., & Knesting, K. (2001, December). Zero tolerance, zero evidence: An analysis of school disciplinary practice. *New Directions for Student Leadership, 92*, 17–43.

> There is little to no evidence that zero-tolerance policies are effective for stopping school violence. Alternative models are recommended.

Smokowski, P. R., & Kopasz, K. H. (2005, April). Bullying in school: An overview of types, effects, family characteristics, and intervention strategies. *Health & Social Work, 27*(2), 101–110.

> Bullying affects approximately one in three children. The authors discuss risk factors and the impact on adult mental health including anxiety, depression, substance use, and conduct disorders.

Solberg, M. E., & Olweus, D. (2003, June). Prevalence estimation of school bullying with the Olweus Bully/Victim Questionnaire. *Aggressive Behavior, 29*(3), 239–268.

> Examines variables important for assessing anti-bullying program efficacy.

Solberg, M. E., Olweus, D., & Endresen, I. M. (2007). Bullies and victims at school: Are they the same pupils? *British Journal of Educational Psychology, 77* (part 2), 441–464.

> The study examines the prevalence of male and female bully-victims when compared with those who are only victims or only bullies.

Strøm, I. F., Thoresen, S., Wentzel-Larsen, T., Sagatun, A., & Dyb, G. (2014, October). A prospective study of the potential moderating role of social support in preventing marginalization among individuals exposed to bullying and abuse in junior high school youth. *Adolescence, 43*, 1642–1657.

> Those exposed to multiple forms of abuse including bullying are at greater risk as adults for depending on welfare or other sources of economic support. Social support from families and peers reduce the likelihood that victims will depend on welfare benefits.

Swearer Napolitano, S. M. (2008, November 10). Bullying and depression. *Educational Psychology Papers and Publications, 134.* Special issue of Education.com. Retrieved from https:// digitalcommons.unl.edu/cgi/viewcontent.cgi?article=1133 &context=edpsychpapers

> It is a misconception that bullying others does not result in negative long-term consequences. Those who bully tend to face a host of psychological difficulties, including oppositional defiant disorder, attention deficit hyperactivity disorder, and depression.

Taillieu, T. L., & Brownridge, D. A. (2013). Aggressive parental discipline experienced in childhood and internalizing problems in early adulthood. *Journal of Family Violence, 28*, 445–458.

> When parents use corporal punishment and/or psychological aggression with their children, these youths are more likely to exhibit problem behaviors.

Teglasi, H., & Rothman, L. (2001). Stories: A classroom-based program to reduce aggressive behavior. *Journal of School Psychology, 39*, 71–94.

> The authors discuss a fifteen-session program called STORIES that includes open communication, reflection, experiential learning, and social problem-solving. They

found it improved problem-solving skills in aggressors, victims, and bystanders.

Teisl, M., Rogosch, F. A., Oshri, A., & Cicchetti, D. (2012, March). Differential expression of social dominance as a function of age and maltreatment experience. *Developmental Psychology, 48*(2), 575–588.

Children who are maltreated are more likely to bully others than those who have not been maltreated. The authors discuss the influence of maltreatment on children's social development.

Thoits, P. A. (2011). Mechanisms linking social ties and support to physical and mental health. *Journal of Health and Social Behavior, 52*(2), 145–161.

Social support, including empathy and coping assistance, from significant others tends to be effective in reducing the physical and/or emotional impact from stress factors.

Thoresen, S., Jensen, T. K., Wentzel-Larsen, T., & Dyb, G. (2014). Social support barriers and mental health in terrorist attack survivors. *Journal of Affective Disorders, 156*, 187–193.

Lack of social support for those who experience traumatic events predicts a greater likelihood for post-traumatic stress disorder and psychological distress.

Ttofi, M. M., & Farrington, D. P. (2011). Effectiveness of school-based programs to reduce bullying: A systematic and meta-analytic review. *Journal of Experimental Criminology, 7*(1), 27–56.

The authors analyze school anti-bullying programs and find that successful programs decrease bullying by 20 to 23 percent on average. More intensive programs are most effective, especially those that include parent meetings, disciplinary methods, and improved playground supervision.

Twenge, J. M., & Campbell, W. K. (2003, February). "Isn't it fun to get the respect that we're going to deserve?": Narcissism, social rejection, and aggression. *Personality and Social Psychology Bulletin, 29*(2), 261–272.

> Those identified as narcissists were angrier and more aggressive after experiencing a social rejection than those who were not identified as narcissists. Narcissism and social rejection predict aggressive behavior.

Vaillancourt, T., Hymel, S., & McDougall, P. (2003). Bullying is power: Implications for school-based intervention strategies. *Journal of Applied School Psychology, 19*, 157–176.

> Many students who bully are perceived to be powerful, popular leaders who feel good about themselves and their interactions with peers. Powerful bullies tend to be viewed as having more competencies and assets, including being physically attractive, wearing stylish clothing, and being good athletes.

Vaillancourt, T., Hymel, S., & McDougall, P. (2006, August). Aggression and social status: The moderating roles of sex and peer-valued characteristics. *Aggressive Behavior, 32*(4), 396–408.

> Aggressive students who were accepted by their peers tend to be perceived as popular, powerful, and likable.

Van der Valk, A. (2013, fall). There are no bullies. Just children who bully—And you can help them. *Teaching Tolerance, 45*, 38–41.

> There are children who bully, but rarely is anyone only a "bully." Youths may bully others in one situation and act respectfully and with kindness in another.

Woods, S., Done, J., & Kalsi, H. (2009, April). Peer victimization and internalizing difficulties: The moderating role of friendship quality. *Journal of Adolescence, 32*(2) 293–308.

Victims of relational violence, such as social exclusion, report higher levels of loneliness than nonvictims. Victims of more direct violence tend to have higher quality friendships and less loneliness.

Youth Violence: A Report of the Surgeon General. Retrieved from https://www.ncbi.nlm.nih.gov/pubmed/20669522.

The report describes research regarding factors that increase risks for youths to commit violence. It makes recommendations for preventing youths from considering violence as an acceptable response to challenging life events, and it reviews strategies and programs designed to prevent and decrease youth violence.

Zapf, D., & Gross, C. (2001). Conflict escalation and coping with workplace bullying: A replication and extension. *European Journal of Work and Organizational Psychology, 10,* 497–522.

Workplace bullying victims tend to respond with constructive conflict-solving strategies and continue trying different approaches until they finally attempt to leave the organization. Sometimes they use conflict avoidance methods including frequent absenteeism. Successful victims fought back and were more successful at avoiding escalating behavior. Unsuccessful victims contributed to bullying escalation.

Zottis, G. A. H., Salum, G. A., Isolan, L. R., Manfro, G. G., & Heldt, E. (2014). Associations between child disciplinary practices and bullying behavior in adolescents. *Jornal de Pediatria, 90,* 408–414.

When parents discipline children and adolescents with punishment, their children are more likely to bully others. Parents are encouraged to find different ways to discipline their children in order to decrease bullying.

Popular Writings

Blad, E. (2014, July 1). Cyberbullying law violates free speech, New York court rules. *Education Week.* Retrieved from http://blogs.edweek.org/edweek/rulesforengagement/2014 /07/cyberbullying_law_violates_free_speech_new_york_court _rules.html

> A New York law meant to curb cyberbullying was ruled unconstitutional on First Amendment free speech grounds.

Comaford, C. (2016, August 27). 75% of workers are affected by bullying—Here's what to do about it. *Forbes.* Retrieved from - http://www.forbes.com/sites/christinecomaford/2016/08/27 /the-enormous-toll-workplace-bullying-takes-on-your-bottom -line/#705bb2de386e

> Seventy-five percent of workers are affected by bullying. The authors describe workplace bullying, the financial costs to companies, and ways to stop it.

Fox News. (2016, January 21). Parents outraged over controversial anti-bullying program. Retrieved from http://video .foxnews.com/v/4715318476001/parents-outraged-over -controversial-anti-bullying-program/?#sp=show-clips

> A parent class-action suit focuses on outrage over an anti-bullying program in a Pennsylvania school.

Goldman, C. (2014, October 10). How do I know what's bullying and what's normal conflict? *New York Times.* Retrieved from https://parenting.blogs.nytimes.com/2014/10/10/how-do -i-know-whats-bullying-and-whats-normal-conflict/

> The author discusses her child's experience with teasing and bullying and the differences between them.

Guldberg, H. (2011, November 24). Anti-bullying campaigns: Doing more harm than good? Retrieved from http://www .heleneguldberg.co.uk/index.php/site/article/109/

Anti-bullying campaigns may pathologize normal behavior. Some children become more resilient and stronger after experiencing bullying. The author suggests that the statistics related to the persistence of bullying are overestimated.

Hartnig, S. (n.d.). Student bullying on increase, federal statistics reveal. News Reporting and the Internet. Retrieved from http://students.com.miami.edu/netreporting/?page_id= 1269
Discussing the National Center for Education Statistics (NCES) data, the author writes that the percentage of students aged twelve through eighteen who report being bullied at school has increased by almost 25 percent since 2003.

Klein, J. (2011, May 25). Bully rage: Common school-shooter misery. *Huffington Post.* Retrieved from https://www .huffpost.com/entry/bully-rage-common-schools_b_46548
School shooters often plan their attack in response to being bullied.

Klein, J. (2012, March 5). My view: It's time to change schools' culture of misery. CNN. Retrieved from http:// schoolsofthought.blogs.cnn.com/2012/03/05/my-view-its -time-to-change-schools-culture-of-misery/
Bullying and school shootings are related to high rates of depression, anxiety, and social isolation.

Klein, J. (2016, October 17). How to deal with bullying—Prevention or penitentiary? The Hill. Retrieved from http:// thehill.com/blogs/pundits-blog/healthcare/301396-how-to -deal-with-bullying-prevention-or-penitentiary
Discusses the controversy between putting those who bully through the criminal justice system and helping to correct behaviors by developing more compassion in schools.

Saxon, R. (2005, February). Kindness curbs kids' name-calling. *Education Digest: Essential Readings Condensed for Quick Review, 70*(6), 8–13.

Name-calling and verbal bullying and harassment can create a hostile school environment that decreases the academic performance of youths being bullied. To reduce assaults, the author recommends strategies that teachers can use to create acceptance and appreciation for different people.

Schaps, E. (2009, March/April). Creating caring school communities. *Leadership*, 8–11.

Strategies are recommended for teachers and school leaders to build community, including implementing professional development resources that build caring school communities.

Schwabe, S. (2013, November 13). News, controversy over school's anti-bullying program. *KKTV 11 News*. Retrieved from http://www.kktv.com/home/headlines/Controversy-Over -Schools-Anti-Bullying-Program-231851731.html

A Colorado school sparked controversy when the principal launched an anti-bullying program for fourth through sixth graders. Some students were given a sticker on their collars and other students were told that they should shun the students with the stickers. The principal hoped that by engaging in this activity, students would feel empathy for others and be kinder to one another. Some parents felt it made their children into targets and created unnecessary emotional stress.

Simplicio, J. (2013, spring). Suck it up, walk it off, be a man: A controversial look at bullying in today's schools. *Education, 3*, 345–349.

The author writes that children are overprotected by parents who refuse to allow them to fail and that this contributes to bullying.

Wachtel, T. (2012, June 6). Social bonding is key to limiting bullying. *Education Week, 31*(33), 31.

> As president and founder of the Institute for Restorative Practices, the author suggests that people refer to hurtful behaviors rather than talk about "bullies" and "victims." He writes that people who bully have often been abused or bullied themselves. Restorative work repairs relationships and makes it less likely that bullying will reoccur.

Books

Bazelon, E. (2013). *Sticks and stones: Defeating the culture of bullying and rediscovering the power of character and empathy.* New York: Random House.

> The author gives a definition of bullying. She suggests that sometimes intervention is essential and that at other times youths should be encouraged to work out their own difficulties. Discusses interventions, including focusing on empathy.

Dillon, J. (2015). *Reframing bullying prevention to build stronger school communities.* New York: Corwin.

> To prevent bullying, the author discusses ways to build school empathy and compassion as an effective alternative to traditional discipline.

Einarsen, S., Hoel, H., & Zapf, D. (Eds.). (2003). *Bullying and emotional abuse in the workplace.* New York: Taylor & Francis.

> Discusses the different ways European countries and the United States address workplace bullying. The authors write that European countries have laws against "workplace bullying." The United States has no federal prohibition against workplace bullying and refers to the same behavior as "mistreatment."

Espelage, D. L., & Swearer, S. M. (Eds.). (2004). *Bullying in American schools: A social ecological perspective on prevention and intervention* (pp. 187–210). Mahwah, NJ: Lawrence Erlbaum.

> Researchers from developmental, social, counseling, school, and clinical psychologists write about school bullying in the United States and they suggest evidence-based interventions.

Garbarino, J. (2007). *See Jane hit: Why girls are growing more violent and what we can do about it.* New York: Penguin.

> Violence perpetuated by girls is increasing. The author explores cultural developments that gave rise to this phenomenon.

Goldman, C. (2012). *Bullied: What every parent, teacher, and kid needs to know about ending the cycle of fear.* New York: HarperCollins.

> The author presents school bullying research and shares stories of children who have been bullied. She suggests strategies for helping children speak up for themselves, resolve conflicts, and cope with teasing and physical abuse.

Heitner, D. (2016). *Helping kids thrive (and survive) in their digital world.* New York: Bibliomotion.

> Parents and school staff are guided on how to raise "responsible digital citizens."

Juvonen, J., & Graham, S. (Eds.). (2001). *Peer harassment in school: Theplight of the vulnerable and victimized.* New York: Guilford.

> The authors present research on chronically bullied children and adolescents and recommend school-based prevention and intervention models.

Kimmel, M. (2008). *Guyland: The perilous world where boys become men.* New York: HarperCollins.

> The author explains the role of the "Guy code" on young men and the way that it often propels them to commit

sexual assault and other violence. The "Guy code" also delays adulthood, including getting married and having a family.

Klein, J. (2012a). *The bully society: School shootings and the crisis of bullying in America's schools*. New York: NYU Press.
Bullying and related school shootings develop from a culture that promotes aggressive and competitive behavior, especially among males. Conventional masculinity rationalizes assaults against girls and against boys perceived to be less masculine and/or gay. School shootings magnify the daily bullying students experience around gender and sexuality. Recommendations are offered for helping schools shift from a "bully society" to a "compassionate community."

Klein, J. (2012b). *For educators: The bully society: School shootings and the crisis of bullying in America's schools, U.S. school shootings data, 1979–2011*. Retrieved from https://dhjhkxawhe8q4 .cloudfront.net/nyupress-wp/wp-content/uploads/2019/06 /18204640/resources-dataonschoolshootings.pdf
Examines 195 school shootings between 1979 and 2011, including any incident when a person fired a gun in a K–12 school or college. It includes names and ages, location, numbers killed and wounded, motives, and a school shooting frequency analysis. Reports and graphs show the relationship between school shootings and issues such as homophobia, dating violence, racism, looksism, and class.

Messerschmidt, J. W. (2000). *Nine lives: Adolescent masculinities, the body, and violence*. New York: Westview.
Interviews with nine adolescent boys: three who committed sexual offenses, three who attacked other students physically, and three who were nonviolent. The boys were largely influenced by how their male role models defined

masculinity. Those who committed assault were influenced by adult males who associated masculinity with violence. Male adults important to the nonviolent boys defined masculinity more peacefully.

Olweus, D. (1978). *Aggression in the schools: Bullies and whipping boys.* Oxford: Hemisphere.
In pioneering bullying research, the author presents results from five large empirical studies and finds that bullying rates are higher than previously known. The author proposes a program to make positive changes.

Olweus, D. (1993). *Bullying at school: What we know and what we can do.* Malden, MA: Wiley-Blackwell.
The author discusses his scientifically evaluated bullying-intervention program that reduced bullying by 50 percent in the schools where it was implemented.

Orpinas, P., & Horne, A. M. (2006). *Bullying prevention: Creating a positive school climate and developing social competence.* Washington, DC: American Psychological Association.
To reduce bullying and aggression, the authors discuss how to create a positive, caring school environment and develop children's social competence skills for engaging in healthy relationships.

Perry, B. D., & Szalavitz, M. (2011). *Born for love: Why empathy is essential—And endangered.* New York: William Morrow Paperbacks.
Explores the importance of empathy in human evolution and its significance for children and society. The authors write that love is essential and increasingly rare.

Simmons, R. (2002). *Odd girl out: The hidden culture of aggression in girls.* New York: Harcourt.

Relational aggression, including social exclusion, is a serious problem in girls' friendship circles. Popularity contests are destructive and dangerous.

Spina, S. U. (Ed.). (2000). *Smoke and mirrors: The hidden context of violence in schools and society.* New York: Rowman & Littlefield.
Educators and cultural theorists address the socioeconomic and social conditions that play a role in school violence. The essays address issues such as poverty, racism, inequality, gender, and the role of the media in glorifying violence.

Willard, N. (2007). *Cyberbullying and cyberthreats: Responding to the challenge of online social aggression, threats, and distress.* Champaign, IL: Research Press.
Examines cyberbullying and recommends constructive responses.

Wiseman, R. (2016). *Queen bees and wannabes: Helping your daughter survive cliques, gossip, boys, and the new realities of girl world.* New York: Harmony.
Discusses the anatomy of girls' social cliques, including the "Queen Bee" (leader) and "Target" (bullied students, such as those excluded from social events). The author provides suggestions on how parents can help their daughters navigate the challenging culture of girls' friendships.

Films

Fey, T. (Writer), & Waters, M. (Director). (2004, April 19). *Mean Girls.* Los Angeles: Paramount), 97 minutes.
The film based on R. Wiseman's best-selling book *Queen Bees and Wannabees* features Cady Heron who returns from Africa and enters a new school in Evanston, Illinois. She meets classmates who describe the school's social

cliques. The most popular group takes an interest in Cady, invites her into their circle, and then makes her into a social outcast.

Hirsch, L. (Director), & Foudy, S., Hirsch, L., Lowen, C., & Waitt, C. (Producers). (2011, April 23). *Bully*. New York: Weinstein, 99 minutes.
This documentary film follows five U.S. students who endure daily bullying. The film is used to launch anti-bullying programs.

Moore, M. (Writer, Director, Producer). (2002, November 21). *Bowling for Columbine*. Beverly Hills, CA: United Artists Distributors, MGM Distribution Company, 119 minutes.
Political documentary filmmaker Michael Moore examines possible causes for the 1999 Columbine High School massacre. He compares circumstances in the United States with those in other countries to understand high rates of U.S. gun homicide.

Newson, J. S. (Director, Producer). (2005). *The mask you live in*. United States: Representation Project.
The film explores how a narrow definition of masculinity harms boys, men, and society and is implicated in high rates of men's violence.

Simmons, R. (Writer), & Richmond, R. (Producer). (2005, April 4). *Odd girl out: The hidden culture of aggression in girls*. United States: Lifetime, 84 minutes.
Based on Rachel Simmons' book *Odd Girl Out*, the film depicts devastating bullying in the form of social aggression and its relationship to suicide.

Organizations

Campbell Collaboration, https://campbellcollaboration.org/

A nonprofit promoting evidence-based social-science policy; they disseminate systemic reviews focused on helping people make informed decisions about educational, social, and behavioral interventions.

Center for the Study and Prevention of Violence in Colorado (CSPV), Blueprints for Healthy Youth Development, https://cspv.colorado.edu/

To promote effective interventions, the organization provides a registry of youth-focused evidence-based programs, practices, and policies that are recommended for promoting health and decreasing antisocial behaviors. It also provides publications that promote "highly scientific standards" for choosing strategies meant to prevent crime and build social health.

Office of Juvenile Justice and Delinquency Prevention (OJJDP), https://www.ojjdp.gov/

Sponsors research programs and trainings, and sets goals and priorities for national juvenile justice issues.

Note: Information is taken from Supreme Court reports, books, news articles, and other reputable sources.

1973 In Scandinavia, pioneering researcher Dan Olweus publishes *Aggression in the Schools: Bullies and Whipping Boys*, a landmark study on bullying. The English edition is released five years later.

1982 In Las Vegas, Patrick Lizotte, age seventeen, kills one teacher and wounds two students. He says he was bullied, taunted, teased, picked on, and physically and verbally tormented by his classmates and teachers.

1983 The bullying-related suicides of three youths in Norway prompt the Ministry of Education to launch a national anti-bullying campaign.

1983–1985 Olweus develops a school-based intervention program in Norway: the Olweus Bullying Prevention Program (OBPP). Studies report that it reduces bullying by about 50 percent.

1985 In Goddard, Kansas, James Alan Kearby, age fourteen, kills his junior high school principal and three students he says were bullying him.

Montana officials sign the Bully-Free Montana Act, April 25, 2015. Montana is the last state to pass state anti-bullying legislation. (AP Photo/Lisa Baumann)

1987   Nathan Ferris, age twelve, an honor student in Missouri, brings a pistol to school and uses it to commit suicide after he kills a student who was teasing him.

1988   Nicholas Elliott, age sixteen, in Virginia, kills a teacher and a student. As one of twenty-two black students in a school of more than five hundred, he was frequently taunted by other students because of his skin color.

1991   In a Houston high school, a sixteen-year-old wounds another student. Just before he shoots the gun, the victim teases him about his Spanish accent.

1992   The Supreme Court rules in *Franklin v. Gwinnett County Public Schools* that students who have been the victims of sexual harassment or abuse by school officials may sue for monetary damages under Title IX.

1993   Gary Scott Pennington, age seventeen, in Grayson, Kentucky, kills a teacher and a school custodian. An honor student from a poor family, he was teased because he stuttered and read a lot. One student admits after the attack that he beat up Pennington while fifteen other students watched. Just before the attack, Pennington's girlfriend breaks up with him, and he has a conflict with a teacher.

1994   In a suburban Atlanta high school, Brian Head, age fifteen, shoots himself in the head in front of his classmates. He was bullied because of his weight and thick glasses. Just after a classmate slaps him, he shouts, "I can't take it anymore!"

1995   Curtis Sliwa, founder of Guardian Angels, launches CyberAngels. The national volunteer neighborhood-watch reports and intervenes on cyberstalking in chat rooms.

1996   Barry Loukaitis, age fourteen, critically wounds a female student and kills a teacher and two male students. One of the students he kills is a popular athlete who, along with other athletes, called Loukaitis a "fag" because he was an honor student. "This sure beats algebra," Loukaitis says while he was shooting.

1996   The American Psychological Association identifies "cyberaddiction" as a clinical disorder correlated with depression and low self-esteem.

1997   In Bethel, Alaska, Evan Ramsey, age sixteen, kills his principal and a student and wounds two other students. Ramsey kills a popular football player after arguing with him. Ramsey says, "I figured since the principal and the dean weren't doing anything that was making any impression, that I was gonna have to do something, or else I was gonna keep on getting picked on."

1997   Luke Woodham, age sixteen, who was bullied and called "gay," stabs his mother to death and then shoots and kills two female students (his ex-girlfriend and her friend). He wounds seven other students at his school in Mississippi. Woodham was bullied for being short, overweight, smart, and poor and he was seeking revenge against his ex-girlfriend for breaking up with him. He and his friends refer to their group as the "Third Reich." He explains, "They'd always talk about me and push me around and start fights with me and stuff. . . . They'd call you gay or call you stupid or fat or whatever. Kids would sometimes throw rocks at me and push and kick me and hit me and stuff like that."

1997   In a Kentucky high school, Michael Carneal, age fourteen, kills three female students and wounds five others. Described as a "slight, skinny, freshman," he was called "faggot" and "gay" face-to-face and in the school newspaper. He says he wanted to kill "popular, preppie students whom he blamed for his mistreatment." His victims include a girl who didn't return his affections and another girl who wouldn't date him. From prison, Michael declares, "I feel more respected now." He also says, "I thought the shooting would make me more popular."

1998   At a Georgia high school, Jonathan Miller, age fifteen, punches thirteen-year-old Josh Belluardo in the head. Miller kills Belluardo as he gets off the school bus. Miller is known for punching, shoving, and threatening other students. In 1999, in response to this murder, Georgia passes the first state anti-bullying legislation, a three-strikes-and-you-are-out policy. Miller is sentenced to life in prison, after being tried as an adult and found guilty of felony murder.

1998   In Jonesboro, Arkansas, Mitchell Johnson, age thirteen, and Andrew (Drew) Golden, age eleven, kill four female students and one pregnant teacher, and they wound nine other female students, a male student, and a male teacher. Johnson was referred to in school as "pudgy," and Golden was called the "wiry, little boy." Johnson targets his ex-girlfriend, who says that she broke up with Johnson because he was hitting her. Johnson also threatens to kill another girl for speaking about the breakup, and he shoots two girls who refused his advances. He says that he targeted the teacher because she placed him on in-school suspension when Johnson wouldn't remove his hat. Johnson has been paddled at school for cursing. Golden shoots and kills his ex-girlfriend, Jennifer Jacobs.

1998   Andrew Wurst, age fourteen, in Edinboro, Pennsylvania, kills a male teacher and wounds his ex-girlfriend. He wounds another girl who laughed at him when he invited her to a dance.

1998   In Springfield, Oregon, Kipland Kinkel, age fifteen, kills two students he says were "jocks" and two of the many students who teased him for being small and having learning disabilities. He is also upset that a girl he liked didn't like him back.

1998   In Jaspar, Texas, three white supremacists use a pickup truck to drag African American James Byrd, age 49, to his death, decapitating him. Later that year, Matthew Wayne Shepard, a twenty-one-year-old gay student at the University of Wyoming, is beaten, tortured, and left to die near Laramie, Wyoming. The murder is widely seen as a brutal gay-bashing attack and ignites a national and international focus on hate crime legislation. In 2009, the U.S. Congress passes the Matthew Shepard and James Byrd Jr. Hate Crimes Prevention Act, and President Barack Obama signs the legislation into law.

1999   Before killing themselves at Columbine High School in Littleton, Colorado, Eric Harris, age seventeen, and Dylan Klebold, age eighteen, kill eight female students, four male students, and a coach and wound twenty-three others. News reports say that Harris and Klebold were both in honors programs and bullied for being "smart." Reports state that they "hated" the "jocks and preps" who bullied them and who called them "homosexual." In a WNPR interview (2016, February 16), Klebold's mother says that she believes there was a pervasive culture of bullying at the school and that there was "shoving, knocking down, (and) trash thrown on kids." She also believes that her son and Harris were "shoved around and humiliated in front of a group of people." Dave Cullen, in his book *Columbine* (2009), writes that his research indicates that Harris and Klebold were not bullied.

1999   One month after the Columbine shooting, Thomas (TJ) Solomon wounds six students. He was bullied by peers and accused of "doing his homework in homeroom instead of socializing." In the shooting, Solomon targets Jason Cheeks, who Solomon says was a "jock" who brutally bullied him. Thomas had an argument with his girlfriend the day before the shooting, and reports say that he was devastated that she then seemed interested in Cheeks.

1999   In *Davis v. Monroe County Board of Education*, the Supreme Court rules under Title IX of the Federal Education Amendments (1972) that schools can be held liable for student-to-student sexual harassment if school officials are aware of the behavior and do not take reasonable actions to stop it. The case focuses on a fifth grader, LaShonda Davis in Georgia. Her mother filed a lawsuit stating that over a six-month period (1992–1993) a classmate identified as G. F. sexually harassed and abused Davis and others. Davis' mother said that she called teachers and the principal, and nothing was done to protect her daughter. In 1993, G. F. is charged with sexual battery and pleads guilty.

1999   Georgia is the first U.S. state to pass anti-bullying legislation.

2000   Dedrick Owens, at age six (the youngest school shooter to date), kills a six-year-old girl in Flint Michigan's Buell Elementary School. News reports say that Owens tells the girl, "I don't like you." She replies, "So?" And then the boy "swung around and shot her."

2003   After years of online bullying, taunts, threats, and homophobic instant messages, Ryan Halligan, age thirteen, commits suicide. Halligan's death influences his father to lobby for state laws that address bullying and suicide prevention.

2004   Following the Columbine shooting, the Secret Service and the U.S. Department of Education launch a collaborative effort on causes of school shootings and ways to prevent them. The study recognizes the relationship between bullying and school attacks and suggests that educators prioritize anti-bullying efforts and empower students to tell adults if they know of anyone being bullied.

2006   Megan Meier, age thirteen, in Missouri, commits suicide after receiving mean-spirited messages from a fictitious sixteen-year-old boy she has befriended on Myspace. A month after her death, her parents discover that the fabricated Myspace profile was created and monitored by their neighbor Lori Drew, the mother of Meier's former friend. Drew is indicted the following year but is then acquitted of the charges.

2007   Arkansas includes cyberbullying in school district harassment policies.

2007   In an effort to curb internet bullies hiding behind their usernames, South Korea creates an "internet real-name system." This requires users to submit their Resident Registration Number assigned at birth when they wish to join and contribute to a website. The decision is introduced after a spate of website posts about fabricated sex scandals, made-up plastic surgery operations, and false controversies about celebrities. The requirement is struck down by the country's Constitutional Court for restricting freedom of speech. This ruling comes months after China's microblogging services are told to ensure that their members have registered accounts with real names.

2008 Brandon McInerney, age fourteen, shoots and kills Lawrence King, a fifteen-year-old transgender student in Oxnard, California. *Newsweek* (2008) describes the incident as "the most prominent gay-bias crime since the 1998 murder of Matthew Shepard." McInerney uses a "gay panic" defense to say he felt provoked by King's gender expression.

2008 Jessica Logan, age eighteen, commits suicide in Ohio after being harassed by classmates over sexually explicit photographs she sent via text message to her boyfriend. When they broke up, her ex-boyfriend circulated the pictures to hundreds of other people. Many called Logan sexually degrading names. In May 2008, Logan tells her story on a Cincinnati television station, saying, "I just want to make sure no one else will have to go through this again." Logan hangs herself in her bedroom two months later. Her death prompts Ohio's Jessica Logan Act in 2012 (House Bill 116), which prohibits cyberbullying, requires anti-bullying policies, and authorizes schools to discipline students for off-campus misconduct.

2008 California passes a law giving schools the authority to suspend or expel students for cyberbullying via internet, cell phones, or other electronic means. In 2011, the law is updated to include social networking websites.

2010 Phoebe Prince, age fifteen, is brutally bullied before she commits suicide in South Hadley, Massachusetts. The case receives international attention and leads to the criminal prosecution of six teenagers for charges including civil rights violations. The state also responds by creating an anti-bullying task force and then passes stricter anti-bullying laws.

2010 New York State's Dignity for All Students Act is signed into law. The act is intended to provide elementary and high school students with an environment safe from discrimination, intimidation, taunting, harassment, and bullying on school property, school buses, and during school functions.

2010   Dan Savage, gay activist and high-profile journalist, and his husband, Terry Miller, launch the It Gets Better campaign to prevent more bullycides of targeted LGBTQI+ youths. As part of the campaign, LGBTQI+ adults and other supporters post videos of themselves online to tell LGBTQI+ teens that their lives will improve.

2010   Tyler Clementi, an eighteen-year-old student at Rutgers University, commits suicide after a roommate broadcasts on the internet a visual recording of Clementi's sexual encounter with another male in his dorm room.

2011   In *Kowalski v. Berkeley County School District*, the family of Kara Kowalski sues, claiming that Kowalski had the right to free speech when she created a "hate" website attacking the sexuality of another student. The family says that she shouldn't have been suspended from school because it didn't happen on school property. The Fourth Circuit Court of Appeals in West Virginia rules that schools have a legitimate interest in monitoring and regulating cyberbullying, including online student or parent actions and speech that interfere with a students' school experiences, even if the offending conduct takes place off campus.

2011   In New Jersey, the Anti-Bullying Bill of Rights takes effect. The law is considered the nation's strictest anti-bullying law and inspires other states to strengthen their anti-bullying measures. New Jersey passes the bill partly in response to Clementi's suicide and to protect LGBTQI+ targeted students.

2011   Several anti-bullying bills are introduced in Congress, including the Safe Schools Improvement Act, the Anti-Bullying and Harassment Act, and the Bullying Prevention and Intervention Act. None make it into law.

2011   Several countries, including Mexico, Brazil, and France, pass anti-bullying legislation after experiencing bullying-related shootings and suicides.

2011   The documentary film *Bully* premieres at the Tribeca Film Festival. Released in theaters in 2012 and shown on PBS in 2014, the film follows five families that have struggled with bullying in schools and prompts a national movement to end bullying.

2011   In *Mardis v. Hannibal Public School District*, the Eighth Circuit Court of Appeals in Missouri rules in favor of a school that suspended a student for sending threatening text messages.

2011   Chile's Congress approves the Law about School Violence. Bullying is defined as repeated aggression/harassment among peers that causes mistreatment, fear, and/or humiliation. Educational institutions are required to form a Committee of Good School Coexistence to create a nonviolent school community.

2012   Lady Gaga and her mother, in collaboration with the Harvard Graduate School of Education, launch Born This Way, their web-based anti-bullying campaign.

2012   In a long-term study of identical twins, Duke University researchers find that children exposed to bullying or violence exhibit DNA changes similar to aging.

2012   North Carolina becomes the first state to prohibit cyberbullying of teachers and other school employees. Under the School Violence Prevention Act, students can face up to sixty days in jail for crimes like creating fake online profiles.

2013   California's governor, Jerry Brown, signs a bill outlawing "revenge porn." Responding to a growing problem, the new law makes it a misdemeanor to distribute private photos of an ex-boyfriend or ex-girlfriend with the intent of causing emotional distress. The American Civil Liberties Union opposes the bill because it could restrict free speech. Florida initially rejects a similar bill after free speech concerns surface.

2013   NFL lineman Jonathan Martin quits the Miami Dolphins after enduring nearly two seasons of homophobic locker-room bullying including frequent verbal harassment and ridicule. Troy Vincent, the NFL's senior vice president for player engagement, plans a meeting with six groups that represent the gay community to go over the league's policies and to seek ideas for improvements.

2013   In Florida, two girls are arrested because they cyberbully twelve-year old Rebecca Sedwick until she commits suicide. The two girls, ages twelve and fourteen, call her sexually derogatory names and "ugly." They are charged with aggravated stalking and are alleged to have posted messages telling Sedwick to kill herself.

2013   The Philippines pass the Anti-Bullying Act of 2013, requiring elementary and high schools to adopt an anti-bullying policy.

2014   In conjunction with the Department of Education, the Centers for Disease Control and Prevention publish a federal definition of bullying for legal, research, and surveillance purposes. The definition focuses on unwanted aggression, power imbalances, and repetition or the likelihood for behavior repetition.

2014   The U.S. Education Department's Office for Civil Rights (OCR) issues a letter to public schools focusing attention on the prevalence of bullying against students with disabilities. It states that the OCR has received more than two thousand complaints about the bullying of students with disabilities in the nation's public elementary and secondary schools.

2014   Internet security firm McAfee releases findings from its "2014 Teens and the Screen" study that shows that the percentage of youths witnessing cyberbullying has tripled from the previous year, from 27 to 87 percent.

2015   Florida passes legislation similar to the California prohibition against sexting, in spite of free speech concerns.

2015   France establishes a nationwide bullying hotline, where anyone being bullied can report the problem anonymously.

2015   Police make a high-profile arrest tied to Yik Yak, when a white suspect posts threats against some black students (Yik

Yak is an app that allows users to post anonymous messages on forum-like threads).

2015   The governor of Pennsylvania signs a law that allows law enforcement officials to intervene in cyberbullying cases. The bill focuses on the cyberbullying of minors and makes harassing a minor online a third-degree misdemeanor punishable by up to $2,500 in fines with possible jail time.

2015   The New Jersey Supreme Court rules the state's bias intimidation law unconstitutional due to vagueness. The concern is that defendants might not be aware that they have caused another to feel harassed as defined under the law.

2015   Montana becomes the last of the fifty U.S. states to adopt anti-bullying legislation.

2016   In a rare public appearance just days before the presidential election, Melania Trump, wife of candidate Donald Trump, announces her intention to launch a campaign to combat cyberbullying as first lady of the United States. In 2018, she launches her anti-bullying Be Best campaign.

2017   For months, Mallory Grossman, age twelve, in New Jersey, receives taunts in text messages, Instagram posts, and via Snapchats. Just before she kills herself, one of the girls who is harassing her writes, "Why don't you kill yourself?" Her parents sue the school district for ignoring months of their pleas to stop the harassment.

2017   The parents of Brandy Vela, age eighteen, in Texas, report that Vela has put a gun to her chest and killed herself in front of her family after being cyberbullied for her weight and called fat and ugly. One message asks, "Why are you still here?"

2019   There is still no federal U.S. anti-bullying law unless the bullying concerns discriminatory harassment against someone from a protected class, including race, national origin, color, sex, age, disability, or religion. Only if bullying and this kind of targeted harassment overlap are federally funded schools, colleges, and universities obligated to act.

Aggressive   Being forceful or destructive, especially with the intent to dominate, such as an unprovoked attack.

Antisocial   Unwilling or unable to be friendly toward others, often causing them to feel annoyed.

Asexual   Denotes a person without sexual feelings or desires.

Attachment   A bond in which close emotional ties are formed, such as between parents and infants.

Bigotry   Intolerance for different opinions, beliefs, or groups.

Bisexual   Denotes a person who is attracted to males and females and sometimes other gender identities.

Bullycide   Suicide associated with bullying.

Cisgender   Denotes a person whose personal identity and gender correspond with their birth sex.

Compassion   Having understanding and feeling sorrow for others difficulties, often accompanied with a desire to help.

Corporal punishment   Physical actions meant to punish or cause another to suffer due to wrongdoing, such as spanking or paddling a youth.

Culture of bullying   Context in which bullying is seen as ordinary or routine.

Cyberbullying   Bullying that occurs online, via email, chat, social media, instant messaging, or other electronic forms.

Desensitization   A process by which exposure to particular stimuli leads to a decrease in one's ability to respond on a physiological, psychological, cognitive, and/or behavior level.

Emotional abuse (also psychological abuse, psychological aggression, psychological maltreatment, and mental abuse) Non-physical harm including intimidating, manipulating, humiliating, withholding affection, yelling, insulting, swearing, blaming, threatening, isolating, rejecting, degrading, and isolating, often in the form of exploitative caregiving.

Empathy   Identifying with, or vicariously experiencing, another person's feelings, thoughts, or attitudes.

Femininity   Having qualities or characteristics traditionally associated with females, often linked to being gentle, empathetic, and nurturing.

Habituation   The process by which responses to stimuli decline after repeated exposure.

Hegemonic   Having dominance or control over others via social, cultural, ideological, or economic means.

Heterogeneous   Varied or mixed.

Homosexual   Denotes a person sexually attracted to members of the same sex.

Hyper-competitive   An extreme tendency to try to win by defeating or establishing superiority over others.

Hyper-individualism   An extreme tendency to think about and do things one's own way without regard to society.

Hyper-masculinity   Having extreme qualities or characteristics traditionally associated with males, often linked to being powerful and aggressive.

Individualism   Philosophy or moral stance that emphasizes self-reliance and independence; the belief that the individual should receive precedence over the group; the right of the individual to self-expression, freedom, and self-realization.

Instant messaging   An electronic message sent in real time and immediately available on the recipient's screen.

Intersex   Denotes a person whose sex a doctor has a difficult time categorizing as either male or female; relates to a person whose chromosomes, gonads, hormones, internal sex organs, gonads, and/or genitals differs from one of the two expected patterns.

Intervention   The action or process of trying to alter a result or course of events.

Juvenile delinquent   A minor who commits antisocial or illegal acts, for instance vandalism or violence.

Lesbian   A female-identified person who is sexually attracted to other female-identified people.

Mandated reporter   A person such as a teacher or doctor who is legally required to ensure that a report is made when abuse is observed or suspected.

Masculinity   Having qualities or characteristics traditionally associated with males, often linked to being strong, competitive, and engaged in risk-taking.

Minor   A person under the age of full legal responsibility.

Mobbing   A large group of people harassing a victim.

Nature versus nurture   A phrase coined in the 1860s to describe the debate over the effects of biology (nature) versus environment (nurture) to explain why people act the way they do.

Paddling   To hit, spank, or beat a person with a flat object (paddle), often as a punishment.

Perpetrator   A person who commits a harmful or illegal act.

Physical abuse   Any act that causes trauma or injury via bodily contact, especially against youths.

Prejudice   A preconceived notion, either positive or negative.

Queer   A term embracing different sexual preferences, orientations, and habits rather than the heterosexual and cisgender majority.

Resilience   Ability to recover quickly from an illness or event.

Restorative justice   A form of discipline that accounts for the needs of both perpetrators and victims and aims to repair relationships and heal an injured community. It can involve community service, apologies, restitution, and education.

School safety team   A group of school personnel charged with protecting students, usually to prevent harassment and intervene in charges of bullying and other hurtful behaviors.

School zero-tolerance policies   Statutes that require school officials to apply specific, consistent, and harsh punishment (e.g., suspension or expulsion) when students break certain rules. The punishment is mandated regardless of the circumstances.

Self-reliance   Ability to rely on one's own strength and resources.

Sexting   Sending sexual photos, videos, emails, or messages in a digital format.

Sexual abuse   Unwanted sexual activity where perpetrators use force, make threats, or take advantage of victims who are not able to give consent. Immediate reactions may include shock and fear. Long-term symptoms may include anxiety and PTSD.

Statute   Written law or rule.

Transgender   Denotes a person who lives as a member of a gender other than the person's anatomical sex. Sexual orientation varies and is not dependent on gender identity.

Typecast   Assign repeatedly to the same kind of role; stereotype.

Upstander   A person who takes a stand against an act of injustice or intolerance, such as standing up to a bully.

Note: Page numbers followed by *t* indicate tables and *f* indicate figures.

About the Author

Jessie Klein, PhD, MSW, MEd, is an Adelphi University associate professor of sociology and criminal justice and the founder and director of Creating Compassionate Communities (CCC), a predominantly K–12 and college empathy-building bullying prevention and intervention program. She is the author of *The Bully Society: School Shootings and the Crisis of Bullying in America's Schools* (NYU Press, 2012), which was listed in *Choice*'s Outstanding Academic Titles (2013). Her writing appears in scholarly journals and the popular press and is featured in television, radio, and online media.

Previously she served as an acting high school assistant principal of guidance, school social worker, college adviser, social studies teacher, substance abuse prevention counselor, and conflict resolution coordinator. She has also worked as a professor of social work.

You can learn more about Dr. Klein and CCC from her websites, creatingcompassionatecommunities.com and jessieklein .com, and her Adelphi University faculty profile at http://www .adelphi.edu/faculty/profiles/profile.php?PID=0326.